Key Concepts in
Urban Studies

Recent volumes include:

Key Concepts in Sociology
Peter Braham

Key Concepts in Migration
David Bartram, Maritsa V. Poros and
Pierre Monforte

Key Concepts in Crime and Society
Ross Coomber, Joseph F. Donnermeyer,
Karen McElrath and John Scott

The SAGE Key Concepts series provides students with accessible and authoritative knowledge of the essential topics in a variety of disciplines. Cross-referenced throughout, the format encourages critical evaluation through understanding. Written by experienced and respected academics, the books are indispensable study aids and guides to comprehension.

contents

Leslie Budd is Reader in Social Enterprise at the Open University, UK. He is a Fellow of the Academy of Social Sciences in the UK and Chair of the Urban and Regional Economics Seminar Group (URESG). He is currently Special Economic Advisor to the Enterprise Trade and Investment Committee of the Northern Ireland Assembly.

Mark Gottdiener is Professor Emeritus, University at Buffalo (SUNY). He is the leading proponent of the New Urban Sociology, a paradigm of urban analysis that has challenged human ecology since the 1970s. In 2010, Gottdiener received the Robert and Helen Lynd Award for Distinguished Career Achievement from the American Sociological Association.

Panu Lehtovuori is the Professor of Planning Theory in Tampere University of Technology, Finland. He is co-founder of Livady Architects, a Helsinki-based practice, and member of SPIN Unit, an NGO developing new approaches to the analysis of urban space and its use.

key concepts in urban studies

preface to the second edition

The 'rise' of the city and the claims for its universal value in transforming the global socio-economic environment has found a stronger voice among many academic and policy commentators. Their commentaries tend to hype increased urbanization as the silver bullet for sustainable economic growth. Many national, state and local governments around the world have bought into this hype and have employed a number of celebrity academics to advise them. At a time of global geo-political uncertainty, over-urbanization and financial bubbles in China, and the institutionalization of austerity in the European Union, the uncritical acceptance of this hype seems odd and unfounded. This new edition seeks to critically analyze the dynamic changes in the field of urban studies. We do not try to cover all concepts of the field, as this would involve a life of scholarship devoted to many volumes. Rather, we seek to construct a critical narrative of some key concepts whose analysis and relevance we think appropriate. Our commentaries on these concepts also represent our professional and personal perspectives to which we are committed.

In this second edition, a new author with a distinct planning and architectural perspective is included. The authors have together re-written nearly all the entries, condensed and combined some old entries and added new ones on Financial and Fiscal Crises, Globalization and Meltdown, Modern Urban Planning, Planning and Public Space, Sustainable Urbanization, Temporary Uses and Adaptive Urbanism. New examples and cases beyond US and UK experience have been added throughout the entries. In doing so we hope to make a significant contribution to this important field, engaging the reader with a way of thinking that does not seek to underpin and reinforce the conventional.

This book is not meant to be read starting with the first entry, The Chicago School, and proceeding to its last page. It is a reference work that we hope will supplement other books used in courses or projects on urban studies, economics, geography, planning, sociology and architecture. Consequently, it can be picked up and opened to any topic depending on need. Wherever appropriate, we have cross-referenced access to similar topics.

Thanks to Gemma Shields, Katherine Haw, Chris Rojek and the whole SAGE team for their support. We sincerely wish that a new generation of students and scholars will find the Key Concepts 2nd edition useful and inspiring!

Mark Gottdiener
Leslie Budd
Panu Lehtovuori

key concepts in urban studies

The Chicago School

Academic studies of the city as a unique form of settlement space were rare until the 1800s when the German sociologist Max Weber wrote a sophisticated analysis tracing its history as a phenomenon of social organization (1966). Somewhat later, the Anglo-German, Friedrich Engels, also the lifelong friend of Karl Marx, wrote a critique of urban living under capitalism (1973). These efforts stood alone until the turn of the 20th century. Just prior to World War I, the University of Chicago founded the very first department of sociology in the US under the leadership of W.I. Thomas and Albion Small, who had been a student of Weber. Their interests were in general aspects of sociology, but in 1913 they hired Robert Park who possessed a specific and strong interest in the urban condition. Park was a newspaper reporter who had acquired extensive experience in the southern US which conditioned him to the injustice of racial discrimination. He also had experience as an urban crime news reporter in Minneapolis, New York City and Detroit. When he was obtaining his doctorate in sociology, he spent some time at the University of Berlin, Germany, where he studied under Georg Simmel, the European sociologist most responsible for writing about urban life (see entry on *The City*). When the Chicago department hired another sociologist with an interest in the city, Ernest W. Burgess, the two set about to study Chicago as an urban laboratory. Together they founded the first 'school' of urban analysis, the Chicago School, and both they and their students published a prolific amount of research until the 1940s, including the first systematic field studies and ethnographies written by professional sociologists.

The members of the Chicago School were uniquely concerned about city life. They called their approach *Human Ecology*, because they were influenced by Darwin to consider human social adjustments to the urban environment as similar to the way plant and animal species attuned themselves to their more natural space (for a critique, see Gottdiener, 1994; Gottdiener and Hutchison, 2000). In place of the emphasis on political economy characteristic of the *New Urban Sociology*, the Chicago School preferred a biologically based metaphor typifying human interaction (see entry on *Social Production of Space*; also Gottdiener and Hutchison, 2000). Thus, they avoided the study of capitalism, preferring instead to view economic competition as a manifestation of the general struggle for survival that unites all species on the planet. According to Park, the social organization of the city resulted from this struggle over scarce resources. It produced a complex division of labor because people would adjust to the biologically based competition for survival by finding specific ways they could compete based on their 'natural' abilities.

Other members of the Chicago School took a more spatially sensitive approach, while retaining their emphasis on biological rather than political-economic forces operating in the environment. Roderick McKenzie emphasized the role of location and argued that establishing a physical position within the environment was most important in the struggle for survival. Individuals or groups that were successful took over the best locations within the city – the higher ground, the prime business locations, the preferred neighborhoods. Those that were not as successful in this spatial competition wound up in less attractive locations. Thus, the population sorted itself out within the environment as a consequence of this process. McKenzie studied the patterns that this spatial sorting produced for both social groups and businesses.

Ernest W. Burgess was also a member of the early Chicago School (see entry on *Models of Urban Growth*). For him the spatial competition created by the struggle for survival produced a land-use pattern of concentric rings of settlement around a centralized business district.

Louis Wirth was also a member of the early school (see the entry on *The City*). The Chicago School researchers viewed city life principally in negative terms. They explained phenomena such as crime and family break-up in terms of social disorganization. For them the city broke down traditional primary relations and therefore contributed to various negative aspects of urban living. Later on this approach was criticized for its overly disparaging view of city life. Another criticism was that their work favored the biologically based approach to locational adjustment and ignored the factor of culture or the role that symbols played in determining spatial patterns within the city. In 1945 Walter Firey wrote a critique of Burgess' concentric zone model by showing how the land-use pattern of Boston was an expression of 'sentiments and symbols' in addition to the ecological competition over space. Despite these criticisms, the idea of ecology persisted as American urbanists preferred to ignore issues of class and race, which the political economic approach demands (see entry on *Social Production of Space*).

After World War II the ecological approach was revived, but it ignored the Chicago School's emphasis on spatial competition in favor of a form of technological determinism. The new perspective was called *Contemporary Human Ecology*. Urban land-use patterns and the distribution of population and activities were a product of communication and transportation technologies. As the technology of these means of interaction changed, human ecologists argued that so did the patterns of social organization. For example, it was claimed that, although the process of suburbanization had been present since the late 1800s in American cities, it did not become a mass phenomenon until after the automobile became a consumer good that many people could afford. Subsequent research reversed this claim and established the fact that 'while the street car, electric trains and automobile may be credited with lowering initial density levels in cities ... they were not responsible for "emptying out"' urban areas on a mass scale.

Another argument by human ecologists in the 1970s claimed that while cities expanded in size their central business districts also had to grow in administrative functions. This was so, they argued, because the command and control activities of the urban area had to increase as the size of that region grew, just as a cell's nucleus expands when the cell develops. A similar argument was advanced in the 1990s when Saskia Sassen (1991) claimed that globalization had produced 'world cities' through the concentration of command and control activities. Upon closer examination, the human ecology argument was shown to be false (Gottdiener, 1994). Command and control functions in the form of corporate headquarters had been dispersing throughout multi-centered metropolitan regions as those agglomerations themselves expanded. In the 1960s, for example, New York City was home to over 120 national and international corporations. By the 1990s that figure had dropped to slightly less than 90, at the very same time that globalization advocates were calling New York a 'global city'. Later on Sassen's argument about the effects of command and control concentration was also proved false (see entry on *Inequality and Poverty*). There is no evidence that these activities require a central city location, as the human ecology approach maintains. However, global financial activities possess components that still do prefer such inner business district locations (see entries on *The City*; *Globalization and Meltdown*).

There are many things wrong with the ecological perspective, both the old and contemporary schools, in addition to its false biologically based conception. Ecologists avoid any mention of social groupings belonging to the analysis of late capitalism, such as class and race. They see social interaction as a process of adaptation to an environment, in keeping with their biological or ecological emphasis, rather than being produced by relations deriving from powerful factors in economic, political and cultural organization, as the socio-spatial perspective suggests. Although they emphasize location, they ignore aspects of the real estate industry (see entry on *Real Estate*) and its role in producing spatial patterns of development. Finally, human ecologists completely ignore the role of political institutions in channeling resources and in regulating competition over scarce resources in a market-based, capitalist economy. With regard to the latter, they focus on the demand-side view of markets, which emphasizes individual decisions, rather than the supply-side that highlights the role of powerful actors in manipulating the market for desired ends.

REFERENCES

Engels, F. 1973. *The Condition of the Working Class in England*, Moscow: Progress Publishers.
Gottdiener, M. 1994. *The Social Production of Urban Space, 2nd Edition*, Austin, TX: University of Texas Press.
Gottdiener, M. and R. Hutchison 2000. *The New Urban Sociology, 2nd Edition*, New York: McGraw-Hill.
Sassen, S. 1991. *The Global City*, Princeton, NJ: Princeton University Press.
Weber, M. 1966. *The City*, New York: The Free Press.

The City

A city is a bounded space that is densely settled and has a relatively large, culturally heterogeneous population. The history of cities dates back to the Neolithic period. The oldest known city is Catal Höyük (7500–5700 BC) in present-day Turkey, while Erbil (founded 6000 BC) in Iraq is the oldest continuously settled city. Today, Erbil is the capital of Kurdistan with 1.3 million inhabitants. In contemporary Urban Studies, the term 'city' is often used in loose or confusing ways (see entries on *The City and Beyond; Classifications and Definitions of Places; Multi-Centered Metropolitan Regions* and *Urbanization and Urbanism* for more discussion).

Cities are important principally because of their political clout. A US city, as an incorporated municipality, has the power to tax and the power to raise money via bonds and other financial instruments. Legally it can hire its own police force and provide for all social services to its residents. Cities have the power of self-governance and they have their own elected officials. As a consequence of the latter, city administrations have political power nationally. Mayors of cities have national political clout, much more so than their suburban counterparts, and this is why cities themselves are important.

In Europe, unlike the US, the formal municipal situation varies enormously depending on different systems of government and governance. In France, the big five cities, Paris, Lyon, Marseilles, Lille and Bordeaux exert enormous formal and informal power. In Germany, the City-Länder of Hamburg, Bremen and Berlin operate with a regional system of government that boosts their position relative to other cities. In the UK, London is the dominant city and its power and influence formally and informally outstrips other cities. The system of sub-national government also has tended to change frequently in the UK. Currently, there has been a shift back to notions of city-regions and ideas of regional balance in the UK.

The political power of cities is related to their position as sites of economic activity. Despite the apparent remorseless march of globalization and digitization, certain activities of large transnational firms still crowd into some of the world's major cities. The benefits of co-location are expressed as agglomeration economies in the form of specialist labor markets, transport accessibility and access to shared lifestyle aspirations. The City of London retains its position as one of the world's leading financial centers as a result of these agglomeration benefits (Budd and Whimster, 1992).

Cities are also considered to be important because they are the site of 'urban culture'. In the past, this characteristic was easy to understand because of its contrast to the culture of the countryside, i.e. rural areas. However, decades of suburbanization and the ubiquitous influence of national media have considerably blurred this distinction so that it has limited value today. One feature of cities that is not characteristic of other areas is the presence of a viable street and pedestrian culture. The urbanist, Jane Jacobs (1961), claimed that the urban street is the fundamental aspect of city life (see entries on the *Neighborhood; Planning and Public Space*). Often this distinctive pedestrian feature is simulated by purposely constructed environments, such as mall arcades and city-themed amusement parks like Universal Studios' *CityWalk*. In London, in the 1970s, the former fruit and vegetable market Covent Garden was transformed into an ersatz urban village, complete with *faux* Georgian arcades, as an exercise in simulation much like the one at Universal Studios in Los Angeles.

Since World War II, US cities have gone through enormous changes; industrial decline, crumbling homes and schools, overcrowded neighborhoods, rigid segregation and racial trauma, rising crime and violence, and an alarming drain of revenues have all contributed to creating a troubled urban landscape. In Europe, re-building the sense of historical urban identity has been a key focus after World War II. Vienna described as the *City as Pleasure Principle* and Paris as the *Capital of Light*, because of their identification with music and art in the late 19th and early 20th centuries, still resonates today in the re-forming of the urban landscape (Hall, 1998).

LOUIS WIRTH AND THE CITY AS A WAY OF LIFE

Wirth defined the city as the combination of three key variables – size, density and heterogeneity or diversity of population. He proposed a theory that, the more intense were the three variables, the more urban the place would be. For example, the larger the population, the more formal, secondary and tertiary social relations would be, replacing the primary relations of a traditional community; the more anonymous would the crowds be. The greater density would accentuate the effects of anonymity and also produce a blasé attitude due to the need to turn out excessive stimulation. Greater density produces greater tolerance of strangers but also greater stress – both attributes of city living. Heterogeneity also creates tolerance because there are so many different people interacting.

Despite many years of research, there is no evidence to support Wirth's theory. Clearly, size, density and heterogeneity all define urban places, especially when these variables are large, but increasing any of these, singly or in combination, does not necessarily produce more 'urban' effects. Some relatively smaller cities, like San Francisco, are highly urban and diverse, other larger ones, like Indianapolis or Nashville, are much less urban. Wirth's theory does not consider how different national cultures determine the path of urban development. In the UK, Glasgow could be considered the only true urban city, with high levels of centrally located flats (apartments) and residential services. In England, the nostalgia for a 'green and pleasant land', expressed strongly in Constable's painting, *The Hay Wain*, and in William Cobbett's book, *Rural Rides*, has until recently created an anti-urban culture and promoted the 'ideal' of suburbia. The dominance of owner-occupation in UK housing markets also tended to encourage suburbanization.

Meanwhile, there has been a counter tendency towards increasingly urban housing preferences in places like London and Paris. Population influx was occasioned by a combination of active cultural resources, new immigration (especially from Asia or North Africa), and real estate interests re-developing office buildings often overlooking watersides as up-market and gated apartments for the affluent. In many European countries, for example Germany and Sweden, distinctly urban qualities have become sought after in medium-sized cities as well, leading to urban densification. The demographic shift is statistically significant, so that only some cities of the nation with 'urban' character grow, and the previously dynamic suburban municipalities stagnate or even suffer population loss. Time will show if this counter tendency is lasting, or turns out to be an outcome of the cyclical development of regional housing markets.

One important contribution made by Wirth involves identification of different kinds of relationship. Any definition of the city must distinguish among *primary, secondary* and *tertiary social relationships*. Wirth accepted the view that rural, community areas were dominated by *primary*, that is, face-to-face and personal relationships. In contrast, cities were less personal and dominated by *secondary* and *tertiary* relations. *Secondary* relations are those based on infrequent but direct interpersonal contacts. At the bank, for example, the tellers are courteous to customers, but a customer may not get the same teller every time. *Tertiary* relations are the most formal types of business relations. When individuals have business with a firm, they may speak to a person, but he/she is only a representative of the firm itself. Increasingly tertiary relationships occur as indirect contacts through telephone or the Internet.

In Wirth's theory he believed that urban life was quite different from rural, community existence because of the dominance in the city of secondary and tertiary relations. He did not live long enough to witness the appearance of the new kind of Internet relationships we have in society today. Cyber interaction involves non-face-to-face, disembodied relations that range from the very personal to the tertiary depending on individual circumstances. Thus, the Internet constitutes a separate dimension of interaction that can either reinforce or transcend the culture of the impersonal urban life, which Wirth believed characterized all cities.

LEWIS MUMFORD AND THE CITY AS THE SITE OF CIVILIZATION

The US urbanist, Lewis Mumford (1961) had a different view of urban life from that of Wirth. Mumfordian ideas stressed the interactive and social role cities fostered in behavior. He did not make the Wirthian distinction that cities nurtured impersonal relations. Instead he believed that important primary relations were established in cities that led to social innovations. For Mumford, urban life was creative and theatrical and the city was the site of civilization which, over the centuries, produced countless innovations. 'The city is a theater of social action' he said. All urban functions were greatly intensified by having to take place on the stage set of city street life.

Mumford's view that dense social interaction was the very life blood of city living influenced an entire generation of urbanists. Jane Jacobs, for example, argued strongly for walkable cities and the important role of street culture, as did William H. Whyte (1988). The French urbanist, Roland Barthes, viewed the compact life in the city center as a kind of eroticism where diversity prevailed and people could observe others from a safe distance (Gottdiener, 2001). This stimulated fantasies and excitement. The planners, Allan Jacobs and Donald Appleyard, resonated with these ideas as well by urging designers to emphasize street life (2003). Their work was extended in concept by the New Urbanists (see entry on *Planning and Public Space*).

Like Mumford and Whyte, the public places of the city were stages upon which residents could act out and interact to the benefit of urban culture.

In one sense Mumford and Wirth agreed. In the city, which was conceived by both of them as a limited space (for a critique see entry on *Multi-Centered Metropolitan Regions*), social relations were also organized into groups and social associations. There were families, neighborhoods, as well as voluntary and business associations. Many of these groups produced fixed sites as they were housed in organized, physical structures, like homes, government bureaucracies and office buildings. According to Mumford:

> The essential physical means of a city's existence are the fixed site, the durable shelter, the permanent facilities for assembly, interchange and storage; the essential social means are the social division of labor, which serves not merely the economic life but the cultural processes ... The city in its complete sense, then, is a geographic plexus, an economic organization, an institutional process, a theater of social action, and an aesthetic symbol of collective unity. (2003: 94)

We see here a kind of old-fashioned thinking that has been turned into nostalgia by current writers. Mumford equates the city with civilization, which was once a very trenchant but is now a dated observation in the US. Once an important conception of the city, at a time when the only other alternatives were rural life or immature suburbs, Mumford's idea, as universal, is now archaic. Furthermore, his glorification of metropolitan culture was based on the limited evidence of early history, the history of ancient civilizations alone. But, all of the claims for the city's uniqueness in these terms are proved false by considering the same importance that suburban regions play in contemporary society (see entries on the *Suburbs and Suburbanization; Multi-Centered Metropolitan Region*). Furthermore, now much of this kind of theatrical social interaction takes place in the social media, although the virtual stage can by no means replace interaction on the street or in the many centers of the 'multi-centered' and fully urbanized region (Gottdiener, 2001; Gottdiener and Hutchison, 2000).

Surprisingly, in contrast, Mumford's thesis of the city as the 'site of civilization' has been revived recently in Europe by the European Union. It has been running a yearly competition for a decade called The City of Culture, or Cultural Capital, that has highlighted the centrality of European cities in regard to their nations' patrimony. Furthermore, current ideas about reviving cities place an increased emphasis on the creativity of the people that specifically live in dense urban areas. This idea was not only articulated first in the US by Richard Florida, but is becoming quite popular in Europe. Yet, whether urban development depends primarily on the creativity of the city population alone remains a thesis that still has to be proved, although no one can deny that artists, designers, computer innovators, and other creative people, such as those working in finance and trade, are critical to a nation's economy. These same people are usually found in cities, although mature suburbs in the US, such as Silicon Valley or the region centered around Seattle, also possess their fair share.

SOME RELEVANT ASPECTS OF CITY LIFE TODAY

Another unique aspect of cities, compared to suburban and rural areas, in addition to pedestrian culture and interaction, is the presence of night-time activities. The social aspects of this world were revealed when academics began to study contemporary subcultures and discovered a variety of socially marginalized groups that had colonized the night-time by creating personalized spaces of participation in the city. It was not street life per se, as in Mumford, Jacobs and Whyte, which created this dynamism, but the enacting of subcultural practices within the city, especially at night when the more conventional population was at home and asleep (Chatterton and Hollands, 2003). (See entry on *Nightscapes and Urban Escapades.*)

Yet another unique aspect of cities resides in their architecture, especially the tall structures known as skyscrapers. The tall building was not a contribution of a particular place, but is viewed, rather, as an evolutionary innovation resulting from the unique city aspect of limited locationally valuable land. Now these structures are valued again for their cultural meaning and the sense of place they give cities. Signature architecture and the creation of hallmark urban landscapes are important elements in the marketing of place during the current phase of globalization. Combined into a tableau, the city 'skyline' is an important marker for place. When that skyline is instantly recognizable, such as the case of Paris, it creates an important tool for the valorization of location in a global economic system.

Housing also represents a difference between the city and suburbia. In the city, housing tends to be of high density. If single family homes are built, they are usually on small lots. Many structures are multi-family apartments, some of which are actually skyscraper in scale. Suburbs possess a contrasting land use with larger size plots and an emphasis on single family home construction that results in considerably less social density. Historically, it is within the city that new forms of housing have been innovated. The emergence of the tenement in the 1800s, for example, marked the transformation of cities into centers of manufacturing, with a working class of renters.

Today cities remain important, as do their contributions to society. However, a true understanding of the city must involve its relationship with other areas of urbanized regions, such as suburbs and the networks of locations that are tied together through electronic means in the information economy. Consequently, the subject of urban studies is no longer confined to the study of the city alone. The next entry on *The City and Beyond* develops the argument further.

REFERENCES

Budd, L. and Whimster, S. (eds) 1992. *Global Finance and Urban Living: A Study of Metropolitan Change*, London and New York: Routledge.

Chatterton, P. and R. Hollands, 2003. *Urban Nightscapes: Youth Subcultures, Pleasure Spaces and Corporate Power*, London: Routledge.

Gottdiener, M. 2001. *Life in the Air: Surviving the New Culture of Air Travel*, Lanham, MD: Rowman and Littlefield.

key concepts in urban studies

Gottdiener, M. and R. Hutchison, 2000. *The New Urban Sociology, 2nd Edition*, New York: McGraw-Hill.

Hall, P. (1998) *Cities in Civilisation*, London: Weidenfeld and Nicholson.

Jacobs, A. and D. Appleyard, 2003. 'Toward an Urban Design Manifesto' in R. LeGates and F. Stout (eds) *The City Reader, 3rd Edition*, London: Routledge. pp. 437–47.

Jacobs, J. 1961. *The Death and Life of Great American Cities*, New York: Modern Library Edition.

Mumford, L. 1961. *The City in History*, New York: Harcourt Brace.

Mumford, L. 2003. 'What is a City?' in R. LeGates and F. Stout (eds) *The City Reader, 3rd Edition*, London: Routledge. pp. 93–6.

Whyte, W.H. 1988. *City: Rediscovering the Center*, Garden City, New York: Doubleday.

The City and Beyond

As hinted in the previous entry, too many urbanists focus on the city in itself and for itself rather than analyzing the complexity of metropolitan regions and their conceptualization and classification. 'City' is still a common discursive reference point, even though the actual analysis is about different and much larger units (e.g. Brenner and Keil, 2005; LeGates and Stout, 1996; Watson and Bridge, 2010). Partly this reflects their own locational experience: often in large metropolises within the developed world. However, they are insufficiently critical of the problem of induction, which they face. That is, generalizing from their experience in an effort to impose a standard template by which to structure the process of urban development. The LA School is perhaps the prime example of this, and its members appear to often take their cue from the futuristic offerings of film directors whose narrative is often that, rather than all the world being a stage, it is a version of the tinsel town they inhabit (see Gottdiener (2002) for an insightful critique of this phenomenon). However, if we raise our eyes above and beyond the vista of the city we find irregularities and differences, which are the meat and drink of any urban analyst and urban studies in general.

The City and Beyond takes two lines of enquiry. One is the analysis of the boundaries of classifications of city and urban forms. The second is how the discussion of urban development goes beyond these forms.

As other entries in the book show, we all have to challenge our assumption about the habitats we occupy (for example see the entry on *Multi-Centered Metropolitan Regions*). If we look at the classification of Polycentric Urban Regions (PURs), we find that they are aggregations of a multiple number of centers that are not geographically contiguous. The nodes of the PUR are linked, but alongside urban activities are semi-rural and agricultural ones. Even within Multi-Centered Metropolitan Regions (MMRs) and Polycentric Mega-City Regions (PCRs) we see this apparent paradox. For example, anyone flying into London's Heathrow may

the city and beyond

9

be surprised to see agricultural land that is being farmed below them, rather than a contiguous urban space

Apart from the classifications of the urban form discussed, there is also the manner in which large metropolitan regions have been classified as 'mega-cities'. A mega-city is defined as a metropolitan area with a population in excess of 10 million. In some classifications, it has to have a minimum population density of 2000 people per square kilometer. In 1990 there were 10 urban agglomerations classified as 'mega-cities'. In 2014 that number had risen to 28 (United Nations, 2014). A number of these cities, however, are claimed to be 'global cities' by the proponents of this classification (see: www.citypopulation.de). The mega-cities range from Tokyo at the top through to Karachi, Sao Paulo and Lagos at the bottom. The United Nations predicts that by 2030 three out five people will live in cities, as the world's population rises from 7 billion in 2015 to nearly 9 billion in 2025, with urbanization the major trajectory of development. However, there are many similarities and differences between the 25 mega-cities, and classifying them according to some size template appears to be a rather crude exercise.

Within the metropolitan area that covers a mega-city there are manifold forms of socio-spatial arrangements, some of them within and beyond the city. Too often, urbanists tend to want to dovetail their classifications of the urban to cities of their choice, and then engage in arcane disputes of whether, say, Kolkata is a mega-city, a global city, a post-colonial city, or just a dense city. The official population count of the municipality of Kolkata is 5.14 million (2010 estimates), while the metropolitan area covers a population of 16.6 million. Similarly in the mega-cities league table London is ranked 23rd with a population of 12.5 million, but this covers the whole metropolitan area. The population of the administrative area known as Greater London is 7.5 million, so the degree to which a city is mega depends on the size of the area that is included. Given the differences between the municipal and metropolitan counts of population, one can infer that the difference between the city and beyond within the outer boundary is similarly large. This brings us on to the nature of urban development and the relationship of the hinterland to metropolitan areas.

The concept of development is a generic one whose definitional basis is frequently elastic. In development studies two types of definition are often advanced.

- *Immanent Development*: the spontaneous development as in the historical trajectory of capitalism; and
- *Intentional Development*: attempts to improve material conditions in response to the consequences of immanent development, for example, poverty and unemployment.

The two are symbiotic, but are subject to lags and leads depending on the economy and geography of places to be studied. But, the fundamental conceptualization of development remains, as Cowen and Shenton have shown in their scholarly contribution:

Development seems to defy definition, although not for want of definitions on offer. ... Thus, development is construed as a 'process of enlarging people's choices'; of enhancing 'participatory democratic processes' and the 'ability of people to have a say in the decisions that shape their lives'; of providing 'human beings with the opportunity to develop their fullest potential'; of enabling the poor, women, and 'free independent peasants' to organise for themselves and work together. Simultaneously, however, development is defined as the means to 'carry out a nation's development goals' and of promoting 'economic growth', 'equity' and 'national self-reliance'. Given that there is scarcely a 'Third World' dictatorship which does not at least in part attempt to legitimise its mandate to rule in the name of development nor a development agency which does not espouse the rhetoric of popular empowerment, it is little wonder that we are thoroughly confused by development studies texts as to what development means. (Cowen and Shenton, 1996: 1)

The same logic underpins our analysis of the classification of cities and metropolitan areas. Thus we have to be pragmatic in looking at general and particular cases, rather than falling into the inductive trap of generalizing the complexity of urban development from a singular case. Shanghai in China and Lagos in Nigeria provide us with two examples to pursue our second line of enquiry.

During Mao Tse-Tung's period in China, 'the city in the countryside, the countryside in the city' became part of the modernization reforms of the Chinese economy from the late 1970s onwards. That is, peasant farmers were encouraged to respond to market reform but also establish small-scale industries in the countryside, run by State Owned Enterprises (SOE), which themselves were to become subject to liberalization. Similarly, the importance of sustaining some food production in the cities was part of the early reforms. The subsequent reforms of the 1990s centered on the growth poles of the 14 coastal cities, which became the manufacturing hubs of China's trajectory to global economy status. The tension between the city and the countryside has been a constant feature of China's history, with the People's Republic reversing some of the urban development of the pre-Communist Republic. In the post Mao-era the city and the re-emergence of modernity has been central to China's rapid growth and urban development. The development of large urban growth poles has attracted what is effectively a reserve army of labor in order to fill the factories that serve the demands of consumers in the set of the world economy. The take-off phase of economic development has created difficulties for the rapidly growing metropolitan regions, with unofficial populations, drawn from the countryside, frequently matching the size of the official populations.

In the case of Shanghai, the regional planning authorities are preparing for an official population of 20 million, up from 13 million in 2010. The metropolitan structure appears to correspond to a combination of central place theory and E.W. Burgess' Model of Urban Growth 3 (see entry on *Models of Urban Growth*) (Burgess, 1925; Parr, 1973), in which a central urban area is linked to a number of satellites. It could be argued that this corresponds to a PUR which, given the pace and scale of urbanization, may develop into an MMR. The challenge for planning authorities and policy-makers is that the total population of Shanghai is likely to reach 40 million, given that the current total population is nearly 20 million and as marginal populations with no formal civic rights are drawn in from the countryside.

Rural exodus appears to be a general condition of economic modernization and intentional development. For the city boosterists, it is the source of economic growth *qua* economic growth, as exemplified in Edward Glaeser's *The Triumph of the City*. This book has been lionized and taken up by politicians and commentators around the world. Its approach is a-historical, however, and seems to focus on 'the city' and not 'beyond'. The relationship between urban settlements and their hinterlands is a complex and long-running one, no matter what the current cultural or fashionable urban turn is. In the case of Shanghai, it has a very fertile rural hinterland, which makes it more sustainable, compared to other metropolitan areas at the same stage of development. But, the pressure from urban development has seen peasant farmers evicted from their land, often without reference to how a potential population of 40 million is to be supported or without recourse to the significant increases in food imports that will be needed to sustain such a large increase.

A similar picture has been the experience of Lagos in Nigeria. It is the second most populous metropolitan area in Africa and the continent's fastest growing one (8.1 million people, set in the wider Lagos State of 21 million in 2012). Lagos City is similar in size to London but with about a 40% higher population density. Its economy had grown rapidly, forecast to average 6.14% per annum between 2010 and 2025 (IMF, 2013), because the bounty of nature means that it is rich in mineral deposits, particularly oil and gas However, the ability to exploit monopoly rents from these assets has had a distorting effect on the Nigerian economy, with people flooding into the urban areas from the rural ones, with all the resulting problems of a growing poor and economically marginal population. Although agriculture accounts for 26.5% of the country's Gross Domestic Product (GDP) and two-thirds of employment, the productivity of this sector is low, with the output of cotton, for example, about half of its potential (World Bank, 2013). Given the imperative of income from exports, tensions over the balance with domestic production are a continual feature of the country's socio-economic development path. The draw of metropolitan areas for those who exist at the level of economic and social subsistence in the rural areas is difficult to resist, which in itself is a general development challenge. Given the immanent development of Lagos and beyond, a more rational intentional development path in respect of negotiating and managing urbanization presents itself. However, the ideology of market reform, structural adjustment and being reliant on monopoly rents from a global energy industry constrain this possibility.

Yet, in the case of both these cities (or city-states?) they are often lionized as global cities, mega-cities and now smart cities, without reference to the challenges presented by their respective development paths.

In part these conceptions are influenced by the advent of new technologies that open up the possibility of different forms of agglomeration, rather than those based on the classic Chicago School central business district (CBD)-dominated urban center, surrounded by successively less dense zones. This development tends to come under the rubric of cyber-cities which vary in definition. One way of defining this space comes from the invention of the matrix of computers known as cyberspace, this being likened to a virtual megapolis, structured by digital technologies (Graham, 2004). Airports are one manifestation of this evolution. This airport space is a 'space of transition' that facilitates the shrinkage of the globe and the transcendence of time and space (Gottdiener, 2001). It is also marked by the intersection of digital technologies and human flows in which the constituent elements of any economy – production, consumption, supply-chains; the built environment (real and virtual); and finance – operate. Yet, airports can be seen as parallel virtual economies which would not be out of place in a Second Life universe (Hannam et al., 2006).

Smart cities are ones that appropriate information and communications technologies (ICT), knowledge and social structures (in the form of human and social capital) in order to enhance their competitiveness. The issue of place competitiveness as an intellectual *canard* notwithstanding, cities have used technologies, knowledge and their supporting social structures as the bases of their development throughout history. Cities may use smart technologies, for example, in utility metering, traffic and water control, public information systems, and so on; but using smart technologies to manage the operation of everyday urban activities operations is not the same as being a smart city. In the European Union (EU), smart has become the buzzword for public policy, based upon the 10-year *Europe 2020: A Strategy for Smart, Sustainable and Inclusive Growth*. Within this framework, the concept of smart specialization is being promoted for cities and regions, and used to maximize knowledge development based upon smart policies that promote research and innovation (Foray and Goenaga, 2013). Unpacking this marketing speak, we find a vacuum of explanation on how this is to be achieved. At a time when unemployment in Greece is over 25% and youth unemployment is over 50% in Spain, due to the crisis in the Eurozone (see entry on *Financial and Fiscal Crises*), the promotion of yet another fashionable neologism by Europe's political elites is hardly the response needed by the inhabitants of its cities and regions under stress.

In the light of the global financial crisis and the complicity of rentiers in its causes and consequences, one could say that so-called smart cities were actually dumb in character; that is, as a result of speculative real estate development and its financing, inequality has significantly increased in the world's leading cities. Classification, like abstraction, is a useful way of organizing a framework of analysis. This should not be a substitute for understanding the often fine-grained complexity of urban development, its history, structure and processes, and the places in which it occurs. The city and beyond gives one starting point, but like the suffix 'post', 'beyond' is often a substitute for examining the history and social narratives of cities and regions. In this entry, a particular line of enquiry has been pursued in order to tease out some general implications about the city and beyond, but we do not claim it is the only one nor that is provides a universal template, unlike those propagandists for global cities, mega-cities and smart cities.

REFERENCES

Brenner, N. and R. Keil (eds) 2005. *The Global Cities Reader*, New York and London: Routledge.

Burgess, E.W. 1925. 'The Growth of the City: An Introduction to a Research Project' in R.E. Park, E.W. Burgess and R.D. McKenzie, *The City*, Chicago: University of Chicago Press.

Caragliu, A., C. Del Bo and P. Nijkamp 2009. 'Smart Cities in Europe', Series Research Memoranda 0048 (VU University Amsterdam, Faculty of Economics, Business Administration and Econometrics).

Cowen. M. and R. Shenton 1996. *Doctrines of Development*, London: Routledge.

Foray, D. and X. Goenaga 2013. *Goals of Smart Specialisation*, S3 Policy Brief Series No . 01/2013, Luxembourg: European Commission.

Glaser, E. 2011. *The Triumph of the City*, New York: Penguin.

Gottdiener, M. 2001. *Life in the Air*, Oxford: Rowman and Littlefield.

Gottdiener, M. 2002. 'Urban Analysis as Merchandising: The "LA School" and the Understanding of Metropolitan Development' in J. Eade and C. Mele (eds) *Understanding the City: Contemporary and Future Perspectives*, Oxford: Blackwell.

Graham, S. (ed.) 2004. *The Cybercities Reader*, London: Routledge.

Hannam, K., M. Sheller and J. Urry (2006) 'Editorial: Mobilities, Immobilities and Moorings', *Mobilities*, 1(1): 1–22.

International Monetary Fund (IMF) 2013. *World Economic Outlook (WEO): Transitions and Tensions*, Washington, DC: IMF.

LeGates, R.T. and F. Stout (eds) 1996. *The City Reader*, London: Routledge.

Parr, J.B. 1973. 'Growth Poles, Regional Development and Central Place Theory', *Papers in Regional Science*, 31: 174–212.

United Nations 2014. *World Urbanization Prospects*, Washington, DC: United Nations.

Watson, S. and G. Bridge (eds) 2010. *The Blackwell City Reader, 2nd Edition*, Oxford: Blackwell.

World Bank 2013. *Global Monitoring Report: Rural–Urban Dynamics and the Millennium Development Goals*, Washington, DC: World Bank.

Classifications and Definitions of Places

Classifications and definitions of places are difficult in the sense of governmental and administrative boundaries, often cross-cut social and cultural ones, as well as the roots of identity. For example, in the United Kingdom there had been a shift towards regional government during the Blair administrations dating from 1997, only to be reversed by a new administration in 2010. This shift reflects different political perspectives and seems to be a repeat of the 19th-century reaction to Continental European regionalism by the Conservative Party, as it implemented county councils. These remain part of sub-national government in the United Kingdom today. There has never been a system of regional government in the United Kingdom, unlike that of many of its European neighbors.

Apart from issues of cultural and identity association, there is the political dimension to the classification and definition of place. In France, the region has been a traditional bulwark against the power of the central state. But the region had no political authority until the decentralization legislation of the 1980s.

Similarly in Germany, its federal system from 1956 was based on the American model but incorporates centuries-old traditions. At the Congress of Vienna in 1815, 39 federal states were established as part of the German Confederation. Today Germany has 16 Länder (regions), including the five in Eastern Germany that were absorbed after re-unification in 1990. The metropolitan areas of Hamburg, Berlin and Bremen are designated states, with the last being divided into two city-states. This points to the linguistic and etymological problem of definition of place: whether they are city-states, city-regions, Polycentric Urban Regions, or Multi-Centered Metropolitan Regions (MMRs) (see discussion in entries on these different urban forms).

The historical trajectory of place can be seen in the case of Brazil and China

IN BRAZIL

The Federation of the Republic of Brazil is made up of 27 *Unidades Federativas (UF)*, one of which, the capital Brasília, is a federal district. These federal states are grouped into five geographical regions, corresponding to five of the eight points of the compass.

The 27 UFs are: *Acre, Amapá, Amazonas, Pará, Rondônia, Roraima, Tocantins (North Region); Alagoas, Bahia, Ceará, Maranhão, Paraíba, Pernambuco, Piauí, Rio Grande do Norte, Sergipe (Northeast Region); Goiás, Mato Grosso, Mato Grosso do Sul, Distrito Federal (Central-West Region); Espírito Santo, Minas Gerais, Rio de Janeiro, São Paulo (Southeast Region); Paraná, Rio Grande do Sul, Santa Catarina (South Region).*

Local government consists of a total of 5568 municipalities. Each municipality has an autonomous local government, comprising a mayor, directly elected by the people to a four-year term, and a legislative body (*Câmara Municipal*), also directly elected by the people. These elections take place at the same time all over the country; the most recent municipal elections were held in 2012. Each municipality has the constitutional power to approve their own laws and collects taxes and also receives funds from the state and federal governments. Municipalities do not have a separate court of law, but one organized by the state can encompass many municipalities in a single justice administrative division called *comarca* (county).

IN CHINA

The constitution of the People's Republic of China provides for three *de jure* levels of government. Currently, however, there are five *de facto* levels of local government: the province, prefecture, county, township and village. At the provincial level there are:

- *Twenty-two provinces (shěng)*: A standard provincial government is nominally led by a provincial committee, headed by a secretary.
- *Five autonomous regions (zìzhìqū)*: These regions have a higher population of a particular minority ethnic group along with their own local government, but an autonomous region has more legislative rights in theory than in practice. The governor of the Autonomous Regions is appointed from the respective minority ethnic group.

- *Four municipalities* (*zhíxiáshì*): A higher level of city which is directly under the Chinese government, with status equal to that of the provinces.
- *Two special administrative regions* (SARs) (*tèbiéxíngzhèngqū*): A highly autonomous and self-governing sub-national territory of the People's Republic of China. Each SAR has a provincial-level chief executive as head of the region and head of government. The region's government is not fully independent, as foreign policy and military defense are the responsibility of the central government, according to the constitution.
- *One claimed province*: The People's Republic of China claims the island of Taiwan and its surrounding islets, including Penghu, as 'Taiwan Province'.

At the prefecture level, there are 17 prefectures (*dìqū*), 30 autonomous prefectures (*zìzhìzhōu*), 283 prefecture-level cities (*dìjíshì*) (283) and 3 leagues (*méng*).

At the county level, there are 1474 counties (*xiàn*), 117 autonomous counties (*zìzhìxiàn*), 374 county-level cities (*xiànjíshì*), 852 districts (*shìxiáqū*), 49 banners (*qí*), 3 autonomous banners (*zìzhìqí*), 1 forestry area (*línqū*), and 2 special districts (*tèqū*).

At the township level, there are 14,677 townships (*xiāng*), ethnic townships (*mínzúxiāng*), 19,522 towns (*zhèn*), 6152 subdistricts (*jiēdàobànshìchù*), 11 district public offices (*qūgōngsuǒ*), 181 sumu (*sūmù*) (Mongolian townships), and one ethnic sumu (*mínzúsūmù*).

At the village level, which is much more informal, there are 80,717 neighborhood committees (*jūmínwěiyuánhuì*) and 623,669 village committees (*cūnmínwěiyuánhuì*) or village groups (*cūnmínxiǎozǔ*).

CONTEXT AND CONJUNCTURE

It is apparent that the classifications and definitions of places in these large and complex countries, with their rapidly emerging economies, presents a challenge for comparative analysis. In the case of Brazil, its colonial history and continental position make it more analytically tractable. In the case of China, its rapidly growing economy based on regional growth poles means that at the provincial level there is greater discretion over economic development. With the absorption of Hong Kong as an SAR, in 1997, the Chinese system has been described as 'federalism with Chinese characteristics'. Given a one to five distribution of income and wealth between poorer and richer regions, it means that this form of federalism is currently asymmetrical.

This reinforces the point that the scale and scope of a country, its history and politics, culture and identity, and the trajectory of economic development cross-cut with definitions of place, can make analytical and conceptual classifications difficult. Thus there is a challenge to scholars of urban studies to establish the specificity of their categorizations. Too often neologisms are used whose meanings are neither apparent nor sufficiently explicit to communicate what is being classified. Similarly, one can delineate syllogistic reasoning in a number of propositions: magical urbanism; dead cities; rebel cities; spaces of hope are among, sadly, too many (Davis, 2002; Harvey, 2000).

The traditional Chicago School may have been criticized for being overly functional and empirical, but the lack of an empirical grounding to the classification of places is a weakness of many who would claim a 'post-modern' reading of the urban environment (also see entry on *The Chicago School*). There is an equivalent here to the treatment of nationalism and the nation-state. As Benedict Anderson pointed out in his incisive book, nationalisms are imagined communities that arose with the onset of modernity (Anderson, 1983). In Europe the great empires of the Ottomans and Hapsburgs were undermined by the rise of nationalism and capitalism. A significant outcome is the description of Europe as the 'dark continent' in which its citizens spent the best part of the 20th century engaging in mass genocide on the basis of classifications of ethnicity and identity and viscerally whether communities and individuals conformed to a nationalist straitjacket (Mazower, 1998).

Similarly, the governmental classifications in China and Brazil are an outcome of imperial, colonial and national histories from which their contemporary urban and regional governmental classifications have been formed. In his insights on the imagined communities of nationalisms, Anderson (1983) offers three paradoxes:

1. Modernity versus antiquity in regard to the nation as an objective outcome of modernity against the romantic delusions of traditional nationalists.
2. The subscription to nationalism as a universal socio-cultural concept versus the concrete outcome of being a particular nationality, say, Malian, Malaysian or Maltese.
3. The political power or nationalism versus its lack of philosophical or intellectual coherence in respect of the manifestation of a nation's interest (economic, political, military) set against legitimizing it to a diverse range of citizens (for example, the War on Terrorism and Internet surveillance) that have challenged how these interests are pursued.

Similar arguments and paradoxes can be made for the imagined communities that comprise urban places. Too often urbanists ignore the way in which places represent the historical crossroads of economic and political systems, multiple cultures and identities; insiders and outsiders. However, all these component categories require some empirical measure and not recourse to a set of vague or fashionable conceptions. For example, the revival and promotion of the notion of the city-state has been supported by the intellectual *canard* of urban and regional competitiveness (see Budd and Hirmis (2006) for a critique). As Paul Krugman has pointed out, at the national level 'firms compete, nations don't' and this sentiment equally applies to sub-national as well supra-national places (Krugman, 1994). John Maynard Keynes, the British economist, opined that:

> The ideas of economists and political philosophers, both when they are right and when they are wrong, are more powerful than is commonly understood. Indeed the world is ruled by little else. Practical men, who believe themselves to be quite exempt from any intellectual influence, are usually the slaves of some defunct economist. (Keynes, 1936)

Similarly, many urban and regional political leaders are prisoners of some fashionable (and ultimately defunct) urbanist (be it Richard Florida in his promotion of 'creative classes' for American cities or Walt Rostow's invocation of growth poles taken up in Chinese cities) (Florida, 2002; Rostow, 1960). At least in Rostow's case there is an empirical basis to his growth pole classification, which formed the basis of China's rapid growth since the early 1980s. Similarly, the urban fashionistas should perhaps look to more traditional attempts at classification and definition, as in the case of Lewis Mumford, the American historian, who, writing in 1937, asked *What is a City?* (Mumford, 1937): a starting point for us all.

REFERENCES

Anderson, B. 1983. *Imagined Communities*, London: Verso.

Budd, L. and A. Hirmis. 2006. 'Conceptual Framework For Regional Competitiveness', *Regional Studies*, 38(9): 1015–28.

Davis, M. 2001. *Magical Urbanism: Latinos Reinvent the U.S. City*, London and New York: Verso.

Davis, M. 2002. *Dead Cities*, New York: The New Press.

Florida, R. 2002. *The Rise of the Creative Class: And How It's Transforming Work, Leisure, Community and Everyday Life*, New York: Basic Books.

Harvey, D. 2000. *Spaces of Hope*, Edinburgh: Edinburgh University Press.

Harvey, D. 2012. *Rebel Cities: From the Right to the City to the Urban Revolution*, London and New York: Verso.

Keynes, J.M. 1936. *The General Theory of Employment, Interest, and Money*, London: Macmillan and Co.

Krugman, P. 1994. 'Competitiveness – a Dangerous Obsession', *Foreign Affairs*, March/April, 73(2): 28–44.

Mazower, M. 1998. *Dark Continent*, London: Penguin.

Mumford, L. 1937. 'What is a City?', *Architectural Record*, LXXXII , November, 58–62.

Rostow, W.W. 1960. *The Stages of Economic Growth: A Non-Communist Manifesto*, Cambridge: Cambridge University Press.

Community Development Programs

A community is a group that perceives itself as having strong and lasting bonds, particularly when the group shares a geographic location. One measure of community is regular participation by individuals in its activities. Another is the strength of identification among members with the perceived social bond of the group. A third is the specific physical space and location that is commonly understood as the group's territory. This space provides its own set of material markers to which community members have strong emotional ties.

Often community is discussed in terms of its 'attachments' – the attachment of the individuals who are part of a community to each other and to the physical location; the feeling of belonging to a community. In this sense, the concept 'community' refers to a deep psychological and emotional relationship to a group and/or a particular space. Attachment is also often based upon on race; ethnicity; religion; and gender and sexuality. The original meaning of this term has been attenuated to describe a collectivity (Brubaker, 2005). In the UK, gay and lesbian people are often referred to as a community as though their sexuality implies the same socio-economic, psychological and cultural characteristics. Other groups of individuals, who are excluded from the mainstream of society, may seek to campaign for equal rights by presenting themselves as communities as a political expedient to resolve their grievances, but this does not make them communities in any ecological sense. These and other groups may have common attachments, but this does not mean that their objectives or the realization of their interests mark them out as a homogeneous community.

This concept of community is also used in relation to defining an organized unit of the society that performs certain functions. The so-called 'community' of school teachers would be one example. When this form of the concept is tied to a particular territory by forms of government we have the concept of community as a unit of city, suburban or rural life. The neighborhood sections of the city, for example, are often referred to as 'communities' whether they possess strong social ties and attachments or not. A Community Development Corporation, in the US, is a localized group situated in a particular section of a city and organized to promote economic and social development, while the term 'community policing' refers to programs in which the police work with community residents to address crime.

In the UK, the concept and notion of community is varied and this is reflected in community development programs. In 2010, the Prime Minister, David Cameron, heading the newly formed coalition government, launched *The Big Society*. This initiative, premised on the economics and politics of austerity that asserts that big government has failed, appears to be intellectually vacuous. At the level of programs proposed, there was a central assumption that the non-profit sector would step in and help socially and economically marginalized communities, without state support or underwriting; which is naive (at best) and disingenuous (Charlesworth, 2010).

The concept of community owes much to the ideas of the European sociologist, Ferdinand Tonnies, who wrote in the 1930s. His term for community was *gemein-schaft*, which is a close-knit spatial unit in which tradition, extended family and religion structure social life. This concept was opposed by that of *gesellschaft*, in which impersonal, secondary relations prevailed and which was governed by formal codes of conduct (Tonnies, 1957). Louis Wirth used these ideas to discuss the types of relationships characteristic of urban life (see entry on *The City*) (Wirth, 1938). Today, Tonnies' concept of a traditional community is overused as applicable to modern societies, while the term 'community' is itself so loosely used as to have little specific meaning. According to one observer, there are at least 100 different definitions (Berger, 1978).

Some urbanists today understand that the closely knit network of friendship ties often referred to as 'community' no longer requires a specific spatial location. This concept of 'community without propinquity', as it is sometimes called, means that the way the term is loosely applied to particular sections of the city may be quite misleading in its social, if not political, implications. The concept of community as a far-flung sparsely-knit network of ties stretching beyond the boundaries of neighborhood or kinship solidarities may be more relevant to our society because many people have only the loosest link to their neighbors, yet retain strong family and/or friendship networks. For this expanded definition of community, its essence lies in its social rather than its spatial structure. Rather than being full members of one physical neighborhood, people in contemporary city and suburban environments enjoy limited memberships in multiple social networks extending throughout space. Furthermore, their ties to others are no less strong than that of the more traditional and spatially limited concept of community (see entry on *Neighborhood*).

Perhaps the best example of how community has changed involves the advent of the Internet and the many ways it is used to connect people on a regular basis across the globe. ICT software and e-mail features allow families and friends to remain in constant contact through the virtual space of the Internet. To speak of 'community' in some localized way, as many academics still do, in the face of these new 'space-less' manifestations of social networks may be somewhat absurd. Explorations of urban relations and Internet flows have given rise to the concept of the 'cyber city' (see entry on *The City and Beyond*). We believe this term is misleading, because its use of the term 'city' has no meaning in this context (see entry on the *Multi-Centered Metropolitan Regions*).

The political scientist, Robert D. Putnam, believes that community life has drastically declined in the US, with corresponding disturbing implications. Whereas cities once held out the promise of a wider, higher form of human community, Putnam argues that contemporary urbanites now follow a path of less, not more, civic engagement and that our collective stock of 'Social Capital' – the meaningful human contacts of all kinds that characterize true communities – is so dangerously eroded that it verges on depletion (Putnam, 2000). Putnam uses the concept of 'bowling alone' as a metaphor for the decline of community participation in America. By his measure, the participation of individuals in local bowling leagues, and other localized group organizations, has drastically declined since the 1960s. This, according to Putnam, indicates a general decline in connection to neighborhoods and communities themselves.

For Putnam, the close ties that neighbors have with each other constitute a powerful social resource that he defines as 'social capital'. The more social capital a community possesses, the greater is their ability to preserve and strengthen their way of life in the city. Thus, for followers of Putnam, the decline of urban areas in the US can in part be reversed by strengthening participation in local organizations.

Putnam's argument that people today have much less involvement in politics and local political clubs is extremely well taken. Yet, the concept of neighborhood 'social capital' is not dependent on the scope of local resident participation alone, as he suggests. In many cases, having a few politically influential residents in a given neighborhood is all that is needed for there to be a response by city government to community concerns. Putnam may overrate the power of communal associations. Furthermore, the 'weak ties that bind' in an organizational setting may equally apply to communities that have developed links through digital media (see di Maggio et al. (2001) for analysis of this concept on organizations). For example, the evolution of online learning, Facebook, and so on, can create almost instantaneous, but albeit unstable, community associations.

Putnam's ideas have been transferred across the Atlantic to Europe and have influenced development academics in other parts of the world. Many of the community development programs undertaken in these other contexts attempt to encourage the creation of bridging capital in order to combat the drawbacks of bonding capital, particularly among ethnic minority and deprived economies. Bonding capital is based upon the exclusive social ties of people around homogeneity of, *inter alia*, identity, culture, religion, etc. Bridging capital is based on voluntary associations and horizontal ties based on common interests transcending class, race, ethnicity and heterogeneous differences within and between communities and networks. This form of social capital is derived from linking capital, which is based on vertical relations that help individuals gain access to resources from formal institutions of socio-economic development (Coleman, 1988). This form suggests government intervention of which community development programs are one part.

In Thailand the Urban Community Development Office (UCDO) was set up in 1992 as an organization in charge of managing the Urban Community Development Fund with resources granted by central government. Before 1996, UCDO granted loans to community organizations in a rather scattered way, by dealing directly with individual community groups. Since 1996, the emergence of community networking has brought a new dimension and development vision to the way UCDO operates. Supporting community networks and building up local partnerships to broaden community development activities have become the leading new development directions. While UCDO still supplied and actively supported communities with various kinds of community development loans, UCDO also acted as a facilitator for larger city collaborative development activities. In the period after the East Asian Crisis, community development programs were more orientated to housing and credit and savings provision in city environments (see Budd and Parr (2008) for reflections on this crisis). Community organizations also became more integrated with local authorities as part of the response to the crisis in order to sustain a number of programs. However, the upsurge in political opposition and violence in Bangkok during the 'Red Revolution' of 2010, shows the vulnerability of these kinds of programs to economic and political crisis.

Are civic associations and other community associations on the decline? Perhaps in many areas of the city, but there is an unevenness to this decline. Yet, the overall participation in politics has eroded. If this is what Putnam means by community social capital, then he is right. However, he is wrong if he necessarily believes that people are more isolated today than in previous periods of our history. They may not care much about politics, or even about the bowling leagues that Putnam loves so well, but they continue to have viable social networks and these are most often spread out in space.

The British political scientist, Benedict Anderson, points to the nation-state as a 19th-century phenomenon that has created imagined communities of different nationalities (Anderson, 1983). The concept of social capital is similarly elastic: from the US economist Gary Becker's location of social capital within individuals' choices, to the French social theorist Pierre Bourdieu's location of social capital within networks, particularly the family, giving rise to the potential concentration of 'symbolic capital' in terms of prestige or honor (for example in the marriage potential of children) (Becker, 1964; Bourdieu, 1986).

Cell phone use and Internet e-mail are positive indicators of the persisting close ties among individuals in society, as are sustained social networks that exist without the need for proximity (Graham, 2004). Now, in fact, the surge in the global use of mobile telephony and new forms of ICT and social media, which seem to be ubiquitous these days, facilitate conversations and discussions in virtual space. The death of distance through virtual means, however, is not a new phenomenon. During the English Civil War of the 16th century, scholars formed part of the 'Invisible College': a forum for the exchange of ideas away from the prying eyes and punishment of Cromwell's Puritan order (Wersykey, 1978). The importance of Putnam's community organizations, in short, may be exaggerated. To what extent do localized groups keep social capital alive, or are they simply limited to consumption practices and chit-chat? And, finally, most cities today face a heavy legacy of deindustrialization and the flight of substantial economic resources. These are hardly problems that greater social capital of local neighborhoods can alleviate.

In critiques of contemporary living, such as Putnam's, there is a subtext, an implied assumption, that we need proximity and density for cities and suburbs to work. But this is a premise, derived from Louis Wirth, that is quite out of date in an environment that is termed the information society (Wirth, 1938). Furthermore, there is another and more important counter-trend that is not discussed by Putnam. Since the late 1990s, many urban areas in the advanced economies of the world have joined the 'sustainable city' movement which requires a revival of civic associations and activism in order to promote environmentally sound growth. Portland, Oregon and Chattanooga, Tennessee in the US and cities in Europe like Gdansk are examples of a turnaround in both environmental quality and in civic life (Satterthwaite, 1999).

The problem is particularly acute in the emerging economies, where rapid industrialization and urbanization form a pressing challenge. The combination of air pollution and a lack of clean water is a challenge not only in cities like Taijuan in Chinab or Dhaka in Bangladesh, but some of the poorer parts of cities in more advanced economies when threatened by environmental disasters (New Orleans in 2005, Fukushima in 2011). All these factors threaten socio-economic sustainability as well as the environmental forms. Community clean-up programs are, however, often a response to short-term expedients. Prior to *Expo2010* held in Shanghai, the largest Chinese steelmaker Bao Steel retro-fitted pollution-reducing machinery to its local plants. The more fundamental problem of environmental damage and its long-term effects on citizens' well-being is not being universally pursued in China, given its economic development model (Byrne et al., 1996). This conclusion holds in spite of experiment with creating eco-cities (Hald, 2009).

In this movement, the issue is not a revival of the social basis of neighborhood participation, as it is in Putnam's conception, but the organization of all local residents into a strong force that can push for control of development in order to make their local space a better place to live in. Such values are more important to society than the stress on neighboring chit-chat and common consumption practices that discussions of 'social capital' often entail. The concept of sustainability has entered the global policy environment, as seen in the sub-title of the European Union's *Europe 2020* strategy. But if the concept of sustainability is to be sustained within community development programs, then the complex ecologies of cities and regions have to be recognized in the formulation of these programs.

REFERENCES

Anderson, B. 1983. *Imagined Communities*, London: Verso.

Becker, G. 1964. *Human Capital: A Theoretical and Empirical Analysis, with Special Reference to Education*, Chicago: University of Chicago Press.

Berger, J. 1978. 'Ways of Remembering' in J. Berger, N. Hedges, G. Pritchard, S. Read, E. Barber, B. Jay and D. Lyon, *Camerawork*, no. 10, July, London: Half Moon Photography Workshop.

Bourdieu, P. 1986. 'The Forms of Capital' in J. Richardson (ed.) *Handbook of Theory and Research for the Sociology of Education*, New York: Greenwood. pp. 241–58.

Brubaker, R. 2005. 'The "Diaspora" Diaspora', *Ethnic and Racial Studies*, 28: 1–19.

Budd, L. and J.B. Parr 2008. 'Neglected Aspects of the East Asian Financial Crisis', *Twenty-First Century Society: Journal of the Academy of Social Sciences*, 3(1): 31–48.

Byrne, J., B. Shen and X. Li 1996. 'The Challenge of Sustainability: Balancing China's Energy, Economic and Environmental Goals', *Energy Policy*, 24(5): 455–62.

Charlesworth, L. 2010. 'England's Early "Big Society": Parish Welfare under the Old Poor Law', *History & Policy* (online).

Coleman, J.S. 1988. 'Social Capital in the Creation of Human Capital', *American Journal of Sociology*, 94: 95–120.

Graham, S. 2004. *The Cybercities Reader*, London: Routledge.

Hald, M. 2009. *Sustainable Urban Development and the Chinese Eco-City: Concepts, Strategies, Policies and Assessments*, FNI Report 5/2009 Lysakre: Fridtjof Nansen Institute.

di Maggio, P., Hargittai, E., Neuman, W.R, and Robinson, J.P 2001. 'Social Implications of the Internet', *Annual Review of Sociology*, 27: 307–336.

Putnam, R. 2000. *Bowling Alone: The Collapse and Revival of American Community*, New York: Simon and Schuster.

Satterthwaite, D. 1999. *The Earthscan Reader in Sustainable Cities*, London and Sterling, VA: Earthscan Publications Ltd.

Tonnies, F. 1957. *Community and Society*, East Lansing: Michigan State University Press.

Werskey, G. 1978. *The Invisible College*, London: Allen Lane.

Wirth, L. 1938. 'Urbanism as a Way of Life', *American Journal of Sociology*, 44: 1–24.

Cultures and Lifestyles

Urbanization is a consistent feature of immanent development of late capitalism and modernity. The biannual United Habitat Report, *State of the World's Cities*, notes that, by 2050, 70% of the world's population will be urban dwellers, and, moreover, that mega-cities and mega-regions will dominate the global economy (United Nations, 2013). These forecasts notwithstanding, too many urbanists assume that this process is universal in respect of culture and lifestyle. A Starbucks coffee tastes pretty much the same in Shanghai as in London, but this globalization of beverage standards is often confused with globalization of culture and lifestyle. In the UK, extending the opening hours of pubs and restaurants in the late 1990s was meant to usher in a continental European style 'café society'. Yet the prevailing Friday night culture in many metropolitan areas is binge drinking – something Samuel Johnson the great narrator of London chronicled in the 18th century in his 1738 poem 'London' (Johnson, 2000).

The essential problem of many urbanists is their lack of understanding of the anthropological and sociological roots of examining culture. They have a tendency to lay a homogeneous template over complex and different urban forms. In his book, *Reason and Culture*, the anthropologist Ernst Gellner debates Reason versus Culture by reference to the work of the philosophers Descartes, Hume and Kant (Gellner, 1992). In many accounts of urban culture there is often no reference to reason through any investigation of the material rationality of different places; for example, the role of rent as a special form of surplus value and the real estate sector in the secondary circuits of capital (Gotham, 2006; see entry on *Real Estate*). Similarly, the cultural theorist Raymond Williams has sought to establish a sociology of culture. He points to the convergence of anthropological and sociological constructs of culture based upon two positions (Williams, 1980): first, the manifestation of national aesthetic histories in an institutional setting that represents the interests and values of a people; and, second, the discovery of a general social order by means of identifying its cultural manifestations.

Williams also noted that modernity is directly connected to urbanization, so that this convergence is generally apparent in urban settings. A related issue is the increased professionalization of the production of culture and the manner in which culture is a signifying system that is intrinsic to the economic structure of an economy and its social relations. Too often this point is forgotten by the urban culturalists.

A multiple perspective on culture and urbanization is that identified by Michael Borer that he terms the *Urban Culturalist Perspective* (Borer, 2006). It consists of six domains of research:

1. Images and representations of the city;
2. Urban community and civic culture;
3. Place-based myths, narratives and collective memories;
4. Sentiment and meaning of and for places;
5. Urban identities and lifestyles;
6. Interaction places and practices.

In this view, culture is not just a by-product of the economic and political structures and processes of urban settlements; rather it emphasizes that urban agglomerations are sites of the interaction between individuals' values and meanings in which community engagement can be realized (Borer, 2006). In this perspective urban places have function as well as meaning. This equally applies to the relationship between lifestyles and culture, whereby the function of lifestyles is often expressed in the meaning of local cultures. The danger with this perspective is that it stresses agency often at the expense of structure in that the examples cited overlook the material roots and locations of many of the communities studied.

In the UK, in the 1960s, youth cultures developed a lifestyle based upon African-American urban cultures of music and clothing. Adherents to this style were known as Mods. The lifestyle developed from an adoption of modernity (hence Mods) and as a reaction against a conservative and conformist culture. In particular, rising real wages and opportunities in new industries for young working-class (mainly) males, created cultures of conspicuous consumption. Devotion to this urban-based culture and lifestyle also created a set of meanings and informal practices that went beyond the buying of music and clothes, and that still re-surfaces in different British cities from time to time.

The Beatles first sang 'All You Need is Love' in 1967, while Richard Florida wrote *The Rise of the Creative Class* in 2002. In the latter case, the exposition was almost as simple. All you need is creative individuals to locate in a city for its economic fortunes to be transformed (Florida, 2002). Florida lacks a theory, the evidence is patchy and the data very variable. His argument is part of the design-led urban regeneration discourse. This is based on real estate developments, centered on signature architecture and street landscaping, with bars, restaurants and retail outlets catering for the professional service employees who occupy the commanding heights of commercial real estate. This development encourages forms of appropriating social production and consumption around imagined life-styles, which in themselves provide fertile ground for corporate place promotion and other signifiers (Bell and Jayne, 2004).

The recycling of conspicuous consumption in business and financial districts creates opportunities for developers to create arts quarters, and aesthetic and tourist spaces. It is the latter which is the source of claims about culture and lifestyles being the driver of intentional development in metropolitan areas (see entry on *Gentrification and Urban Redevelopment*). Yet this is a secondary outcome of the primary driver of real estate accumulation strategies. In the case of cities whose propulsive industry (manufacturing, etc.) has disappeared, 'creatives' exploiting low rents are not the condition for revival and redevelopment, as Florida and other creative-boosters claim. The essential problem is that Florida and his acolytes confuse correlation with causation (Peck, 2005). The central issue is that creatives are drawn from professional classes who have higher levels of wealth and income than average. Attracting them to some new previously unexploited area of a metropolitan region does not of itself lead to an increase in regional income and wealth. Moreover, in many cities in the world, bohemian and creative lifestyles (whatever their meaning) are marginal. The rise of the use of unpaid interns and unstable short-term freelance work contracts in the 'creative industries' (sic) in London is one example. The political repression of Pussy Riot in Moscow is another that makes Florida's creative arcadia seem fanciful. These are the kinds of claims that the urban culturalist perspective is critical of in that the creative classes thesis rest upon a functionalist view of how these classes transform a place without reference to the meanings and values inherent in the cultures and lifestyles of a place.

There is also a complete mis-specification of creative classes. In all cities around the world, their histories are replete with immigrant communities who have transformed downtowns. In the US, after the Balkans War of the 1990s, a large number of Bosnians escaped the conflict by migrating to the downtown of St Louis, helping to revive some its former dynamism. In other literatures, this would be called entrepreneurialism – you pay your money and take your choice of discourse.

Once you begin to look at the urban informal economy, a rather different creative and lifestyle economy begins to emerge. John Rennie Short distinguishes different kinds of informal economy in the 'urban order'. These include the *illegal informal economy*, the *communal economy* and the *domestic economy* (Rennie Short, 1996). All these forms have creativity at their heart, but as they encompass marginal populations they appear below the radar for the creative class promoters like Florida and his ilk. It is clear that in the ghettos, the slums and the barrios, a relatively high degree of creativity is needed to survive. Moreover, many metropolitan areas survive on a reserve army of an underclass, displayed dramatically in the film *Slum Dog Millionaire* set in Mumbai. Similarly, a number of *favelas* in Brazilian cities are developing themselves as tourist destinations. The Santa Marta favela in Rio de Janeiro attracts 40,000 visitors a year. Once a violent zone for drugs wars, it was 'pacified' in 2008 with the installation of a Pacifying Police Unit. Consequently, the means and values of this community have altered as its culture and lifestyle have adapted in an apparently creative manner. However, lionized by business magazine like *Forbes* as a zone for entrepreneurial opportunities, the material reality of the drugs economy and state enforcement of pacification are never far away.

It is the material basis of urbanization and not its aesthetic manifestation per se that establishes culture and lifestyles, and thus it ever was. This point is admirably demonstrated in James Boswell's *London Journal* written in the late 18th century. This intimate account of daily life in London has become a classic as it portrays the lifestyles and culture of an imperial city near the height of its power (Boswell, 1992).

REFERENCES

Bell, D. and M. Jayne (eds) 2004. *City of Quarters: Urban Villages in the Contemporary City*, Aldershot: Ashgate.

Borer, M.I. 2006. 'The Location of Culture: The Urban Culturalist Perspective', *City & Community*, 5(2): 173–97.

Boswell, J. 1992. *The Journals of James Boswell: 1762–1795*, New Haven and London: Yale University Press.

Florida, R. 2002. *The Rise of the Creative Class: And How It's Transforming Work, Leisure and Everyday Life*, New York: Basic Books.

Gellner, E. 1992. *Reason and Culture*, Oxford: Blackwell Publishers.

Gotham, K. 2006. 'Reconsidered: Globalization and the US Real Estate Sector', *American Journal of Sociology*, 112(1): 231–75.

Johnson, S. 2000. *Major Works*, Oxford: Oxford University Press.

Peck, J. 2005. 'Struggling with the Creative Class', *International Journal of Urban and Regional Research*, 29(4): 740–70.

Rennie Short, J. 1996. *The Urban Order: An Introduction to Urban Geography*, Oxford: Blackwell Publishers.

United Nations 2013. *State of the World's Cities 2012/2013: Prosperity of Cities*, New York: United Nations.

Williams, R. 1980. *Problems in Materialism and Culture: Selected Essays*, London: Verso.

De-Territorialization and Re-Territorialization

Recently, urbanists have been concerned about large-scale migrations of particular people as a result of war, famine, political oppression, religious intolerance and enduring poverty. This phenomenon is referred to as 'de-territorialization' and often the people themselves are known as 'refugees'. When such mass movements of people are accompanied by the persisting organization of daily life centered on cultural practices of the place of origin, urbanists refer to this phenomenon as 're-territorialization'. These twin aspects are important topics for an understanding of changes in the ethnic composition of urban places throughout the world since World War II because of the profound impact that modern political unrest, global economic changes and warfare have had on local peoples (Appadurai, 1996).

The processes of de- and re-territorialization can be illustrated by the effect of the Holocaust on European Jewry. As a consequence of mass murders and mass dislocations of Jews within the nations of Europe attacked by the German Nazi regime, age-old aspirations for a specific Jewish homeland in the ancient Holy Land, known as Zionism, were given world-wide credence and power resulting in the creation of a Jewish State – Israel – in 1948. The de-territorialization of radically diverse ethnic groups, all of whom were Jews, in both European and Middle Eastern countries, resulted in a subsequent re-territorialization or in-gathering within the State of Israel and a consequent, and qualitatively new, emergent culture once this process was institutionalized.

Unfortunately, many de-territorialized ethnic and religious groups have only experienced limited success in re-territorializing, if at all. Among these people, the Tibetans are one of the most long-suffering. After the Chinese invasion of Tibet in 1950 and the consequent crackdown on Tibetan religion and culture, a steady stream of refugees escaped to other countries, principally India. Arriving in foreign locations, religious leaders have recreated centers of Tibetan culture on a limited basis, such as the community in Darjeeling. Tibetans, however, can be found in many countries around the globe. For the most part they remain de-territorialized because, having once possessed their own country, they now find themselves living elsewhere and without a state of their own. This makes their case more politically extreme, if not as harsh, as other refugee groups that have been de-territorialized in modern times but who have never possessed a state of their own, such as the Palestinians, Biafrans or Kurds. Nevertheless, the latter groups, as well as many others that have large populations in other lands, but which retain a certain level of ethnic identity, are examples of the displacement of people on a mass basis and on a world scale characteristic of 20th-century upheavals.

In other cases, refugees in large numbers can transform cities. This has been true of Miami, Florida, after the Castro-led revolution in Cuba. An area once called 'Little Havana' became too small to contain all the Cubans fleeing their native land. In the process, the city of Miami, once a curious blend of white and black southerners mixed together with predominantly retired Jews from the north, became Hispanic (Portes and Stepick, 1993).

In the UK, migration from the former Commonwealth countries (the successor of the old colonial empire) has transformed British cities. The ebb and flow of finance and population between the colonial core and former dependent territories has been a feature of globalization since the 17th century. Now London contains over 300 different languages. Some ethnic communities have moved from the urban core to the suburbs as they have flourished economically, just as they have in the US. In other cases, the de-territorialization of many ethnic groups, for example in the Balkans or in Afghanistan, has led to re-territorializing many parts of European cities. The failure of host cities to fully absorb these populations and their failure to share the socio-economic benefits of the larger society has made many of their young men susceptible to recruitment by criminal groups and even terrorist organizations. The culture of Paris, for example, has been altered forever by the influx of immigrants from former North African colonies.

The issues of de- and re-territorialization for people from Asia, Africa, the Middle East and Latin America are also linked to contemporary processes of immigration and globalization, colonialism and post-colonialism. See the entries on *Globalization and Meltdown* and *Immigration, Migration and Demography* for more information.

REFERENCES

Appadurai, A. 1996. *Modernity at Large: Cultural Dimensions of Globalization*, Minneapolis, MN: University of Minnesota Press.

Portes, A. and A. Stepick, 1993. *City on the Edge: The Transformation of Miami*, Berkeley, CA: University of California Press.

Financial and Fiscal Crises

Financial crises are endemic to capitalist economies and appear to be closely related to real estate development and speculation (Krugman, 2003; Roach, 2009) (see entry on *Real Estate*). The roots of the credit crunch and subsequent crisis and recession, beginning in late 2007, lay in the sub-prime market in the US, leading to the effective economic implosion of cities like Detroit. Similarly, the 1997 East Asian Crisis came out of speculative commercial real estate development and speculation and the consequences of how it was financed. Even nearly fifteen years on cities like Bangkok and Manila are suffering from a serious overhang of commercial real estate developments. The US$9.5 billion bailout of Dubai World, the major development company in Dubai in late 2009 by some of the United Arab Emirates governments due to real estate speculation on a massive scale is another manifestation (*Times of India*, 2009). We also see signs of the crisis in the rise of Chinese cities, accompanied by an explosion in urban development, as the country seeks to build its world market share. At the end of 2014 China's debt accounted for over 250% of the country's production, up from 147% in 2008 and marking a record high. The ratio has grown 34% over the past five years, sparking concerns about the country's future, since the United States saw growth of roughly 30% immediately prior to the 2008 crisis. The rapid increase in the price of housing is a major warning of a possible financial crisis, according to many financial analysts. The average house price in China's cities grew 113% between 2004 and 2012 compared to 84% growth in the United States between 2001 and 2006 (*Want China Times*, 2013).

Ultimately the argument that the root causes of financial crisis are found in real estate development is persuasive on the grounds of size in that over 90% of net wealth in the world's largest economy is tied to real estate (Case and Schiller, 1988; Fenn and Cole, 2008). One of the problems with the analysis of financial crises and the justification of austerity in response to fiscal crises is the misunderstanding and misspecification of financial markets, assets and their measurement. For example, market capitalization is merely the number of stocks of a company multiplied by the price they are traded at in any one moment, while turnover of trading in stocks in markets, for example the New York Stock Exchange, is a measurement of activity on these markets. Too many politicians and academics proclaim changes in these measures as being some signifier of apocalyptic change in the global economy, when they are essentially comparatively static accounting changes to fit particular circumstances. In a financial crash, all stock prices fall rapidly and vice versa.

What was exceptional about the financial crisis that began in late 2007 was that it was so explicable and hence acts as an exemplar of financial crises in general. A catenation of events came together to burst a financial bubble and bury the myth that the business cycle (boom and bust) had been conquered once and for all. The litany of financial crises includes, among others: 17th-century Tulip mania; the 18th-century South Sea Bubble; railway booms in Europe and the US in the 19th century; the 20th-century Great Crash and East Asian Crisis; and the dot. com crash at the turn of the millennium. These crises represent the pantheon of this self-evident fact (Budd and Parr, 2008; Goldgar, 2007; Kindleberger, 1984; Sprague, 2009). Will it happen again? Almost certainly, only the timing, scale and scope will be unknown until the crisis is upon us.

There appear to be some general rules about the nature of conditions from which financial crises will develop, and those prevailing in the world's largest economy, the US, at the onset of the 2007 crisis were no different. These include: a large trade deficit; a large fiscal deficit, which is mainly funded externally; and very overvalued currency. The underlying processes that allowed these conditions to be fulfilled included the following (Budd, 2012):

- Global imbalances between creditor and debtor nations reinforced the role of the US as the consumer of last resort in fuelling global demand. This was underpinned by large external and internal deficits of the US funded by countries with large trade surpluses, such as China, who bought private and public US$ denominated assets.
- Global imbalances fuelled commodity and other asset booms, as financial institutions sought to exploit the rising demand for natural resources in the emerging economies.
- A global deflationary environment brought about the expansion in the supply of goods produced in the emerging economies which lowered the cost of capital and encouraged financial institutions to seek higher investment returns from riskier assets.
- Regulatory changes, for example governments in the US and parts of Europe encouraging the extension of home ownership and financial de-regulation including the scrapping of the *Glass-Steagall Act* (introduced in the US after the Great Crash of 1929), which had separated the functions of commercial and investment banks, encouraged more speculative behavior.
- A low cost of capital encouraged financial institutions to lend to consumers with low creditworthiness and encourage them to apply for mortgages they had no hope of repaying. In the US, these loans to this section of the population

became known as 'Ninjas': no income, no job and no assets. The assumption was that a continuing rise in house prices would generate a wealth effect that could be capitalized into an income stream that would cover loan repayments.

- The bundling and mixing of mortgage-backed assets (especially Ninja ones), with different risk profiles, to produce new financial assets (for example, Structured Investment Vehicles (SIVs) and Collateralized Debt Obligations (CDOs)), which were sold by investment banks with the highest credit ratings.

For many commentators the bankruptcy of Lehman Brothers, in September 2008, tipped the global economy into recession. The turning point of the whole financial crisis rests on what is called a 'Minsky Moment', named after the late American economist, Hyman Minsky (Minsky, 1993). He developed a five-stage model of financial crises:

1. *Displacement:* An external shock leads to profitable opportunities in one sector leading to a boom, for example the dot.com and commodities booms;
2. *Boom:* Expansion in money supply leading to rapid expansion of channels of credit, which in turn creates opportunities for speculative investment;
3. *Over-trading:* Over-trading in financial assets created by over-borrowing and over-investment;
4. *Revulsion:* The perception that the top of market has been reached leads to large and rapid selling of assets which creates a stampede and mania leading to crisis and panic;
5. *Tranquillity:* The lender of last resort role of central banks and government monetary easing creates the perception that the crisis can be managed.

The Minsky Moment occurs between stages three and four, but we can add two more stages which appear to describe current circumstances:

6. *Retribution:* The 'fictional' markets created among the financial institutions themselves through new instruments (SIVs, etc.) are in free-fall. This leads to a blame game aimed at central banks, as they exercised their lender of last resort function and the financial regulators rapidly reached their limits. The financial system descends into chaos as the new instruments unravel because the underlying assets are found to be close to worthless;
7. *Revisionism:* The ideology is promoted that it is not market irrationality but 'Big Government' that is distorting market behavior, creating the potential inflationary impulse of a rise in budget deficits and national debts as the state underwrites the losses incurred in the system. The financial institutions at the heart of the crisis seek to return to 'business as usual' (Budd, 2012).

Part of the 'business as usual' ideology includes the assumption that banks can take public money and run by deciding who they will lend to, irrespective of governmental support and pressure. The total public support for the global financial system, including capital injections, government guarantees, asset purchases and liquidity provisions, reached 29% of total world income in 2008 (International Monetary Fund (IMF), 2010). Estimates at the end of 2014 suggest that US$4 trillion was spent by governments in the world's leading economies bailing out the financial system (IMF, 2014).

The emerging economies of Russia and China escaped relatively lightly from the consequences of the global recession of 2008/09, except for the impact of lower demand for exports in the case of the latter. But, both economies are engaged in the over-production of the built environment and neither is a full market economy nor has an internationally convertible currency. In the event of them fulfilling the latter characteristic, the former may provide the ingredients for future crises. Similarly, the attempt in the Gulf States in the Middle East to create a post-oil development path through a real estate-based strategy has been undermined by the financial crisis (see the *Global Cities and Regionalization* entry)

Fiscal crises occur because of a tendency for a structural gap to appear between state expenditure and state revenues. The 'fiscal crisis of the state' was a term conceived of by Joseph O'Connor and manifested in the fiscal crisis of New York in 1975 (O'Connor, 1973). These kinds of crises evolve from the twin roles of the capitalist state: to facilitate capital accumulation and to legitimate the accumulation process. The state achieves this in two ways: socializing the cost of social consumption and that of social investment. The former encompasses welfare systems and expenditure on goods such as education and health, which would be under-provided by private capital. The latter includes infrastructure such as transport links, utilities and, very importantly, the urban built environment.

The development of what seems to be a financial mode of production and associated processes and institutionalization during the latter part of the 20th century appears to have expanded the role of the state in socializing the costs of risk of capital (Budd, 1995). The variety of state rescue programs aimed at ameliorating the impact of the recent global credit crunch and financial crisis is a manifestation of this extended role. This issue is pertinent to the relationship between the financial system and the real economy. Many public commentators and politicians had assumed that the credit crunch could be contained within the financial system and only bear marginally on the real economy. They could be forgiven for this fundamental misunderstanding of how market economies operate because the growth of a financial mode of production and financialization had created the impression that the financial economy had spun-off from the real one. This bears doubly on urban development and sustainability.

Fiscal crises are symptoms of the general decline in city economies. This pattern has been visible since the 1950s as a consequence of metropolitan deconcentration and the shift of people and industries both to suburbia and the sun belt. Because those areas, in turn, grew rapidly, they too suffered a fiscal crisis and an inability to fund adequate infrastructure and public services. The massive shifts in population began in the 1950s. Propped up by state and federal programs, it took over 20 years for the shortfalls in revenue to make themselves felt in a noticeable way. But, when that occurred, in the 1970s, it became clear that both cities and suburbs suffered from the inability to provide the kind of services and quality of life that most Americans and Europeans desired. The fall of communism in Europe and the rapid development of cities and regions in the emerging economies, suggest that this pattern will be continually repeated.

If you want evidence of this symbiotic relationship between financial and fiscal crises and their urban manifestation you only have to look at metropolitan regions and real estate developments within them. In 2010 Meredith Whitney, the US research analyst, predicted that 100 US cities faced bankruptcy, with debts totaling $2.1 trillion (about the size of the British economy) (*The Guardian*, 2010). According to the magazine *Governing: The States and Localities*, there have been 47 city bankruptcies since 2010, with Atlantic City possibly filing in 2015 after its bonds were downgraded to junk status. Similarly, we find a number of Chinese local governments are effectively bankrupt because of urban over-development.

The largest municipal default in US history is Detroit with pension liabilities of $9.2 billion, $1.9 billion owed to creditors and $18.5 billion total debt (at 2013 prices). Eight other cities are on the verge of bankruptcy, including California's two largest and Baltimore, the setting for the intelligent and insightful TV series *The Wire*, that documented the city's decline. All eight share an unemployment rate above 10% – the consequence of economic decline exacerbated by the financial crisis. In Europe, local and regional government debt was set to peak at US$1.9 trillion in 2010 but has increased further. At the end of 2012, Spain's 17 regions were €42 billion in debt (25% of GDP).

In Europe, there are different forms of fiscal multi-governance, with cities and regions depending on debt issuance or local taxes, but their fiscal room for manoeuver is constrained by the central state. Consequently, in attempting to manage the fall-out from the financial crisis of 2007, the ensuing fiscal crisis is borne most heavily by urban areas and impacts most strongly on the urban form. This was exacerbated by the fiscal rules underlying the Eurozone – the single currency area of the European Union that limits the total debt to GDP ratio to 60% and a budget deficit to GDP ratio to 3%. But in 2012, in the zone, sovereign debt/GDP varied, from 148% and 127%, in Greece and Italy respectively, to less than 60% in Finland, the Slovak Republic and Slovenia. The problem in the advanced economies of Europe is the pursuit of austerity *qua* austerity to pay down public debt. The cost to governments of bailing out the banks has been huge. For the main countries involved, it is estimated by the International Monetary Fund (IMF) that the cost of direct support initially exceeded $1.5 trillion, equivalent to at least 5% of global GDP, rising in 2015 to $4 trillion, as stated above. In the case of the Netherlands, Ireland and Germany more than 10% of their combined GDP was spent (Kitson et al., 2011). The Troubled Asset Recovery Program (TARP) and other rescue measures in the US, the quantitative easing program in the UK, and the European Union-wide packages amounted to US$300 trillion (at 2008 prices) (IMF, 2010). However, some of these amounts are what can be termed 'funny money' – in that they represent financial guarantees, similar to insurance policies, and the money may never have been spent.

Moreover, the full and partial nationalization of banks and financial institutions in the developed economies suggest that forms of state directed and managed, formal and informal intermediation of the financial system are important. Yet, metropolitan regions in the US and Europe are allowed effectively to go the wall, with severe consequences for their citizens, in pursuit of a failed ideological project. In many emerging economies, the knock-on effects have also been very severe. In these economies rapid urbanization, steep increases in the price of real estate and unstable state-supported financial systems are creating the same heady mix experienced elsewhere (Reuters, 2013).

It has taken a global financial crisis to remind us that just as these crises are endemic to capitalist economies, so the accompanying fiscal crisis is endemic to metropolitan regions, with all its consequences for urban economies, communities and cultures. The experience of urban regions in the European Union in late 2013, as the economics and politics of austerity bore down on them, stands as a testament to pursuing a false ideology of fiscal fetishism. There is a certain irony here in that the state creates money in capitalist economies, yet there is a visceral reaction against public debt, with it being viewed as some kind of signifier of a society's morality. This anthropological and cultural reaction goes back centuries to pre-modern times, but the aversion to increased public debt within modern capitalism results in perverse outcomes (Graeber, 2011). In their analysis of the history of financial crises, the US economists, Reinhart and Rogoff, claim that once total public debt reaches 90% of GDP, then an economy will no longer be sustainable at these levels (Reinhart and Rogoff, 2009). Fiscal conservatives and their supporters banded around this ratio as some eternal truth of economics. A smart grad student pointed out errors in their estimations to derive this result, yet this proof did not stop the revisionism.

The consequences of financing rapid over-production of the built environment are readily apparent in the peripheral economies of the European Union. The booming cities of Dublin, Cork and Limerick in Ireland soon went bust as their own local sub-prime crisis took hold. A similar pattern emerged in Spanish cities, for example Valencia, where real estate development, fuelled by a financial bubble, became relatively worthless as the crisis took hold. The legacy of these outcomes can be seen in the ongoing crisis of the Eurozone currency area, in which banks of the core economies underwrote speculative real estate projects. The government bail-out of the rentiers financing this development led directly to the fiscal crisis and the possibility of both countries defaulting on their sovereign debt. It has been argued that the 21st century will be a Chinese rather than American dominated one (Eichengreen, 2012). If this is case, and it remains doubtful, then the lessons of the century of American metropolitan regions should learned in respect of financial and fiscal crises and their relationship to real estate development. The conclusion is that fiscal crises afflicting cities and regions around the world could be relieved by state action, yet the ideology of structural adjustment through market reform and austerity constrain this possibility.

REFERENCES

Budd, L. 1995. 'Globalisation, Territory and Strategic Alliances in Different Financial Centres', *Urban Studies*, 32(2): 345–60.

Budd, L. 2012. 'Re-regulating the Financial System: The Return of State or Societal Corporatism?', *Contemporary Social Science: Journal of the Academy of Social Sciences*, 7(1): 1–19.

Budd, L. and J.B. Parr 2008. 'Neglected Aspects of the East Asian Financial Crisis', *21st Century Society*, 3(1): 31–48.

Case, K.E. and R.J. Schiller 1988. 'The Behaviour of Home Buyers in Boom and Post-boom Markets', *New England Economic Review*, 83–92.

Eichengreen, B. 2012. 'China's Century or America's?', *East Asia Forum* 15/04/13. Available at: http://www.eastasiaforum.org/2012/04/15/china-s-century-or-america-s/ (accessed 18 November 2013).

Fenn, G.W. and R.A. Cole 2008. 'The Role of Commercial Real Estate Investments in the Banking Crisis of 1985–92', *SSRN Working Paper Series*, 1 November (Boston, MA, Social Science Research Network). Available at: http://papers.ssrn.com/sol3/papers.cfm?abstract_id=1293473 (accessed 1 April 2009).

Goldgar, A. (2007) *Tulipmania: Money, Horror and Knowledge in the Dutch Golden Age*, Chicago, IL: University of Chicago Press.

Graeber, D. 2011. *Debt: The First 5000 Years*, Brooklyn, NY: Melville House.

The Guardian 2010. '$2tn Debt Crisis Threatens to Bring Down 100 US Cities', 20 December. Available at: http://www.theguardian.com/business/2010/dec/20/debt-crisis-threatens-us-cities (accessed 24 December 2010).

International Monetary Fund (IMF) (2010) *Global Financial Stability Report: Meeting New Challenges to Stability and Building a Safer System*, Washington, DC: International Monetary Fund.

International Monetary Fund (IMF) (2014) *World Economic Outlook (WEO) Legacies, Clouds, Uncertanties*, Washington, DC: International Monetary Fund.

Kindleberger, C. 1984. *A Financial History of Western Europe*, Oxford: Oxford University Press.

Kitson, M., R. Martin and P. Tyler 2011. 'The Geographies of Austerity', *Cambridge Journal of Regions, Economics and Society*, 4(3): 289–302.

Krugman, P. 2003. *The Great Unraveling*, London: Penguin.

Minsky, H.P. 1993. *Stabilizing an Unstable Economy*, New York: McGraw-Hill.

O'Connor, J. 1973. *The Fiscal Crisis of the State*, New York: St Martin's Press.

Reinhart, C.M. and K.S. Rogoff 2009. *This Time is Different: Eight Centuries of Financial Follies*, Princeton, NJ: Princeton University Press.

Reuters 2013. 'China Faces Social, Financial Risks in Urbanization Push', London: Reuters. Available at: http://www.reuters.com/article/2013/03/07/us-china-parliament-urbanisation-idUSBRE92607K20130307 (accessed 18 November 2013).

Roach, S.S. 2009. *The Next Asia: Opportunities and Challenges for a New Globalization*, Hoboken, NJ: Wiley.

Sprague, O.M. 2009. *History of Crises Under the National Banking System*, Charleston: BibiloBazaar.

Times of India 2009. 'Dubai Debt Fears Hit World Markets Hard', *Times of India*, 26 November. Available at: http://timesofindia.indiatimes.com/business/international-business/Dubai-debt-fears-hit-world-markets-hard/articleshow/5272611.cms#ixzz12446M9m0/ (accessed 18 November 2013).

Want China Times (2013) 'Signs of Financial Crisis Evident in China: Economists'. Available at: http://www.wantchinatimes.com/news-subclass-cnt.aspx?id=20130322000081&cid=1202 (accessed 18 November 2013).

Gendered Spaces

The masculine and the feminine, as cultural qualities, are related to each other in the form of superordinate/subordinate relations. Men possess power in our society that is manifested as the ability to define situations and to control social outcomes.

Often, men are situated in the positions of leadership and control in the powerful organizations of the economy and the political structure. This hierarchically structured system of gendered dominance is manifested in urban space and practices.

Thus, spaces within our built environment are gendered. Places that can be characterized as 'masculine spaces' facilitate the expression of male-biased activities and power. Produced by material as well as non-material aspects of society, gendered spaces exhibit biases towards one or another sex. Aspects of the material environment, such as masculine associated theming in a sports bar, help define the space according to dominant gender use. Behaviors that are socially acceptable within that same space, or which are not easily sanctioned according to gender, comprise the non-material social practices that also help define dominant gender use. Together these two dimensions articulate with social practices creating a 'gendered space'.

Importantly, the gendering of urban space can be challenged. Koskela (1997) studies how the 'bold' street behavior of women in the Scandinavian context broadens their night-time spatial rights and builds self-confidence. Koskela shows that fear is socially constructed. If the fear is negotiated, a confident appropriation and possession of previously 'masculine' urban space is actually possible for women. In her classical text on gendered spaces, Wilson (1991: 7–8) suggests that:

> ... male and female 'principles' war with each other at the very heart of city life. The city is 'masculine' in its triumphal scale, its towers and vistas and arid industrial regions; it is 'feminine' in its enclosing embrace, in its indeterminacy and labyrinthine uncentredness. We might even go so far as to claim that urban life is actually based on this perpetual struggle between rigid, routinised order and pleasurable anarchy, the male-female dichotomy.

While such a 'dichotomy' may be exaggerated, Wilson correctly points towards the possibilities for 'alternative' living arrangements in cities – the advantages of anonymity, spontaneity and freedom associated with the city in contrast to suburb or countryside. She asserts that these are important liberating and empowering qualities for women. For Wilson, women are not 'victims' of urbanization, but rather its beneficiaries.

FEMININE SPACE

The subordinate social status of women produces environments where females have power. These are examples of 'feminine space' (Spain, 1992). Consider the following observations by Lara Zador (2001: 1):

> My notion of womanhood is tied to space, I have a fear of taking up too much space as though space is masculine and the more feminine I am, the less space I consume ... My anorexic friend sent me a note apologizing for the size of the letters she used, she was sorry for taking up so much space with her words. Women only shout when they say 'NO', which means no when a very private space is about to be violated – one of the only spaces women can call their own.

The exploration of feminine space includes representational or virtual spaces. It is possible to speak of a 'feminine space' in literature, in films, in advertising. Ellen McCracken (1999) discusses how the religious space of the Catholic Church is re-interpreted by Latina authors and expropriated in the syncretistic practice of Santería. This is a case common to women in their response to the male domination of space. Environments themselves are not changed; their symbolism and significance are only altered by the different, subversive reading of feminist discourse. The significance of such writing is that it acknowledges the importance of spatial transformation as well as symbolic re-readings in the critical practice of feminism.

The voice of women has been heard but little recognized and rarely acknowledged in architecture and urban planning. Dolores Hayden's (1981) path-breaking book details the contribution of women to design in homes, cities and suburbs. Women's roles were defined as stay-at-home housewives in the 1920s, after once participating actively in the industrial labor force. This shift to the middle class made the domestic kitchen and the single family suburban home the new environmental domain of women. Today's suburban culture, especially styles in automobiles, reflect the persistence of the mothering role for many middle-class women who also must chauffer their children to everyday suburban activities in environments relatively devoid of mass transportation. It may still be possible to say that large supermarkets, shopping malls and the middle-class, single family home are examples of 'feminine space'.

According to the Matrix Collective (1984), control by women over the decoration of the single family home has enabled them to express themselves and to influence others by their environmental choices. This milieu stands in contrast to the space outside that is and remains controlled by men. As Benard and Schlaffer (1993: 338) remark about the street:

> Whether you wear a slit skirt or are covered from head to foot in a black Chador, the message is not that you are attractive enough to make a man lose his self-control, but that the public realm belongs to him and you are there by his permission as long as you follow his rules and as long as you remember your place.

These spatial distinctions play a significant role in the continued socialization of young people into separate gender roles that reproduce society's gender bias. There are other disadvantages to society revealed by a spatial analysis sensitive to gender:

> Community planning invariably assigns the major portion of open space to traditionally male-dominated activities, such as sports. Places for mothering are rarely considered at all, and often are restricted to playgrounds. Creating safe environments for children and mothers requires some planning. In Columbia, MD, one of the totally planned New Towns in the US, pedestrian and automobile traffic are separated by the segregation of space. This feature of Columbia makes it easier for mothers to protect children at play. (Gottdiener and Hutchison, 2000: 167)

Other countries, such as those in Scandinavia, make explicit provision in public space and on public transportation for mothers with children. Their cities are safer for them than are ours.

MASCULINE SPACE

Masculine spaces are places where traditionally men have congregated more commonly than women and where males are at a distinct advantage regarding the deployment of power. Bars are excellent examples, as are sports stadiums, although places like restaurants where men and women act out typical dominant/subordinate social roles also qualify. The offices of white collar labor have long been associated with male dominance and can also be considered masculine spaces. In fact, in most of the corporate world, if not virtually all of it, men resist the 'feminization' of office decor and interior design. A final and graphic example of a 'masculine space' would be any public mass audience facility within which the equal numbers of bathrooms for the sexes painfully obscures the fact that women need many more times the amount of bathroom space when they are among a crowd than do men. The pathetically long lines of women outside their restrooms at up-scale classical concert halls illustrates this negative bias perfectly.

There is an implicit understanding that the domestic realm is a feminine space while places of action and public meeting are masculine ones. Yet, typically male gendered spaces have recently been under attack by female attendance and transformation (Petty, 2003):

> To a great extent, the Western male has been driven out of spaces once considered exclusively male. The workplace, the pub and the club are all spaces that have seen an increasing level of female participation and inclusion.

According to this report, however, the increasing 'bisexuality' of previously male-gendered spaces has contributed to the redefinition of maleness that reinforces excessively masculine traits:

> The erosion of the exclusively male space of the past and the failure to redefine new, healthy spaces for men has led to a redefinition of masculinity that is overtly sexual, aggressive and, at times, violent ... The ideal male, no longer the SNAG (Sensitive New Age Guy) of the mid-nineties, is now the aggressive 'new lad' popularized by such magazines as *Maxim* and *FHM*, and re-enforced through sports culture, schools, television and music. (Petty, 2003)

Now, as real masculine spaces retreat under social pressure to have them accommodate both sexes, virtual masculine spaces of a certain, exaggerated kind have proliferated in movies, magazines, virtual video games, 'extreme' sports and on television (see for example, Comedy Central's *The Man Show*, as well as all the ultra-violent or extreme video games on the market that are played through the home TV set). One cannot be physically present in these virtual spaces, but they do reproduce the exclusively male discourse, albeit in an exaggerated and, most certainly, an alienated fashion. Petty concludes the assessment of the disappearance of masculine spaces in our society with the following:

This is not a call for exclusive men's clubs, segregating boys and girls in the classroom, or creating a new gender hierarchy. It is, however, a cry for constructive definitions of masculine identity, and the provision of venues (cultural, literary, political) in which men are encouraged to examine their masculinity in honest, unclouded terms. The disappearing man is being replaced by what is increasingly becoming a walking penis with fists. A troubling sight indeed. (Petty, 2003)

The above observations are interesting precisely because they introduce the important concept that spaces in our culture are both real and virtual (see entries on *Nightscapes and Urban Escapades* and *Social Production of Space*). However, the claim that, actually, existing environments are increasingly bi-sexually controlled, may be an exaggeration. Societies still invest men with the power to dominate. That fact alone implies that, in most spaces, it is male-biased activities and influence that will prevail. Thus, the creation in society of spaces that are uniquely feminine or which cater to the sensitivities and needs of children, for example, remains an important consideration in social planning.

REFERENCES

Benard, D. and E. Schlaffer 1993. 'The Man in the Street: Why He Harasses' in L. Richardson and V. Taylor (eds) *Feminist Frontiers III*, New York: McGraw-Hill. pp. 338–91.

Gottdiener, M. and R. Hutchison 2000. *The New Urban Sociology, 2nd Edition*, New York: McGraw-Hill.

Hayden, D. 1981. *The Grand Domestic Revolution*, Cambridge, MA: MIT Press.

Koskela, H. 1997. 'Bold Walk and Breakings: Women's Spatial Confidence Versus Fear of Violence', *Gender, Place and Culture*, 4(3) 301–19.

Matrix Collective 1984. *Making Space*, London: Pluto Press.

McCracken, E. 1999. *New Latina Narrative: The Feminine Space of Postmodern Ethnicity*, Tuscon, AZ: University of Arizona Press.

Petty, J. 2003. *Entrepot*, 1 (1 January 2003).

Spain, D. 1992. *Gendered Spaces*, Chapel Hill, NC: University of North Carolina Press.

Wilson, E. 1991. *The Sphinx in the City*, London: Virago.

Zador, L. 2001. www.soapboxgirls.com, April.

Gentrification and Urban Redevelopment

This process involves the inflow of capital investment into the real estate of an already existing place in a metropolitan region whose values are depressed. Related to the decay of place, both gentrification and urban redevelopment (or 'renewal') are cycles of capital investment in urban real estate. Gentrification in the US and many parts of Europe is usually characterized by the convergence of apartments into condominiums (studios) and the renovation of select homes in a specific area. As more upscale residents move in, candle-lit restaurants and stores catering to people with higher incomes displace convenience and bargain shopping stores. Rents rise as landlords realize they can attract professionals and business people as tenants. Older residents on limited incomes then have to move out. In London, the predominance of owner-occupation has seen the professional classes appropriate large three-floor Victorian houses or developers convert them into apartments and studios. The combination of predominant owner-occupation and the widespread cosmopolitan nature of London makes it more complex than its US counterparts (Hebbert, 1998). However, quite large tenure changes, from low-income private rental to higher-income owner-occupation, have been a consistent feature of gentrification over the last 30 years. In other UK cities, competition for international sporting and cultural events, for example the Olympics, Commonwealth Games, the European City of Culture, city marketing and the location of cultural centers has led to a rise in gentrification in the last 10 years. The central agency of this change has been real estate interests marketing waterside developments and associated lifestyles to urban professionals. Waterside developments appear to be a consistent feature of contemporary gentrification in most cities, for example Sydney.

> The housing market tends to sort the population by income into different areas. Racism may add another type of sorting. If an area is increasingly filled by lower income residents, landlords have an incentive to not maintain their properties. It they were to invest in upgrades, they'd need to charge a higher rent to make this a profitable investment. People with higher incomes who could pay the higher rents may not be willing to live in that neighborhood. So landlords simply 'milk' the decaying buildings of their rent. By putting off repairs, they can save money to buy other buildings elsewhere. (Wetzel, 2002: 1)

London has not suffered the level of ghettoization experienced in other cities. The level of inter-racial marriage is high and there is a complex social and cultural geography. However, as older residents of Asian or Afro-Caribbean extraction move out of gentrifying areas, they tend to be replaced by younger, mainly white, professionals (Wetzel, 2002).

The failure to continually upgrade buildings and replace the worn-out building site with inflows of new cash amounts to a process of disinvestment – a shrinkage of capital – in an area. As a space becomes more of a low-rent district, some houses may be cut up into separate rooms or apartments to increase the rental revenue. This leads to further deterioration of the housing stock and the community environment. If a declining area is close to centers of employment, the availability of cheap housing and novel aspects, such as interesting architecture and small restaurants nearby, are incentives for capital to re-enter the area and invest in real estate, thus starting the investment cycle all over again. To make investment in new construction and rehabilitation profitable, developers must be able to attract residents that can pay higher rents, such as professionals (the 'gentry'). Once this process gets underway, the less affluent residents are pushed out of the area.

When an area gets 'gentrified' prices go up for all neighborhood services. Writing about the changes that took place in the 'Hell's Kitchen' section of Manhattan, on the west side, Michael Gwertzman focuses on the little things that are so costly to previous residents, they are forced to move. 'He remembers eating at a restaurant … which served Cuban-Chinese food for $3 a plate. Six restaurants later in the same space, a new "Latino" restaurant serves the same food for $10 a plate' (1997: 2).

The process of displacement that often accompanies gentrification may result in political struggles as older residents resist the incursion of new capital. Thus the process of dis-investment and re-investment results in cycles of decline and gentrification that afflict the housing stock of the city. Community concern and resistance accompanies these changes, including the emergence of political protests and, occasionally, social movements (see entry on *Urban and Suburban Politics*).

Gentrification and urban redevelopment are not necessarily the same thing. Looking at the rapid growth of urbanization in Asia one sees a variety of redevelopment programs; for example, in Seoul in South Korea the Joint Redevelopment Programs seek to transform shanty-type settlements into high-rise commercial housing estates in urban areas. The driver is not gentrification, *sui generis*, but real estate interests exploiting rent gaps, underwritten by a central state whose commitment to social redistribution is limited.

Too many of the academic commentators on gentrification take it as read that gentrification is a parameter and not a variable in urban redevelopment. That is, it is assumed that regeneration in itself improves urban habitats as a whole rather than creating different forms of tensions and conflicts between groups and individuals within them. For example, the East Asian Crisis of 1997 had less impact on South Korea than on Thailand because of the latter's exposure to a real-estate-induced financial bubble created by speculative office and housing developments. Similarly, the distinction between structural and cyclical changes in the urban habitat is often either overlooked or conflated

Too often urbanists display category errors in their attempt to analyze urban change. That is, a property is ascribed to a thing that could not have that property. Unfortunately, gentrification and urban redevelopment are examples among rather too many of this type of error.

gentrification and urban redevelopment

REFERENCES

Gwertzman, M. 1997. 'Keeping the "Kitchen" in Clinton'. Available at: www.hellskitchen.net (accessed 25 June 2003).

Hebbert, M. 1998. *London*, Chichester: John Wiley.

Wetzel, T. 2002. 'What is Gentrification?' Available at: www.uncanny.net/~wetzel/gentry.htm (accessed 25 June 2003).

GLOBAL CITIES

The debates about global cities have attracted affirmation and opprobrium in varying measures. The essential challenge for the concept of global cities is that it has become an increasingly elastic one. Furthermore, it no longer seems clearly to pass what is called the *Gottdiener Test*:

- Where's the theory;
- Where's the evidence; and
- Where's the data.

Global cities are ones that are characterized by being integrated into global networks of business financial and information flows, out of which knowledge economies are created, developed and sustained. At the heart of these economies are advanced producer services (including financial and business services) that are internationally tradable through digital networks that overcome the constraints of time and place. The most well-known exponent of this view is the US sociologist, Saskia Sassen.

The contemporary use of the term global city in urban studies stems from the work of Heenan (1977). He located the development of global cities in the globalization and regionalization of Multinational Companies (MNCs). For Heenan, MNCs created a need for global cities as a result of their organizing themselves on a regional basis. In this view these cities need to be 'knowledge command posts' in the evolving system of globalized production (Heenan, 1977: 82). The basis of Sassen's thesis was founded on the subsequent work of Cohen (1981) in emphasizing the dominance of advanced producer services in a few key cities. He states that 'global cities act as centers of corporate control and co-ordination for the new international system' (Cohen, 1981: 288). In other words, a few global cities exercise strategic control over the global economic system.

Sassen's thesis is a development of the World City Hypothesis advanced by Friedman and Wolff (Friedman and Wolff, 1982). They established a research agenda that put a few dominant cities at the heart of the formation of a world-wide economic system. In 1986 Friedmann claimed that there were now world cities that were either primary or secondary in the core or semi-periphery of the world economy (Friedmann, 1986). In further developing this hypothesis, Sassen proposed a poly-nodal world system based upon the primary nodes of New York, London and Tokyo (Smith, 2014).

The main characteristics of a global city as outlined in Sassen's 1991 book *The Global City* are:

- Command and control points in the organization of the world economy;
- Key locations and marketplaces for the leading industries of the current period, which are finance and specialized services for firms;
- Major sites of production for these industries, including the production of innovations (Sassen, 1991: 4).

These characteristics underpin Sassen's 'social polarization' thesis – reducing the city to dual populations, one increasingly affluent, the other mired in low-level service jobs. Nearly 15 years since the first publication of the book, social polarization is more complex and heterogeneous in the cities she calls global. In particular, the role of housing has been a more powerful factor in creating and sustaining inequality (see the entry on *Housing*).

In spite of subsequent work in which she claims the concept now encompasses the cities of the South, definitional clarity has hardly improved (Sassen, 2005). She has tended to dissemble on the characteristics of the global city, the number of which she has increased. If we look at her work more closely and that of other US-based urban sociologists, for example Manuel Castells, we find they seriously over-estimate the contribution of financial services, by confusing market capitalization and turnover of stock exchanges (Castells, 1996) (see the entry on *Financial and Fiscal Crises*). Market capitalization is the price of stocks multiplied by the number available to buy or sell at any one time. Turnover is the amount of revenue produced by the buying and selling activities on stock exchanges at any one time. Whether these individuals are suffering from category error or ignorance is an open question, but this fundamental misinterpretation does blow a hole in their thesis, as the monopolization of financial markets distributed among a few large locales is central to it.

The problem is that mayors and leaders of metropolitan regions and cities would also like to promote each of their places as a 'global city'. In May 2009 a report was published, *Philadelphia 2040: A New Kind of Global City*. It listed five characteristics (University of Pennsylvania, 2009):

- Diverse population;
- Internationalism;
- Interconnected;
- Webs of commerce; and
- Rich/poor disparities.

These five characteristics are global, in the sense of being universal, for almost any city. In fact, a number of cities in the PricewaterhouseCoopers top-10 global cities list do not completely conform to these characteristics (PWC, 2009). Consequently, a standard classification of what constitutes a global city may be hard to find. Unfortunately, regional and urban politicians are often suckers for the snake-oil charm of consultants and celebrity academics, who are selling them a brand, as part of place marketing, but not the material means to transform the economies within their jurisdictions. So what we are left with is that global cities have large populations, economic activities in which advanced business and financial services account for a significant share, and have populations drawn from the world's diasporas. Moreover, as the cities and urban regions of the emerging markets grow, the number of cities that could be termed global also grows. Consequently, the global command and control characteristic of a few is severely weakened by the growth of many cities.

It is true that the world's major metropolises are so connected to each other through the organization of international finance that they are often seen as being disconnected from their national contexts. Manhattan, the City of London and the business/Ginza district of Tokyo have more in common with each other than with other cities in their respective countries. Hong Kong is a Special Administrative Region (SAR) within the Peoples' Republic of China, as a result of it effectively being an off-shore (in the regulatory sense) global financial entrepôt, combining financial and real estate trading and speculation as its main activities. Shanghai is now added to this list, as its futures exchanges based in the Pudong district have become the world's largest. It is also true that these cities' local economies and regional hinterlands are equally susceptible to the cycles of growth and decline of that financial sector. Thus, while many of the older centers prospered in the 1980s, they suffered a decline in the early 1990s that resulted in increased job loss, foreclosures on real estate, and substantial declines in corporate taxes that help float government spending. Many of these outcomes have come home to roost in the aftermath of the 2007 financial crisis which has generated a fiscal crisis (see entry on *Financial and Fiscal Crises*).

Similar arguments apply to the global networks created in industries like fashion, but also social media. Yet in spite of the claims for an information society, we find airline and shipping traffic has increased dramatically: much of it inter- and intra-regional, rather than global. For example, Las Vegas has more flights arriving and departing at weekends than any other airport in the world. The reasons are obvious, but equally apply to a range of activities in other metropolitan areas around the world. It follows that a global city thesis appears to be one in which its original regionalized basis is reappearing

Furthermore, the trend away from the centralization of financial activities in specific cities towards a set of electronically based networks further undermines the global city hypothesis. These changes are a consequence of the very same innovations in information and communication technologies (ICT) that have made the global city thesis possible in the first place. Writing in the 1990s one observer noted:

> For example, the National Associated Automated Dealers Quotation System (NASDAQ) has emerged as the world's fourth largest stock market: unlike the New York or Tokyo exchanges, NASDAQ lacks a trading floor, connecting half a million traders worldwide through telephone and fiber optic lines. Similarly, Paris, Belgium, Spain, Vancouver and Toronto, all recently abolished their trading floors in favor of screen-based trading. (Warf, 1996: 670)

This trend has continued in the third millennium as the European stock exchanges have gone digital and merged with each other. NASDAQ has taken over the Nordic digital exchange OMX and has expanded into the Arabian Gulf through NASDAQ Dubai, which was outsourced to the Dubai Financial Market (DFM) in 2010. Effectively, many of the stock and commodity trading exchanges in the dominant financial centers have become like MNCs competing globally, as they have ended their mutual status. In 2013, the Hong Kong Exchange took over the London Metal Exchange (LME) that sets the contract prices of global base metals prices. The Hong Kong Exchange also established HK-Connect in order to give international investors access to buying and selling stocks on the Shanghai Stock Exchange. Rather than a small set of global command centers there is now a larger number of regionally distributed financial centers (see 'Regionalization' below).

The fact that there remains an international hierarchy of financial centers is the result of the interaction of still powerful external economies of scale and scope and the role of real estate in investment banks' balance sheets, not simple command and control functionality (Budd and Parr, 2008; Parr and Budd, 2000). There is also a distinct hierarchy of financial functions, with many lower order activities being digitized or decentralized. London has seen a significant decline in financial services employment in the last 10 years, to be compensated by a growth in business services as London takes on the appearance of what could be called a rentier rather than simply a global city. That is, a metropolis now characterized by real estate and commodity speculation underpinned by new financial intermediaries (hedge funds and private equity firms) primarily engaged in a process of financialization (Palley, 2007). Yet London's labor markets are not dominated by global activities. Gordon estimates that 60% of employment in the London economy serves local and national rather than global demand. Financial services account for 22.3% of London's Gross Value-Added (GVA) compared to 7.9% for the whole of the UK. But the dominant areas of economic activity are wholesale and retail, accounting for 40% of London's GVA, most of which is driven by local and regional demand (Buck et al., 2003).

The narrowness and limited conception in the conventional literature on global cities is explained by the economic geographers, Henry Wai-chung Yeung and Kris Olds:

> [W]e would like to reiterate that there are varieties of global cities and differential pathways to global (or world) city formation. Their processes of transformation and development must be situated within historically and geographically specific contexts. Having said that, the existing literature on global cities seems to have focused too narrowly on a few 'champion examples', in particular London and New York. Furthermore the global city literature fails to shed enough light on the complex inter-relationships between global city formation and the state. (Yeung and Olds, 2001: 28)

In other words, cities and regions become globalized in the sense that their economic and financial networks may determine their intentional development path. But this is in a large part shaped by the degree to which the immanent development of each *habitus* can respond to these global networks through state underwriting and/or support. In Yeung and Old's analysis of the established and emerging urban areas of Asia, it is more productive to analyze them as globalizing cities than global cities, thereby focusing on agency rather than structure, per se.

REGIONALIZATION

In contrast to global cities, regionalization appears to have greater analytical resonance and purchase. We can distinguish regionalization at two geographical scales: supra-national and sub-national. The former encompasses economic and/or political groupings, for example the European Union (EU), North American Free Trade Association (NAFTA) and the Association of South-East Asian Nations (ASEAN), among a number of others. In the United States, the state is more important than the region, at the sub-national level, while in many European countries the region remains the locus of socio-economic activity and cultural identity.

The boundaries of sub-national regions may be administratively formal, but are frequently economically functional and travel-to-work areas. They also are contiguous with metropolitan areas and have given rise to a number of concepts, for example city-regions, Polycentric Urban Regions (PURs) and Multi-Centered Metropolitan Regions (MMRs) (Gottdiener and Hutchinson, 2000; Hall and Pain, 2006; Parr, 2004). The definition of a PUR is not precise but implies a number of centers within an urban region that are physically separate. Examples include the Ranstaad in the Netherlands, Raleigh, Chapel Hill and Durham (The Research Triangle) in the US and the Kansai area in Japan, but the difficulty of definition has led Parr to devise seven characteristics of a PUR (Parr, 2004).

It has been argued that London has moved from being a city-state to a city-region, or from a metropolis to a region but with some characteristics of a PUR (Budd, 2006; Mogridge and Parr, 1997). For others, the wider London region is a Polycentric Mega-City Region (PCR), but this specification tends to conflate a city-region and a PUR.

An MMR is similar to a PUR, but there is a contiguity of space in that at its heart are two processes of recentralization and decentralization. It can be claimed that London is more an MMR than a PUR, while the metropolitan regions of Sao Paulo, Hong Kong, Houston, Las Vegas and Phoenix in Arizona all correspond to this classification

MMRs may appear to be a more appropriate definition for a number of American and Asian cities, including Shanghai, but looking at different metropolitan regions through the lens of PURs, PCRs and MMRs provides a more fined-grained analysis than that provided by the globalist boosterists. It may seem arcane to devise this kind of classification, but different urban regions do have different characteristics: an important detail that is often missing in the global cities literature (see entry on *Multi-Centered Metropolitan Regions* for a fuller discussion of this issue). Moreover, debates about whether an urban agglomeration is a city or a region, or both, are a continual part of the challenges for urban and regional scholars.

In China, the coastal cities were at the heart of Deng Xiaping's economic reforms and development strategy under his *socialist market economy* program from 1978 onwards. These cities and their hinterlands were regenerated as growth poles based upon Walt Rostow's growth theory of economic development, that proceeds using five stages (Rostow, 1960). Growth-pole theory has made a comeback in the analysis of European cities and metropolitan regions, to which Parr's comment below is also apposite:

> If the Rostow framework is to be applied at the regional level, there is a need for the stages to be defined in more general terms, so as to accommodate the distinctive nature of the regional economy and the diversity of forms which regional development takes. (Parr, 2001: 8)

This comment reinforces the nuances that have to be understood in applying classifications of regional and urban development in different territories. The rapid urbanization of the emerging and emerged economies, especially that of China, provide rich material to investigate. These classifications also include those proposed by the Chicago School (see the entry on *The Chicago School*).

It is at the supra-national regional level that much recent comment and discussion has occurred as the emerging supra-national regions of the world have come to the fore. In the same way that the differences between cities and metropolitan regions tend to create analytical confusion, supra-national regionalism is often conflated with multilateralism. The former coalesces around a number of neighboring states who develop economic and trade relationships as part of a process of greater integration. Multilateralism implies states signing up to discrete but not integrated agreements over, say, trade, defense, intellectual property rights, and so on. However, many multilateral agreements are purely regional. Often they originate in limited or ad hoc arrangements that may then be extended and become more institutionalized over time. The existence of 80 Regional Trade Agreements (RTAs) involving 133 member countries of the World Trade Organization (WTO), gives some indication of the scale and significance of regional multilateralism. The importance of such groupings is obvious when transnational economic activity is considered.

In the last two decades, the claims for greater globalization appears to have been found wanting, as the universalism of socio-economic and cultural activity has not emerged (see the entry on *Globalization and Meltdown* for a fuller treatment of this argument). Rather, a strong regional distribution is apparent, with most trade taking place within the three dominant regions of North America, Europe and East Asia with the three regions accounting for about 30% of the world's trade in recent decades (Budd, 1995; Budd and Parr, 2008).

The distribution of national incomes measured by Gross Domestic Product (GDP) shows a similar picture. In 1980, the relative share of GDP was 27% for North America, 29% for the European Union (EU) and 14% for East Asia. By 2000 the distribution was 35%, 25% and 23% respectively (Fujita and Mori, 2005) and by 2014, the outcome was 20.5%, 17.8% and 45.9%, reflecting both the impact of the eastwards shift of regional economic development and the outcome of the global financial crisis for the advanced economies (IMF, 2014). In the three decades that supposedly constituted the most global ones in our time, the regional structure of the world economy has remained intact, albeit with a different distribution within it. In other words, globalization (as the mechanism for integrating the global economy) is still incomplete and has displayed signs of fracture (Dumas, 2010).

Total GDP figures are misleading as indicators of economic welfare, however, and would tend to distort the urban distribution of economic welfare in the world's major regions. Furthermore, the rapid growth from a relatively low base in the emerging economies of Brazil, China, India and Indonesia, among others, in the last decade also tends to distort the picture. According to the PWC index, in 2008 the top five cities of the European Union had a GDP per capita of US$52,909, the top five North American cities US$54,309, and the top five East Asian cities US$28,112. The figures for South America and Sub-Saharan Africa were US$21,398 and US$1541 respectively, thereby reinforcing a distinctly regional rather than global distribution of wealth and income. The dominance of this regional triumvirate is supported by a number of material and institutional factors, as shown in Table 1. This table gives a simple overview of the key factors of the global economy and their distribution among the dominant regions. Like globalization, this regional structure is under challenge with the rise of what the British economist, Jim O'Neil, terms the BRICs countries (Brazil, Russia, India, China) (O'Neil, 2001). The first three are important commodity economies, while the demand for their output is sustained through China's significant growth over a long period. Furthermore, the rapid growth of the BRICs has been accompanied by the creation of their own MNCs, who invest in cities and regions around the world (for example, the Brazilian mining company taking over Canada's INCO, based in Toronto). Thus we are starting to see the emergence of a more distributed form of spatial economic development structured by rapidly growing cities and regions within and outside the formerly dominant regional triumvirate.

Table 1 Distribution of activities in regional reference zones

Zone	Americas	Asia	Europe
Reference currency	$	¥/Rmb	€
Dominant/largest economy	USA	Japan/China	Germany
Dominant/global financial centers	NY/Chicago	Hong Kong/Tokyo/Shanghai	London/Frankfurt
Location of main economic activities	New England/California/sun belt	China/Japan/Korea/rest of ASEAN	Northern EU economies
Dominant political center	Washington/New York	Beijing/Tokyo	Berlin/Paris
Dominant foreign exchange flows	Dollar/euro/yen/renimbi	Yen/dollar	Euro/dollar/sterling/renimbi

Source: Adapted and updated from Budd (1995).

Globalization and global cities may have a certain utility in place marketing, and have a resonance for the political elites attempting to discipline their populations to the ideological claims they espouse. These variable concepts act as a certain short-hand for policy-makers in navigating the complexities of an uncertain world. For the urban and regional scholar contending with weak theory, contradictory evidence and patchy data, these concepts and forms of would-be praxis tend to lead to an academic and analytical cul-de-sac. Rather, there are more sophisticated and nuanced forms of intellectual enquiry to make sense of spatial and territorial structures and processes.

REFERENCES

Blackburn, S. 1994. *The Oxford Dictionary of Philosophy*, Oxford: Oxford University Press.

Buck, N., I. Gordon, P. Hall, M. Harloe and M. Kleinman 2002. *Working Capital: Life and Labour in Contemporary London*, London: Routledge.

Budd, L. 1995. 'The Growth of Global Strategic Alliances in Different Financial Centres', *Urban Studies*, 32(2).

Budd, L. 2006. 'London: City-state or City Region?' in M. Baker, I. Hardill, P. Benneworth and L. Budd (eds) *The Rise of the English Regions?*, London: Routledge.

Budd, L. and J.B. Parr 2008. 'Neglected Aspects of the East Asian Financial Crisis', *Twenty-First Century Society*, 3(1): 31–48.

Castells, M. 1996. *The Rise of the Network Society: The Information Age: Economy, Society and Culture*, Vol. I (2nd edition, 2000), Cambridge, MA: Blackwell.

Cohen, R.B. 1981. 'The New International Division of Labour, Multinational Corporations and Urban Hierarchy' in M. Dear and A.J. Scott (eds) *Urbanization and Urban Planning in Capitalist Society*, New York and London: Methuen. pp. 287–315.

Dumas, C. 2010. *Globalisation Fractures: How Major Nations' Interests Are Now in Conflict*, London: Profile Books.

Ertürk, S., J. Froud, S. Johal, A. Leaver, M. Moran and K. Williams 2011. 'City State against National Settlement: UK Economic Policy and Politics after the Financial Crisis', *CRESC Working Paper Series*, Working Paper No.101, Manchester.

Friedmann, J. 1986. 'The World City Hypothesis', *Development and Change*, 17(1): 69–84.

Friedman, J. and G. Wolff 1982. 'World City Formation: An Agenda for Research and Action', *International Journal of Urban and Regional Research*, 6(3): 309–44.

Fujita, M. and T. Mori 2005. 'Frontiers of the New Economic Geography', *Papers in Regional Science*, 84(3): 377–405.

Gottdiener, M. and R. Hutchison 2000. *The New Urban Sociology*, Boulder, CO: Westview Press.

Hall, P. and K. Pain (eds) 2006. *The Polycentric Metropolis: Learning from Mega-city Regions in Europe*, London: Earthscan.

Heenan, D.A. 1977. 'Global Cities of Tomorrow', *Harvard Business Review*, 55: 79–92.

IMF 2014. 'Report for Selected Country Groups and Subjects (PPP valuation of country GDP)', October 2014, Washington, DC: International Monetary Fund.

Krugman, P. 1994. 'Competitiveness: A Dangerous Obsession', *Foreign Affairs*, March/April.

Mogridge, M. and J.B. Parr 1997. 'Metropolis or Region: On the Development and Structure of London', *Regional Studies*, 32(2): 97–115.

O'Neil, J. 2001. 'Building Better Global Economic BRICs', *Global Economics Paper No. 66*, London: Goldman Sachs.

Palley, T. 2007. 'Financialization: What It Is and Why It Matters', *The Levy Economics Institute and Economics for Democratic and Open Societies Working Paper No. 525*, Washington, DC: The Levy Institute.

Parr, J.B. 2001. 'On the Regional Dimensions of Rostow's Theory of Growth', *Review of Urban & Regional Development Studies*, 13(1): 2–19.

Parr, J.B. 2004. 'The Polycentric Urban Region: A Closer Inspection', *Regional Studies*, 38: 231–40.

Parr, J.B. and L. Budd 2000. 'Financial Services and the Urban System: An Exploration', *Urban Studies*, 37(3): 593–610.

PWC 2009. *Global City GDP Rankings 2008–2025*, London: PricewaterhouseCoopers, December.

Rostow, W.W. 1960. *The Stages of Economic Growth: A Non-Communist Manifesto*, Cambridge: Cambridge University Press.

Sassen, S. 1991. *The Global City: New York, London, Tokyo*, Princeton, NJ: Princeton University Press.

Sassen, S. 2005. 'The Global City: Introducing a Concept', *Browon Journal of World Affairs*, XI(2): 27–43.

Smith, R.G. 2014. 'Beyond the Global City Concept and the Myth of "Command and Control"', *International Journal of Urban and Regional Research*, 38(1): 98–115.

Taylor, P.J. 2001. 'Specification of the World City Network', *Geographical Analysis*, 33(2): 181–94.

University of Pennsylvania 2009. *Philadelphia 2040: A New Kind of Global City*, School of Design, University of Pennsylvania, Philadelphia.

Warf, B. 1996. 'International Engineering Services in the 1980s', *Environment and Planning A*, 28: 667–86.

Yeung, H.W. and K. Olds 2001. 'From the Global City to Globalising Cities: Views from a Developmental City-State in Pacific Asia', Paper Presented at the *IRFD World Forum on Habitat – International Conference on Urbanizing World and UN Human Habitat II*, Columbia University, New York City, USA, 4–6 June.

Globalization and Meltdown

Globalization lies at the heart of many contemporary commentaries and debates, with proponents and opponents of the process taking strong positions. Martin Wolf, the chief economic commentator at the British newspaper the *Financial Times*, argues in his 2004 book, *Why Globalization Works*, that standards of living and income have increased in nations that have 'globalized'. Wolf supports this argument by using data he has collected since the 1980s to mount a comprehensive defense of globalization (Wolf, 2004). In the opposition camp, the Canadian journalist Naomi Klein published *No Logo* in 2000. This book became a manifesto for the anti-globalization movement. *No Logo* condemns the negative effects of brand-orientated consumer culture by describing the operations of large corporations. Klein argues that their products turn people into walking billboards and that these corporations are also often guilty of exploiting workers in the world's poorest countries in pursuit of ever-greater profits (Klein, 2000). Perhaps more interesting is the intervention of Joseph Stiglitz in *Globalization and its Discontents*. Formerly chief economist of the World Bank and the Nobel Prize winner for economics in 2001,

Stiglitz asserts that the International Monetary Fund (IMF) puts the interests of 'its largest shareholder', the United States, above those of the poorer nations it was designed to serve (Stiglitz, 2002).

By the time that the financial credit crunch had turned into a global recession with the collapse of the US investment bank, Lehman Brothers, on 15 September 2008, Wolf had altered his view with the publication of *Fixing Global Finance: How to Curb Financial Crises in the 21st Century* (Wolf, 2009). The virtual financial meltdown following the collapse of Lehman Brothers led to a contained global depression, as states around the world bailed out their financial and banking systems. In spite of the simplistic and somewhat naive claims for *'financialization'* (confusing the primary and secondary circuits of capital), the real economy depends upon credit creation in the banking and financial systems, as noted by Keynes over 80 years ago (Keynes, 1930; Lazonick, 2013).

The longest recession in economic history has led central banks around the world to undertake monetary easing in the form of near zero or negative interest rates. However, given that the majority of the world's population live in urban areas, where local governments' budgets have been slashed and revenues have fallen drastically, it is there that the impact of the recession is greatest. There are four dimensions to the impact upon European cities and regional hinterlands (Turcu et al., 2015):

Economic: a crisis in real estate, construction and services sectors (Spain, Greece); economic diversification (Italy, Sweden); austerity measures and budget cuts (UK);

Social: a 'social crisis' illustrated by evictions, homelessness, informal economy, curtailing of welfare provision and new forms of urban poverty and vulnerable groups (Spain, France, Italy, Greece, UK);

Environmental: a reliance on 'cheaper' (but 'dirtier') energy resources; relaxation of environmental standards for the industry and a lesser concern with environmental agendas;

Spatial: a 'spatial crisis' in the shape of 'ghost towns' (Spain) and cuts in urban infrastructure provision (Greece, France), but also a wider emphasis at the European level on devolution and city-regions.

The most direct impacts have been on the urban economy; social problems; city governance; urban housing; and urban renewal. The resultant fiscal crises led to the promotion of austerity as the *only* solution to the economic consequences of a possible financial meltdown. The result of over 50% unemployment for the 18–24 age group in Greek and Spanish cities, in particular, has generated social and political consequences . These consequences have impoverished citizens elsewhere in world, the reaction to which has been the establishment of the Occupy Movement in 951 cities in 25 countries across the world. At the same time, the rise of the Pirate Parties, who seek open content and free sharing of information and have contested a number of elections in regional parliaments in Europe, attest to the political reaction to potential meltdown of the global order.

The election of Syriza, a radical anti-austerity political party, to government in Greece has led to conflict with other Eurozone Member States. The possibility of contagion from Greece leaving this currency area may lead to the euro's collapse, the effects of which would be severely damaging for cities in the more peripheral economies of the EU. Similarly, the rise of the Podemos Party in Spain stems from a rejection of externally imposed austerity. The change in the political environment has also promoted pressure for independence from some Spanish regions, in particular Catalonia. In the context of increased geo-political uncertainty on the eastern border of the EU, economic, financial and political meltdown remains a possibility.

Harvey's book *Rebel Cities* points to cities being the historical sites of revolutionary politics, and in citing Henri Lefebvre's *Right to the City* establishes a narrative that explains the provenance of the Occupy Movement (Harvey, 2012; Lefebvre, 1968). Unfortunately, the historical method is rather absent from other contributions led by well-known bourgeois urbanists, who are rather less engaged in urban struggles at the ground level, as they view the world from somewhat different towers than the traditional ivory ones (see Castells et al., 2012).

Returning to globalization, we can see that it is a process that is sometimes seen as an analytical artefact rather than something real. That is, many academics and public commentators use it as a term to examine changes in the world. But it is a term that has limited evidence to support it as a universal phenomenon in the view of a significant number of commentators (see Hirst and Thompson, 1996, among others). In examining the possible impact of globalization on the economy and society, politics and government, culture and identity, a number of preliminary conclusions can be drawn:

- Globalization describes greater interconnectedness between different parts of the world;
- The spatial form of social relations (that is, how people interact in different places, particularly cities and metropolitan regions) becomes markedly changed as the interaction of global and local processes in society become more and more important;
- Power is organized and exercised on a global scale yet has to be exercised locally;
- It is multi-dimensional in being relevant to all aspects of the life of individuals in society: economic, political, cultural – from the music we listen to, to the TV programs we watch; from the food we eat, to sustaining the environment;
- There are as many benefits as there are costs, with debates most divided between globalizers and traditionalists (Cochrane and Pain, 2000).

The American political scientists Keohane and Nye in their aptly titled paper 'Globalization: What's New? What's Not (And So What?)' discuss a more historical context of globalization than many other accounts. They attempt to set out why contemporary globalization may be different (Keohane and Nye, 2000). But, as Keohane and Nye have shown, globalization has been with us for centuries and is not just a characteristic of late capitalism. The Centre for the Study of Globalisation and Regionalisation (CSGR) at Warwick University in the UK has also devised a globalization index constructed from measuring the following components:

Economic Globalisation: Trade; Foreign Direct Investment (FDI); Portfolio Investment; Income of Non-resident workers and returns to non-domestic investors;

Social Globalisation: Foreign stock and flows of population; Worker remittances to familial country; Number of tourists, Density of internet use; International phone call traffic; Exports and Imports of films; Exports and Imports of books and newspapers; Volume of international mail.

Political Globalisation: Number of foreign embassies; Amount of participation in United Nations (UN) missions; Number of memberships of international organisations. (CSRG, 2000)

The contemporary historical trajectory of the economic and financial regimes is set out in Table 2. This categorization, however, tends to neglect important cultural dimensions to globalization. This dimension of globalization is often the most contested and leads to contradictions, particularly as urbanization continues to grow and metropolitan regions are the spaces in which the tensions within cultural globalization are played out. It could be argued that in each periodic regime and as each regime has proceeded, urbanization and regionalization at a sub-national scale have been reinforced as urbanization on a global scale has increased. As the recent crisis has shown, however, there are conditions within each regime that contribute to rupture and possible meltdown.

Table 2 Characteristics of economic regimes in the post-1945 period

Period	Economic and financial regime	Characteristics
Mid-1940s to early 1970s	Embedded liberalism	National regulatory system bound by fixed exchange rates, exchange and capital controls, underpinned by the Gold Exchange System, underwritten by the international convertibility of the dollar
Late 1950s to early 1960s	Regulatory challenge of euro markets	Differences in the national regulatory systems established by the concept of 'regulatory asymmetry' between financial centers and international demand for dollar deposits outside the control of the US Federal Reserve led to a eurodollar market being established in London, which had the most liberal regulatory regime
Mid-1970s to mid-1980s	Successive international deregulation	Aftermath of the Bretton Woods international system created the need for some international 'thermostatic device' to recycle excess, in particular dollar liquidity and new technologies. Financial innovation and the need for risk-managing financial instruments created the environment in which the New York

(Continued)

Table 2 Continued

Period	Economic and financial regime	Characteristics
		stock exchange was de-regulated in 1975, followed by London in 1986 and the other major financial centers in Europe in 1987. The locus of a few international financial centers embeds international flows in these few places
Late 1980s to late 1990s	New re-regulation	Increased systematic risk from increased exposure to derivatives and fall-out from associated scandals, as well as the East Asian Crisis of 1997, leading to demands for global re-regulation. Combination of electronic trading and moves towards regulatory 'level playing field' threatened locational embeddedness of large centers through increase in placeless financial flows
Late 1990s to present	'Financialization' as the only regulatory game	The opening up of the emerging markets to Foreign Direct Investment (FDI), world trade and global financial imparted a deflationary bias into the world economy and lowered the cost of capital. Global investment banks in search of higher returns engaged in investing in riskier assets, particularly in real estate

There is much made about culture and identity. The key question for all of us in respect of globalization is: does it represent my personal and professional identity and express the culture I subscribe to and/or live in? If you work for British Airways, once claimed to be the world's favorite airline, in Delhi are you linked more closely to globalization than someone who works for the city authority in Gdansk in Poland?

Identity is a complex thing but, as noted by the French anthropologist Bourdieu, the employee of British Airway recognizes that he or she works for a global firm, but the local government employee in Gdansk lives and works in an historic city that has been subject to the pressures of globalization, particularly since the fall of communism in 1989. Who is the more global citizen? The cultural theorist Raymond Williams notes the close relationship between globalization, urbanization and modernity. Thus as globalization proceeds, identity and culture are increasingly tied to urban life, that in spite of claims to the contrary, is globally heterogeneous (Williams, 1958).

The near global financial meltdown, which began in late 2007, centered on conventional economic and financial assets and has had an impact on globalization, the dark side of which is seen in the growth of gun-running and drugs and people trafficking, as noted and evidenced in the United Nations sponsored report *The Dark Side of Globalization* (Heine and Thakur, 2011). These outcomes have socio-spatial effects in waves of legal and illegal immigration, as a result of post-colonial change and regional conflicts. In spite of claims to the contrary, immigration into the UK has generated large economic benefits, but many immigrant communities throughout Europe are faced with the dark side of globalization, as they are often the urban interface between the advanced and emerging economies. The drivers are clearly global, as noted by the former UN Secretary-General Kofi Annan speaking in 1998:

> This changing world presents us with new challenges. Not all effects of globalization are positive; not all non-State actors are good. There has been an ominous growth in the activities of the drug-traffickers, gun-runners, money-launderers, exploiters of young people for prostitution. These forces of 'uncivil society' can be combated only through global cooperation, with the help of civil society.

The manifestation of these challenges is clearly felt in many of the metropolises of the advanced economies.

The World Health Organization (WHO) has estimated that this trade reached US$1 trillion (the same size as the Australian economy) in 2010, with the urban centers in the Indian subcontinent developing as key nodes in this trade. A United Nations Office on Drugs and Crime (UNODC) study suggested that nearly 200 million people have been displaced in 2008 because of conflict and shortage of foodstuffs, reinforcing crime, environmental degradation and poverty. This has been an increasing feature of a number of Asian metropolitan regions, exactly the places that have been in the forefront of globalizing forces in the emerging economies (UNODC, 2010). Similarly, the democratic uprisings in a number of cities, as part of the Arab Spring, often against technocratic military dictatorships, have experienced the impact of globalization. Democratic hopes have been dashed as religious fundamentalism and jihadism confront the global strategies of Western powers. Cities in Iraq, Libya and Syria have been effectively destroyed by the conflict against Islamic State. Consequently, any aspiration to re-animating and sustaining civic society and local culture in urban habitats will be thwarted (see the entry on *Urban Violence and Crime*)

These kinds of outcomes tend to be ignored by the adherents of globalization, in their ignorance of its Darth Vader-like impacts.

There are other paradoxes of globalization in the face of meltdown, as noted by a Canadian academic:

- Less equitable income and wealth distribution both within most 'globalized' countries, and between most countries;
- Poor countries lending much more money to rich countries than vice versa;
- Developing countries that borrow capital from the rest of the world growing more slowly than those that lend to the rest of the world;
- No consensus even among democratic, capitalist countries about optimal government involvement in their economies;
- Many people in ex-communist or socialist countries claiming to be worse off under capitalism. (Dean, 2009: 1)

Another paradox is that the economics of austerity, in response to the fiscal crisis, has reinforced the structural adjustment approach to economic development as the

International Monetary Fund (IMF) has organized rescue packages for a number of governments, particularly in Europe. It can be strongly argued that structural adjustment was a major contributor to the global financial crisis and the near meltdown of the world's banking system. From being the globalization boosterist of 2004, Martin Wolf has now stated of 'the second globalization' that it is at an end in the face of meltdown (Wolf, 2009). That is, as the emerging economies rapidly grow and underwrite the trade and budget deficits of the developed economies, the specter of regionalism and regional inequality does not seem to go away.

The relationship of globalization to regionalization remains complex. On the one hand, it is a way of negotiating the maze of apparent global integration, its pressures and challenges, while at the same time preserving local differences and discretion. On the other, it may be complementary to globalization and seen as a stepping stone to full globalization by some commentators (Taylor, 2001). Some authors argue against wholesale support for globalization, in favor of regionalization (Albert, 1999; Budd, 1995; Ohmae, 1995), while others suggest that the universal embrace of globalization is inevitable (Luttwak, 1998; Sassen, 2000).

Globalization is thus a contested concept in both academic literature and public commentaries. Among the communities of politicians, policy-makers, public managers and practitioners it is promoted as an ideology that constrains them in undertaking their national and sub-national roles.

What is clear, however, is that in much of the literature globalization tends to be long on rhetoric and short on comprehensive evidence regarding its universal applicability The poor policy-maker and practitioner in real urban and regional spaces can be forgiven if they feel bombarded by the outcomes of academic fashion and debate. After all, the rapidly and growing Asian cities cited in the Boston Consulting Group Report (detailed in the entry on *Global Cities and Regionalization*), for example, are responding to regional imperatives. However, the ebb and flow of the dark effects of near global meltdown are never far away.

REFERENCES

Albert, M. 1999. *Capitalism versus Capitalism*, New York: Four Wall Eight Windows.

Bourdieu, P. 1984. *Distinction: A Social Critique of the Judgment of Taste*, Cambridge, MA: Harvard University Press.

Budd, L. 1995. 'The Growth of Global Strategic Alliances in Different Financial Centres', *Urban Studies*, 32(2).

Castells, M., J. Caraca and G. Cardoso (eds) 2012. *Aftermath: The Cultures of the Economic Crisis*, Oxford: Oxford University Press.

Centre for the Study of Globalization and Regionalisation (CSGR) 2000. *CSGR Globalisation Index*. Coventry: CSRG University of Warwick.

Cochrane, A. and K. Pain (2000) 'A Globalizing Society?' in D. Held (ed.) *A Globalizing World? Culture, Economics, Politics*, London: Routledge.

Dean, J.W. 2009. 'Paradoxes of the Global Financial Meltdown', Presentation to the ESCAP/WTO Fifth ARTNeT Capacity Building Workshop for Trade Research, 22–6 June, United Nations Conference Centre, Bangkok, Thailand.

Giddens, A. 1999. 'Globalisation', Lecture 1 of the *Reith Lectures 1999: Runaway World*, Broadcasting House, London: BBC.

Guillén, M.F. 2001. 'Is Globalization Civilizing, Destructive or Feeble? A Critique of Five Key Debates in the Social Science Literature', *Annual Review of Sociology*, 27: 235–60.

Harvey, D. 2012. *Rebel Cities: From Your Right to the City to the Urban Revolution*, London: Verso.

key concepts in urban studies

Heine, T. and Thahkur, R. (eds) 2011. *The Dark Side of Globalization*, Washington, DC: United Nations University Press.

Hirst, P. and G. Thompson 1996. *Globalization in Question*, Cambridge: Polity Press.

Keohane, R.O. and J.S Nye Jr 2000. 'Globalization: What's New? What's Not (And So What?)', *Foreign Policy*, 118(Spring): 104–19.

Keynes, J.M. 1930. *A Treatise on Money*, Basingstoke: Macmillan.

Klein, N. 2000. *No Logo*, London: Penguin.

Lazonick, W. 2013. 'The Financialization of the U.S. Corporation: What Has Been Lost, and How It Can Be Regained', *Seattle University Law Review*, 36: 857–909.

Lefebvre, H. 1968. *Le Droit à la ville [Right to the City], 2nd edition*, Paris: Anthropos.

Luttwak, E. 1998. *Turbo-Capitalism: Winners and Losers in the Global Economy*, London: Weidenfeld and Nicolson.

Mishkin, F. 2006. 'Promoting the Next Great Globalisation', *Financial Times*, 10 October: 13.

Ohmae, K. 1990. *The Borderless World: Power and Strategy in the Interlinked Economy*, New York: Harper Business.

Ohmae, K. 1995. *The End of the Nation State-How Region States Harness the Prosperity of the Global Economy.* New York: Free Press.

Robertson, R. 1990. 'Mapping the Global Condition: Globalization as the Central Concept', *Theory Culture Society*, 7: 15–32.

Sassen, S. 2000. 'Spatialities and Temporalities of the Global: Elements for a Theorization', *Public Culture*, 12(1) Winter: 215–232.

Stiglitz, J. 2002. *Globalization and its Discontents*, London: Penguin.

Taylor, P.J. 2001. 'Specification of the World City Network', *Geographical Analysis*, 33(2): 181–94.

Turcu, C., Karadimitriou, N. and Chaytor, S. 2015. The impact of the global financial and economic crisis on European cities', *UCL Briefing for Policy Makers*, March, London: University College.

United Nations Office on Drugs and Crime (UNODC) 2010. *World Drug Report 2010*, Vienna: UNODC.

Williams, R. 1958. *Culture and Society*, London: Chatto and Windus.

Wolf, M. 2004. *Why Globalization Works*, New Haven, CT: Yale University Press.

Wolf, M. 2009. *Fixing Global Finance: How to Curb Financial Crises in the 21st Century*, New Haven, CT: Yale University Press.

Housing

Housing is a resource that is commodified and allocated by real estate markets in capitalist societies (see *Real Estate*). There is a market for rental, private home and commercial real estate. Under capitalism, the type and quality of housing that can be acquired depends, like any other commodity, on the ability of the purchaser to pay the market-determined cost of shelter. As with all consumer purchases, there are also loan-granting institutions available that will aid in the acquisition of goods by providing money in return for interest. In the case of private housing in the US, however, the institutional framework for the provision of loans, or mortgages, is quite complicated and is regulated by the government, in addition to the usual regulation of the banking industry as a whole. Yet, the fundamental restraints remain – you live in a house and in a location that you can afford, whether you own or rent (called type of housing *tenure*). Americans are subsidized in the purchase of single family homes compared to those who live in other capitalist countries. This is because the federal government allows them to make a pre-tax deduction of all interest paid on their mortgage. A similar form of subsidy exists on principal homes in Denmark and the Netherlands, and formerly existed in the UK until being scrapped by the Labour administration in 2000. For this reason, renters are automatically discriminated against because no such comparable provision is available for their tax relief. This discrimination is reinforced because private rental landlords receive tax relief on mortgages in Denmark, Germany, the Netherlands, the UK and the US. This form of tenure accounts for 17%, 54%, 11%, 12% and 30% of total tenure respectively. Social rental landlords, who charge lower rents, also receive this type of subsidy, but given this form's lower share of 20%, 7%, 33%, 18% and 2%, we can see that policy-makers privilege other forms of tenure. In other countries, for example Spain and Ireland, the tax regime has, until the financial crisis of late 2007, privileged housing development over other forms of real and investment assets.

Tax policies on housing are complex and variable in all these countries, all of which tends to reinforce commodification, whose spillover effects can be detrimental to the provision and maintenance of social housing. House prices are capitalized rents in that the calculation of the former is based upon the accumulation of rental yields over a particular period (in the UK the average mortgage of 25 years is used). In the richest part of the UK (London and the South-East) demand has significantly outstripped supply, leading to rising prices and rents. As affordable housing rent is deemed to be 80% of private rents, the young and the poor are being priced out of the market. A consequence has been some local councils in London forcing social housing tenants out of the capital in a process that can be described as akin to 'social cleansing'.

Apart from being a commodity, housing is also a merit good. That is, society considers some goods – education, health and housing – as being sufficiently meritorious as to be a basic right. Hence, the state either directly produces or subsidizes their provision. Many, particularly in Continental Europe, see the existence of subsidized housing as part of redistributive welfare policy. The tighter regulation of private rental markets and their tenure in these countries can also be seen as acting as a restraint on rent levels

In the UK, the housing environment is complicated. The burning issues are accessibility and affordability. Social housing is the main provider of non-owner occupation in the UK. New public housing is negligible and most public housing is being transferred from local authorities to the social housing agencies (Housing Associations).

In 1990 the UK rent levels consisted of:

- 58% owner occupation;
- 10.8% private rented;
- 2.2% social housing; and
- 29% public housing.

In 2011, the figures were:

- 59% owner occupation;
- 18% social housing (combining public and non-profit); and
- 17% private rental.

Owner occupation peaked in 2002 at just over 69% (Department for Communities and Local Government, 2013). The owner-occupied segment of the housing market is both a source of economic growth and economic instability in the UK in that rising house prices create a wealth effect for owner/occupiers that generates extra expenditure and a source of funding for other forms of expenditure (e.g. cars, overseas holidays and household goods). The British model appears to be spreading to other metropolitan regions in Europe, where former more socialized models of housing are giving way to more commodified ones (Scanlon and Whitehead, 2008).

The tipping point of the 2007 financial crisis was the sub-prime market in housing in the United States. Ninjas (no income, no job and no assets) were advanced mortgage loans made on the basis of people being able to repay them from the proceeds of capital gains as house prices continued to rise. These housing loans were re-packaged by investment banks as high yielding and investment grade assets and sold to a range of buyers. This whole mortgage finance house of cards could only be supported if housing continued to rise in value. Once the business cycle was re-established, with defaults on loans increasingly putting downward pressure on prices, the whole edifice began to collapse. This crisis spread to other European economies in which housing had become the driver of economic growth. The subsequent fiscal crises in the single currency area of the European Union has been exacerbated by the housing loans made by French and German banks and, in particular, in Spain and Ireland (see the entry on *Financial and Fiscal Crises*).

A similar situation has been developing in what is now the world's second largest economy, China. In a recent Green Book on housing development in China, published by the Chinese Academy of Social Sciences (CASS), many commentators argue that the housing affordability issue has reached a breaking point. The Chief Economist of the National Bureau of Statistics of China stated:

> House prices in Beijing are absolutely ridiculous. When a young couple purchases a house, parents and grandparents from both sides need to help out. The collective effort of four families is required to support a young family's decision to buy a house. Three generations of savings are thus exhausted in buying a single house. (Quoted in East Asia Forum, 2012)

According to the same Green Book, the current price of an apartment in China's urban centers costs 8.3 times the average income of a household. This figure is significantly higher for China's farmers: a roof over their heads would require roughly 29 times their annual household income. This is similar to the peak of house prices to income ratio in the UK just before the crisis. Apart from the issue of affordability in China, the pace of urbanization in this huge country suggests that the tensions between housing as a commodity and a merit good are likely to be intensified in the near future. This in large part is due to the control over the supply of land for housing. In spite of claims that average house prices could fall by 30% in reaction to the aftermath of the financial crisis, house prices have stabilized and increased in London and the south-east of England because of a lack of public/social housing. In the most economically congested region in Western Europe, this lack of housing supply is distorting economic recovery.

Because the value of urban land is determined by its location and not its intrinsic worth as a resource, the dependency of the type and placement of housing on the ability to pay for it, whether subsidized by a loan or not, leads directly to spatial inequality in the distribution of people within metropolitan areas (see *Inequality and Poverty*). Distinctions produced by the real estate market are more complex than a simple contrast between the more or less affluent. Considerable variation in the prices for shelter results in a rather fine-grained filtering process of people throughout the metropolitan region. Due to the practices of developers in suburban residential areas, for example, single family homes are clustered according to prices that may differ by only as much as $20,000. A family searching for a home that they can afford in the $200,000 price range, for example, may not be able to purchase one in a section of suburbia where homes start at $220,000 and up. The rental market also produces clustering. In any given building or apartment complex, the rents are confined to a narrow range. Those that cannot bear the price in one location must search in other places until they find a cluster with available units that they can afford. In sum, the private real estate market under capitalism allocates housing according to the ability to pay, but construction and development practices cluster like-priced units so that this same mechanism leads to region-wide segregation of individuals by income (there are also racial biases that operate, see below). This clustering is not a separate aspect of location but is an intrinsic feature of the residential real estate market in the US.

REDLINING AND STEERING

Redlining and steering are the two most common discriminatory practices. Redlining is the process by which financial institutional actors (banks, insurance companies) withhold access to resources such as mortgages and insurance policies from specific geographical areas. Mostly the poor and minorities suffer. In the UK, this term would refer to the postcode lottery that also affects education and health provision. Financial institutions track house prices by postcode and supply different levels of finance according to postcode.

Steering is the practice by real estate agents of shunting prospective customers that are a minority or poor to specific areas and away from other opportunities in white and/or relatively more affluent neighborhoods. Similarly, real estate agents will market certain areas to families because of the premium paid to be located within the catchment areas of better performing (usually middle-class) schools.

HOUSING AFFORDABILITY

People may acquire quality housing but, often, they really cannot afford it, as the financial burden consumes an excessive amount of their personal income. According to guidelines from the federal government's Department of Housing and Urban Development, a housing cost burden is defined as paying more than 30% of monthly income, regardless of tenure (i.e. rental or owner occupation). By this measure, over 28% of all US households were cost burdened at the time of the 1990 census, a figure of disturbing magnitude ('Housing Problems', 6/25/03). In many urban areas, renters were disproportionately represented among those paying excessive costs for shelter. Results of this kind indicate another dimension of uneven development. Providing an adequate supply of affordable housing is clearly a problem in the United States, as it is in the UK. The clearest indicator of this problem and the uneven development it personifies is in the presence of homeless populations within metropolitan areas. The question of affordability is closely tied to inequality of wealth and income. In Thomas Piketty's recent book, *Capital in the Twenty-first Century*, he advances the thesis that the rate of wealth accumulation increasing faster than the rate of growth is the cause of growing inequality over time (Piketty, 2014). One of the criticisms of his thesis is that he does not include housing wealth in this calculation. The role of inequality of wealth based upon housing appears to be a growing phenomenon in many of the world's cities. Consequently, housing affordability is becoming a crucial socio-economic issue and one of political resistance as the pace of commodification of housing increases.

HOUSING AND SEGREGATION

There is a dual housing market for those who can and can't afford housing and for those who are white and those who are not. Discrimination in housing occurs through the failure of banks to approve loans and the steering of clients by real estate agents to specific areas or away from specific areas, and so on.

Rental units have their own aspects of discrimination, such as the behavior of landlords in refusing to rent to prospective tenants for racial or other reasons. In the UK, social housing is subject to good tenancy agreements, with the threat of eviction if these are breached. The conditions laid out in these agreements are often onerous and have more to do with social control of poorer families and individuals. Similarly, local authorities have introduced anti-social behavior orders (ASBOs) for public housing tenants. Dysfunctional families and struggling single-parent families (the UK has the highest rate of teenage pregnancies in Europe) are excluded from housing rather than having their health and behavioral problems addressed by appropriate support agencies. There has been a perceptible shift in housing policy in the UK in the last 25 years. Housing wealth is also strongly related to greater life expectancy. Recent research in the UK has shown the following:

- The homeless have death rates which are 25 times the national average;
- Residents in temporary accommodation (cheap hotels who only offer bed and breakfast) have four to five times the death rate of those in permanent housing;

housing

61

- Death rates for hostel residents are seven times greater than those in housing;
- Death rates for those sleeping on the streets are 25 times greater than those in housing.

Those living in households which have significant amounts of housing equity (the difference between the current value and the amount of mortgage debt) are likely to have, on average, more than twice the life expectancy of those sleeping rough on the streets (Dorling and Rees, 2003). There is also a distinct geography of these effects with the south and the south-east of the country, the wealthiest parts, having the highest life expectancy rates. Housing is now a privilege not a right, in the land romanticized by the pomp of the Royal Family and the imagined rural bliss of Constable's paintings.

HOUSING QUALITY

In addition to the issues of affordability and spatial segregation, housing can be a problem when it is not maintained or is deteriorating. Substandard housing is defined by the US federal government's Department of Housing and Urban Development (HUD) according to the kind of physical and structural deficiencies present ('Substandard Housing Defined', 6/25/03). Inadequate shelter may lack hot or cold water or a flush toilet, or both a bathtub and a shower; it may have heating equipment that is broken, or that has broken down at least three times for six hours or more during the previous winter; it may have no electricity or exposed wiring or a room with no working outlet, or has had three blown fuses or tripped circuit breakers in a period of 90 days; it may have no working light fixtures in public areas, such as hallways and staircases; it may have loose or missing steps, a broken elevator or missing railings; it may also have at least five basic maintenance problems, such as water leaks, holes in the floors or ceilings, peeling paint or broken plaster, or evidence of rats, which haven't been fixed after 90 days.

A residential housing unit may be classified as 'moderately' substandard if it has one or more of the following: problems with repeated breaking of flush toilets; unvented gas, oil or kerosene heaters as the primary heating equipment; is lacking a sink, refrigerator or an oven (although microwaves are now allowed); has hallway problems as listed above; has maintenance problems as listed above.

Problematic rental housing is regulated by the federal government (HUD), which can levy fines, and is monitored by the US Census of Housing. According to one survey conducted in New York City in 1998, for example, the census found that over 20% of all rental units in the Borough of the Bronx, over 15% in Brooklyn and over 16% in Manhattan were substandard. This is a high percentage for a 'global city' and shows clearly the quality of *uneven development*. The figures were also high compared to one of the poorest rural areas in the US, the Appalachian Region of Kentucky and West Virginia, which had over 10% substandard units in 1990 ('Housing Problems', 6/25/03).

HOUSING QUALITY AND THE SLUM

(See the entry on *Slums and Shanty Towns*.)

According to the Department of Housing and Urban Development (HUD):

> The most widely used definitions of housing adequacy are based on evaluations of individual homes. But housing quality is strongly influenced by the physical and social context of the surrounding area in which the home is located. Extensive aggregation of substandard and/or informal home construction is called a slum.

HOUSING IN DEVELOPING COUNTRIES

Urban space is highly differentiated by the quantitative and qualitative dimensions of housing conditions, such as size, location, extent of provision for basic services, and accessibility. Accessibility to adequate housing is a critical issue for the urban poor. In most rapidly growing cities of the developing countries, housing is a critical problem precisely because there are too few units. In Brazil, with about 36 million households in 1991, for example, the shortage reached almost 6 million; among the existing dwellings, over 10 million units needed to be repaired. Developing countries were estimated to need 21 million housing units every year for the decade 2000–10, with the figure increasing to 25 million for the following decade, 2010–20, to accommodate additional urban households (UNCHS, 1999). As elsewhere, the more rapidly growing cities tend to have a higher proportion of housing shortages.

The problem of housing is not confined to the absolute number of housing deficits. A more serious problem is the quality of existing and new housing units such as substandard housing and overcrowding. In the developing countries, a very high proportion of the urban housing stock is substandard, being built on illegally occupied land with temporary materials, no authorization, and no access to basic infrastructure and services. About a quarter of the urban housing stock in the developing countries is made up of temporary structures and more than a third of urban housing units have been constructed without compliance to local regulations, while 13% of urban dwellers in the developing countries are cramped in areas without access to safe water, and 25% without access to adequate sanitation (UNCHS, 1999). Overcrowding is another indicator of the quality of housing. When measured by floor area per person, urban dwellers in low-income countries occupy only a sixth of the average living space in high-income countries (UNCHS, 2001: 199). The severity of housing problems in growing cities of the developing world can be illustrated by the 'hotbed' system in Calcutta, India, where two or three tenants rent the same bed in a room to use in turn over a 24-hour period (UNCHS, 1996: 217).

Given these housing conditions, informal or illegal housing is not unusual in most cities of the developing countries. For households on a limited income, the possibility of owner occupation is diminishing and informal housing, including illegal subdivisions and sharing, becomes an important source of affordable, if not adequate,

housing

accommodation. By relying on informal housing, the urban poor may minimize costs and maximize income. Illegal subdivisions are the main source of housing supply for the urban poor, along with housing built in squatter settlements, in many cities of the developing world (see entry on *Slums and Shanty Towns*). Sharing is another type of informal housing. Recent migrants arriving in a city with the help of family members, relatives or friends tend to rely on migration networks for initial accommodation and job information. The recent migrants and urban poor settle in non-standard, poor-quality housing usually nestled on the urban periphery where public utilities and infrastructure are typically not serviced (Peattie and Aldrete-Haas, 1981). Informal settlements are not the same as squatter settlements. Although all people living in illegal settlements are commonly labeled as squatters, most are not squatters because they occupy the land with the permission or implicit approval of the landowner. Unlike squatters, informal residents are not usually threatened with eviction.

PUBLIC HOUSING

Despite the presence of a private real estate market, housing can also be supplied by government sponsored programs at all levels of society, from the local to the national. Public funds can support the construction and/or subsidy of rental housing based on economic need. In addition, subsidized housing can be constructed and run not only by government but also by unions, co-ops and housing associations. But government sponsored public housing is never for profit. In the UK in the 1950s and 1960s, the construction industry was known as the regulator of the economy. If construction grew at 2% per year, so would the economy. When there was a downturn in privately funded activity, publicly funded programs, especially housing, would fill the order books of construction firms.

Around the world countries differ greatly with regard to both the extent of units provided and the success of their public housing programs. In the advanced economies, the provision of public housing is no longer a political imperative. Ideas such as 'homes for heroes' after World War I in the UK, when governments of all political persuasion set targets in excess of 300,000 housing starts per year, have long gone (Barnett, 2001). It will be interesting to note whether a similar situation develops in the emerging economies in Asia and Latin America as they face the consequences of rapid urbanization. The growth of social housing, at the expense of public housing and underwritten by private finance, re-asserts the role of capitalism in the exploitation of land rents, as Adam Smith, David Ricardo and Karl Marx noted two and three centuries ago.

REFERENCES

Barnett, C. 2001. *The Verdict of Peace: Britain between Her Yesterday and the Future*, London: Macmillan.
Department for Communities and Local Government 2013. 'Dwelling Stock Estimates in England: 2012'. London: Department for Communities and Local Government.
Dorling, D. 2003. 'Housing Wealth and Community Health: Explanations for the Spatial Polarisation of Life Chances in Britain'. Available at: http://www.lancs.ac.uk/fss/apsocsci/hvp/projects/dorling.htm (accessed 15 June 2004).

Dorling, D. and P. Rees 2003. 'A Nation Ever More Divided', *Town and Country Planning*, 72(9): 270.

East Asian Forum 2012. 'China's Housing Crisis', 28 January, Canberra East Asian Bureau of Economic Research.

H.M. Treasury, 2004. *Delivering Stability: Securing our Future Housing Needs*, London: Stationery Office.

'Housing Associations'. Available at: www.odpm.gov.uk. (accessed 25 June 2003).

'Housing Problems'. Available at: www.ruralhome.org (accessed 25 June 2003).

Peattie, L. and J. Aldrete-Haas, 1981. 'Marginal Settlements in Developing Countries', *Annual Review of Sociology*, 7: 157–75.

Piketty, T. 2014. *Capital in the Twenty-first Century* (trans. A. Goldhammer), Cambridge, MA: Harvard University Press.

Scanlon, K. and C. Whitehead 2008. *Social Housing in Europe II: A Review of Policies and Outcomes*, London: LSE.

'Substandard Housing Defined'. Available at: www.rental-housing.com/rental/substandard.htm (accessed 25 June 2003).

United Nations Center for Human Settlements (UNCHS) 1996. *An Urbanizing World*, Oxford: Oxford University Press.

United Nations Center for Human Settlements (UNCHS) 1999. *Basic Facts on Urbanization*, Nairobi, Kenya: UNCHS Habitat.

United Nations Center for Human Settlements (UNCHS) 2001. *Cities in a Globalizing World*, London: Earthscan.

Immigration, Migration and Demography

Urban spaces have always grown and been sustained by the constant influx of new people. Historically, cities developed as people who were tied to a prosperous agricultural economy found they could sustain themselves by other means, most commonly associated with a permanent marketplace. As these market locations grew, so they attracted increasingly more people from the surrounding agricultural land. This type of population shift would be considered 'migration' today, because it consists of a movement of people *within* national boundaries. 'Immigration', in contrast, refers to the movement of people *across* national boundaries. In many ways the processes of migration and immigration constitute the very lifeblood of cities, suburbs and, in general, metro regions in countries around the world.

Our task in this book has been to help define concepts in order to avoid terminological confusion. Nowhere is this need more evident than in the proliferation and confusion of terms produced by the new cultural studies discourse on immigration. Most writers, however, seem to embrace each new term, thereby avoiding any need for specificity. Recently, for example, a number of writers have re-conceptualized the phenomenon of immigration through the discourse of cultural studies and by introducing a number of neologisms and/or other terms that were used in the past in different contexts, such as hybridity, diaspora, transnational ethnicities and transculturation. Concise meanings have given way to semiotic confusion and jargon in much of this work (Clifford, 1997: 245). To cite one case, the concept of 'diaspora' originally referred to the forceful scattering of the Jews from the Kingdom of Judea by the Romans throughout their empire after the last of three Jewish Wars (around 80 CE). The political, punitive and forceful dimensions of the term are stripped clean by current writers that use it to refer to any ethnic group that is currently dispersed in a number of different countries as the consequence of a variety of factors over a relatively long period of time. The neologism 'transnational' is another confusing term. Why it is used instead of the more traditional or specific concepts such as immigrant, guest worker, undocumented alien and the like, is hard to say. The concepts of de- and re-territorialization and specific naming of different types of migrants and immigrants are clearer and much preferred, at least by the present authors. (See the entry on *De-Territorialization and Re-Territorialization*.)

At present there are different kinds of immigrants.

LABORERS

In Europe, gaps in the availability of domestic laborers compelled countries to make arrangements for workers to be allowed to leave their home nations on a 'temporary basis', at least in theory, and reside in the host country as a 'guest' without citizenship. This guest worker system was used by Germany extensively in the 1970s and 1980s to import hundreds of thousands of male laborers along with their families, principally from Turkey. In the UK, immigration from the British Empire and the Commonwealth has been a constant feature since the late 16th century. In the immediate post-World War II period, immigration from the new Commonwealth (Indian subcontinent and the Caribbean) accelerated as the 'mother country' cried out for people to fill jobs that the indigenous population deemed beneath them. Most of these immigrants settled in London and its suburbs or in other cities where labor shortages in particular sectors were acute, for example textiles. There have been successive waves of immigrants to the east of London, ranging from French Huguenots escaping the revolutionary terror in the 18th century to Jews escaping the pogroms in Central and Eastern Europe in 19th century, followed by Bangladeshis in the mid-20th century who were recruited for the bottom of the economic pile of an international division of labor in the garment trade (see the entry on *Global Cities and Regionalization*).

Despite their alleged temporary status, guest workers have had a profound impact on European countries. The once relatively homogeneous Germans, and it is not unfair to bring up the nightmare of racial purity murders during the Holocaust by this country, now live in a multicultural society that is part Muslim with ethnic differences that are quite stark. This is especially so for cities like Berlin, Frankfurt and Hamburg which all have their large Turkish sections. The fear of growing Muslim political power in parts of Europe is not exaggerated. Most of these countries do not have a long history of tolerating ethnic minorities.

In the US, guest worker arrangements have been made with Mexico and some Caribbean countries, such as the Dominican Republic and Puerto Rico. Large numbers of Hispanics now reside in the US as a consequence of labor needs. Cities in the US as far north as Minneapolis and Chicago have significant Mexican communities due to the far-ranging extent of agricultural businesses and their need for non-unionized, cheap workers. Hispanics currently comprise a powerful and growing voter base, although their interests remain split among various constituencies, different countries of origin and party affiliations.

Recently, the growth and modernization of the oil-rich Arab states of the Persian Gulf has required a lot of laborers. The Gulf region is now the most popular destination for temporary labor migrants of any world region, surpassing the US, and flows have continued to increase despite economic crises and fluctuations in oil price. Poor people from Pakistan, Bangladesh, India and other Asian countries do construction and service work, often in substandard and harsh conditions. In 2013, one of the Gulf countries, the United Arab Emirates (UAE), had 7.8 million migrants out of a total population of 9.2 million, according to United Nations estimates. In that small country, immigrants thus comprise over 90% of the private workforce (www.migration policy.org)! In addition, high-skilled experts, such as doctors and engineers, move to the region as *professional economic immigrants* (see below).

TRADITIONAL IMMIGRANTS

These are people who have applied for permanent entry into other nations. Often they have limited resources and so they are dependent on friends and relatives in the destination country for aid. Usually, it is these very connections that determine the success of the legal process, for without them the potential immigrant cannot be sponsored. As a result, ethnic communities in host countries continue to grow as the stock of first generation immigrants persists in being replenished by new arrivals over time. The diverse ethnic areas in US cities have continued to make their mark on the urban terrain in this way.

PROFESSIONAL AND MIDDLE-CLASS ECONOMIC IMMIGRANTS

From the late 1970s to the present, the US and many European countries have allowed significant immigration from places elsewhere for people with advanced skills. Recently, these professional and middle-class immigrants have eclipsed traditional ones. For example, in the US at the time of the 1970 census, US-born Asians constituted about two-thirds of the Asian American population. A short time later, by the 1980 census, the ratio had been reversed, with Asians from abroad comprising over 70% of the total Asian American population. More striking has been the change in the composition of this group for the US case. Increasingly after 1970, significant immigration was experienced from India, Pakistan, Hong Kong and South Korea, rather than China or Taiwan and Japan, as had been the case in the past.

Michael Ames observes the following, which is typical of the experience of many city-dwellers in the 1990s:

> In Vancouver, where I live, English is now a minority language among the home languages of school children, 44.5% compared to 31.6% who speak a Chinese language in their homes, followed by Vietnamese, Punjabi, Spanish and Hindi. In fact, I believe that Cantonese is now the second most frequently spoken language in British Columbia, next to English, even though French, like English, is an official language of the country. (1998: 2)

A similar flip-flop in population make-up was experienced in the State of California, where, prior to 1990, people classified as white comprised a majority. By the year 2000 this was no longer the case as mainly Hispanic and Asian populations combined with African Americans to constitute a slight plurality of the total. Such changes are clearly reflected in urban areas because of ethnic place-making which externalizes cultural diversity across the landscape. In London it is estimated that there are 300 languages spoken. At the London office of Goldman Sachs, the US investment bank, it is estimated that 49 different first languages are spoken among its staff.

The de-territorialization and immigration of Asian peoples has brought graphic changes to urban areas in the US, Canada and in the UK in particular. Re-territorialization within cities has produced new ethnic enclaves or expanded traditional ones thereby multiplying the experience of diversity. Place-making by new immigrants and their attempts at forging identities based on dual or multiple nationalities have also greatly influenced the culture of the host countries.

For the most part, this latest wave of immigration since the 1970s is comprised of people that were relatively well educated and/or had significant resources who were looking for better opportunities of advancement abroad. They came to the US voluntarily, as did traditional immigrants. But, unlike the latter, they often retained their citizenship and ties to the country of birth. The outcome of this process has been a new kind of immigrant that is at home in many places and who possesses cross-cultural ties to people and governments in more than one nation.

According to Ames:

> What is strikingly new about the new world order, Arjun Appadurai (1990) suggests, is that it has become a kind of rapid global interactive system never seen before, filled with inconsistencies, differences, disjunctures, alienation and electronic forms of togetherness, inclusions, and exclusions ... This introduces into the world a powerful new force of 'de-territorialization': global movements, new markets, and [a] growing diaspora of intellectuals who are continuously interjecting new peoples into nation states and new ideas into global discourses. (1998: 1)

Although the claim that new ideas are being felt as a consequence of this movement is certainly exaggerated, it is observed that immigration on a global scale of relatively well-educated people with relatively well-paying jobs has resulted in Internet traffic and modes of togetherness that are new, coupled with significant international travel to visit friends and family on a regular basis – all characteristics that differ greatly from the traditional immigration of the past.

MIGRATION IN DEVELOPING COUNTRIES

There is a big difference between the process of migration in the developing countries and that of the developed countries. In Europe and the US, migration from rural to urban areas occurred at the same time as industrialization. In developing countries, by contrast, migration from rural areas is occurring despite unemployment in urban areas. This is so because in developing countries people migrate based on expected income rather than actual income and because rural poverty is so great. It is the 'life lottery'. A rural worker will migrate if he/she expects his average city income will be greater than his rural income despite periods of unemployment. A solution to this kind of migration is to retain resources in rural areas and develop them further.

Rural to urban migration in developing countries is most often viewed as a problem – poverty in rural areas and lack of development leads to a rapid and uncoordinated influx into large cities that cannot assimilate newcomers, leading to an increase in slums and urban poverty. The result is increased crime, substandard housing, congestion, disease, pollution and a loosening of family bonds and loss of traditional cultural practices and values. The most common reasons given for people moving from rural areas to urban ones in the developing countries are family needs and seeking education and jobs. Family is the most common driver in sheer numbers only because the family head usually moves first and then the rest of the relatives follow. By this mechanism, entire family groups have left traditional villages in the countryside of developing countries only to be swallowed up by urban shanty towns (see entry on *Slums and Shanty Towns*). Yet not all migrants to cities are the same. Different groups have different coping strategies for adapting to the city so that there is great diversity in the urban experience of migrants. There is variety in the way groups respond to the job, housing and social dilemmas placed on them. In addition, rather than having to choose between complete assimilation or some variant of an ongoing racial or ethnic orientation, there are a variety of alternatives exhibited by migrants in between the two extremes.

For researchers of immigration from rural to urban areas and/or from developing to developed countries, the basic unit of analysis is the household or family rather than the single individual. That is, in these cases, movement across space is a family affair even if the head of household, whether male or female, arrives first.

DEMOGRAPHIC EFFECTS

Demography concerns the statistical study of human populations. Migration and immigration influence the size and composition of both national and urban populations, together with birth rate and mortality. In the developed countries, populations are rapidly *aging* due to relatively low birth rates and long life expectancy. To take an example, less than 12% of Japan's population was over 65 in 1989. In 2006, the share was 20%, and in 2055 it is expected to reach 38%. Developing countries face the same process. China and even India will become 'grey' societies in the coming decades.

Aging of the population has serious social and economic consequences. In countries that have state-financed social security, the funding of welfare programs becomes increasingly difficult, because the ratio between working-age people who pay taxes and children and the retired population who consume public services becomes less favorable. In any aging country, economic growth slows down because elderly people, on average, earn less and consume less than people with jobs. Immigrants are in many countries seen as a (partial) solution to the problems of aging. Canada and Australia are examples of countries that have a systematic and selective immigration policy with primarily an economic rationale. While immigrants' problems in the country of destination, such as the difficulty of joining the labor market on equal terms with natives, are relatively well known, the economic, socio-cultural and demographic difficulties of the countries of origin are seldom acknowledged. To take an example, post-communist Latvia has lost 13% of its population since its accession to the European Union in 2004. The main destinations are the UK and Ireland. Professor Mihails Hazans refers to the trend as a 'demographic disaster': 'Most emigrants are young – about 80 percent of recent emigrants are under 35 – hence the remaining population is ageing faster' (www.france24.com). In the Latvian countryside, villages and small towns are hollowed out as children and the elderly are left behind.

Both immigration and migration tend to focus on the major metropolitan regions. Because of this, the populations of the largest urban areas tend to be both younger and more multicultural than the national average. In Sweden, 1.33 million people or 14.3% of the inhabitants are foreign-born (2010 figures), but in the industrial city of Malmö as much as 41% of the population has a foreign background: 30% are foreign-born and 11% are born to an immigrant family in Sweden. In the late 19th and early 20th centuries, hundreds of thousands of Swedes emigrated to the US and Canada. After World War II the tide turned, and immigration is now the only reason for Sweden's population growth.

REFERENCES

Ames, M. 1998. 'Museums and the Culture of Uprootedness', unpublished paper, University of British Columbia.
Appadurai, A. 1990. 'Disjuncture and Difference in the Global Cultural Economy', *Public Culture*, 2(2): 1–24.
Clifford, J. 1997. *Routes: Travel and Translation in the Late Twentieth Century*, Cambridge, MA: Harvard University Press.

Inequality and Poverty

Inequality and poverty are not the same. The former is a relative condition usually measured by comparative ratios, such as the Gini or, less commonly, the Theil-L coefficient. These relate high to low levels of income obtained by people living in the same city or region. To be sure, poverty may have its relative components, but it is an absolute condition manifested in inadequacies of various social indicators, such as poor health, poor sanitation, poor nutrition, poor pre-natal care and, equally as profound, limited to non-existent opportunities for bettering one's existing situation in the future.

INEQUALITY

Inequality is typically urban. Friedrich Engels noted the contrast between the wealthy and the poor in the 1850s when he visited the industrial cities of England, and novel writers of the 19th century, such as Charles Dickens, made the same observations in their books. Early Chicago School researchers, such as Harvey Zorbaugh in the 1920s, referred to this distinction as 'The Gold Coast and the Slum'. Indeed, inequality is epitomized by spatial differences in well-being. Less affluent slum residents may be getting along, but take a short walk in most cities to the locations where the more affluent live and the contrast is immediately graphic. Poverty, in distinction, is as much a rural as it is an urban phenomenon. In fact, world-wide, there is more poverty in rural than urban areas. This spatial differential has historically been responsible for the essential demographic component of urbanization, namely, the population movement from the countryside to the city in search of a better life.

The entry on *Global Cities and Regionalization* discusses why Sassen's (1991) 'social polarization' thesis – reducing the city to dual populations, one increasingly affluent, the other mired in low-level service jobs – is wrong. Further evidence comes from an English study by Williams and Windebank (1995), who assert that Sassen's perspective ignores a more relevant way of approaching changes in the occupational structure than by focusing on individuals. They argue that it makes more sense to view urban wage-earners within a household context. Taking a whole economy perspective, UK data reveal that since the 1980s there has been a radical shift in employment practices with a fundamental decline in households that have only one (usually male) wage-earner. 'The stereotypical household of the male breadwinner and the wife at home has suffered a major decline' to less than 25%. While many individuals belong to families that have experienced either increasing affluence or poverty, the vast majority belong to households with two or more wage-earners. Thus the polarization, often spoken about, does not exist. But, there is increasing inequality between households with only one breadwinner and those with multiple ones. The latter are the social units that are becoming more affluent.

In the UK, policy-makers are increasingly turning their attention to households that are 'work-rich' and those that are 'work-poor'. Nick Buck points to six themes that underlie inequality in the UK: changes in state benefits compared with labor market earnings; different rates of growth of earnings in different occupational groups; changes in household composition; changes in the level of unemployment; increases in paid work by married women; and the changing balance of manufacturing and service-sector employment (Buck, 1991).

By adopting the household rather than the employment place as the primary unit of analysis, the process of socio-spatial polarization has been portrayed not as an increasing divide between core and peripheral employment, but, rather, as a division between two types of households: the new 'workhouses' which not only have multiple earners but also conduct more informal work, especially of the autonomous variety; and the 'no longer working' group of households that suffer exclusion from employment and are unable to participate in the informal sector due to mitigating circumstances. Thus, part-time and other forms of so-called peripheral or marginalized work cannot automatically be associated with deprivation, as the individual employment approach often shows.

Clearly, there are more than just two social spheres alive in central cities. Recent immigrants, small business owners, and a persisting segment of the middle class continue to reside in urban areas. Yet, the growing affluence and voracious high-end consumption style of life pursued by the relatively well-off does create the impression of a dichotomous urban terrain existing between the haves and the have-nots in the largest cities. Around the globe, the inequality gap has also been expanding. Urban places in regions like Latin America and Africa have always exhibited this duality. But, lately, with the fall of communism in Eastern Europe, inequality has appeared with a vengeance in the former Soviet societies. When China enacted capitalist reforms in the late 1980s, its social structure also developed an inequality gap. In short, there are virtually no urban places now that are not experiencing the growing difference between the rich and the poor.

Researchers in the US recently completed a four city study of inequality that confirms little to no progress in alleviating aspects of racial and income segregation (Multi-Study of Urban Inequality). Analyses of Atlanta, Boston, Detroit and Los Angeles for the period 1992–4 focused on how changing market dynamics, racial attitudes, and racial segregation act singly and in concert to foster contemporary urban inequality (Bobo et al. 2000). Most strikingly, the patterns observed in the spatial isolation of the African Americans and the less affluent were already substantiated prior to the 1990s. In effect, this most recent research effort confirms that economic prosperity and the 'changing market dynamics' of US cities in the 1990s had little effect on segregation.

Inequality is manifested in residential segregation (see the entry on *Segregation and Hypersegregation*), which, in turn, is manifested in great differences among all school children with regard to their educational performance. Urban school systems suffer because of the concentration of poor and minority students within central cities. On average, among all students in metropolitan areas, whites score 20% higher on standardized tests in grade school than blacks, Hispanics and Native Americans. While attention has been paid in the past to the effects of segregation on black students, it is now clear that Hispanic students are even more disadvantaged by inequality and segregation. Data from 1990 indicate that dropout rates are the highest for the Latino community. These data indicate that something much more than the mere effect of language barriers is going on – Asian students in comparable conditions do not exhibit a remarkable dropout rate. In effect, the spatial isolation of many Hispanics results in the failure of their children to obtain an adequate education, thereby, in turn, reproducing the marginal economic status of their parents.

Taking the multi-centered metropolitan region as a whole, there is an obvious inequality differential between the city and the suburbs. Life chances are enhanced for children by moving from the inner city to the suburbs, when that change can be affected. Often it cannot be because of the limited availability of affordable housing in the suburbs. Spatial differences between the city and the suburb in the US can be summarized by the contrasts set out in Table 3.

Table 3 Contrast between suburbs and cities

Suburbs	Cities
• More homogeneously white	• More minorities who are the majority
• More homogeneously middle class	• Sharp contrast between wealthy and poor
• More residential	• More tourism
• Population is younger	• Concentration of aging population
• More retailing, commerce and industry	• More high-end speciality shopping, banking and professional services
• More affluent	• Significant numbers of poor people

Such a divide between the relatively affluent and the less well off on a regional scale is not characteristic of European metropolitan areas, despite the presence of inequality there as well (Jargowsky, 1997). Rather, the European situation is more complex because of the historic nature of many of its cities. Consequently, the settlement patterns mean that areas of deprivation are found close to areas of affluence. Housing, educational and health differences, as well as cultural and ethnic differences, sustain the inequalities between very proximate areas. For example, the traditional manufacturing district of St Denis in the Paris metropolitan region is now populated by high-tech service firms and professionals sitting cheek by jowl with poor immigrant communities originally from Algeria and Morocco in North Africa, whose young men are mainly unemployed and thus alienated from mainstream secular society (Body-Gendrot, 2000).

POVERTY

Unlike the relative concept of inequality, poverty can be measured directly by social indicators of well-being. Poverty is not only a problem of poor countries; it is found at a significant level in the most affluent societies. Since the 1980s, the number of people around the world living in poverty has increased. In the US, the census defines the poverty level in terms of an annual income for a family of four. In 2012, the census defined poverty as at or below $23,283 (www.irp.wisc.edu). About 15% of Americans were considered to be living in poverty by this measure, a three percentage point increase since 2002. The United Nations' poverty threshold for people living in developing countries is a daily income of either $1 or $2. In 2001, roughly 1.2 billion people were living on less than $1 a day, that is, about 20% of the globe's total population, and there were almost 3 billion people, or half the world's population, living at or below $2 a day. (In 2008, the World Bank revised the line of extreme poverty to a daily income of $1.25 at 2005 purchasing power parity.)

Poverty can be found in rural as well as urban areas. It becomes a metropolitan problem when it is expressed spatially as a concentration of poverty-stricken people in specific places. The census defines poor neighborhoods as tracts with 40% or more of people living at or below the poverty line. As Jargowsky notes:

> The poor, especially minorities, are increasingly isolated in depopulated urban wastelands. Such neighborhoods exhibit severe signs of economic distress, including vacant and dilapidated housing units, high levels of unemployment, high rates of single parenthood, problems with gangs and violence, and widespread drug and alcohol use. (1997: 143)

In the UK, the link between inequality and poverty is generated by health (Davey-Smith et al., 2002). Dorling states:

> Policies which have produced increased income inequality and poverty have helped to drive the polarisation of mortality. The geographical polarisation of health chances has been precipitated by a polarisation of life chances, in terms of employment opportunities, income and living standards. The health gap is now such that, in the period 1994–1997 in Britain, 24% of deaths of people aged 15–64 would not have occurred had the mortality rates of the least deprived decile of the population applied nationally; almost one quarter of all deaths can now be attributed to unfavourable socio-economic circumstances. (2004)

To be sure, problems of gangs, drug and alcohol abuse, and even single parenthood among teenagers, exist in the suburbs as well. But, what distinguishes poverty in contemporary urban society is its concentration at high levels within pockets of severe decline and isolation in the urban landscape. Between 1970 and 1990 the concentration of people living in poor neighborhoods in the US increased from 12.4% to 17.9% (Jargowsky, 1997). 'Poverty concentration is much higher for minority groups. For example, 33.5% of the black poor and 22.1% of the Hispanic poor lived in high-poverty neighborhoods in 1990, compared to 6.3% of the white poor' (Jargowsky, 1997: 143). The cross connection between minority and poverty status is quite graphic for US cities and most troubling. Since the 1970s, there is a pattern of increasing isolation in terms of race and income within the central cities of the nation. For example, between 1970 and 1990 the percentage of blacks in Detroit that were classified as living in poverty increased from 11.3% to 54%. New York City experienced an increase of 27%, Chicago 21.4% and Pittsburgh 21.7%. The concentration of poor Hispanics also increased within large central cities. New York saw an increase between 1970 and 1990 of 18.8%, Philadelphia 48.4% and Detroit 33.8%. According to the UK government, just under one in four people (approximately 13 million people) live in poverty. This figure includes nearly one in three children or around 4 million (Department of Work and Pensions, 2002).

In comparison to the rest of Europe, the UK does not fare well. Over 15% of the UK population is included in the human poverty index, compared to 10.4% in Germany and 11.1% in France (United Nations, 2000). The human poverty index is measured by:

- the proportion of the population living below 50% of national median income (Germany: 5.9%; France: 8.6%; UK: 8.9%);
- the percentage of people not expected to live to age 60 (Germany: 10.5%; France: 11.1%; UK 9.6%);
- the percentage of 16–65-year-olds classified as functionally illiterate (Germany: 14.4%; UK: 21.6%);
- the percentage of long-term unemployed in the labor force (Germany: 4.9%; France: 5.2%; UK: 2.1%).

This significant and troubling increase in the concentration of poverty within central cities is the consequence of several factors, including white flight to the suburbs, an influx of poor migrants and immigrants, and the shift of the economy to more professionally oriented jobs and away from blue collar manufacturing. The concentration of poor and often minority people within spatially isolated areas in the metropolitan region is considered a serious social problem. William J. Wilson (1987) called attention to the 'tangle of pathology' and the reproduction of social problems that this isolation produces. As indicated in the entry on *Segregation and Hypersegregation*, minority and poor concentration is reproduced over time as limited resources prevent people from breaking out of their economic and social constraints. Poverty is not only perpetuated but it seems to be increasing due to the failure of society to overcome this spatial isolation.

Poverty in developing countries is also increasing just as the population of urban areas around the globe continues to increase as well. Not only are cities in developing countries getting bigger, but, with growth, the absolute numbers of the poor living in cities is also growing. Comparable measures of poverty are obtained from quality of life indicators that include availability of adequate housing, health care, potable water, and levels of infant mortality and population morbidity. According to a United Nations study, the percentage of poor people living in cities increased for most developing countries between 1980 and 1993. Some examples are: Ghana – 28.3% from 23.7%; China – 10.8% from 6.0%; India – 23.3% from 19.3%; Pakistan – 28.6% from 23.7%; and Columbia – 37.4% from 35.8%. Among all nations, those located in South America and Africa have the highest levels of urban poor. Furthermore, as in the case of the US, rapid economic growth in the 1980s and 1990s for places like South Korea and Indonesia, did not translate into reductions in the overall percentage of people living in poverty. In addition, as the countries of Eastern Europe abandoned communism and as the Chinese economy shifted to more capitalist features, the percentage of people living in poverty also increased and, in some cases, quite remarkably. According to the United Nations, the percentage of people living on less than $2 a day in Eastern Europe for example, increased from 3.6% to 20.7% from 1987 to 1998 (World Bank, 2000).

Analysts of poverty are alarmed at the extent of its concentration within central cities, as we have already discussed. Other dimensions of poverty are equally disturbing. The high levels of female headed households that are poor indicates a world-wide 'feminization of poverty'. Families are broken up and children are abandoned to a life on the streets in many cities of the developing world as a consequence of this process. Women cannot cope with the dual burdens of raising a family and making a living. In the US, the increase in female headed households living in poverty since the 1980s is reflected in the deterioration of adequate opportunities for children to better themselves and in the absence of positive male role models (see Wilson, 1987). In sum, it is the social aspects of the poverty condition – specifically, the weakness of the family, the deteriorating environment of poor neighborhoods, and the limited chances for social advancement that compound the absolute indicators of poor welfare, such as high infant mortality, poor health care, malnutrition, inadequate shelter and the like – that make the persisting presence of urban poverty such a compelling issue for all societies.

RACIAL SEGREGATION AND POVERTY

There is controversy over the primary cause of the growing concentration of poverty in major US cities. Whereas some researchers attribute it to racial segregation (Massey and Denton, 1993), others insist that social and structural transformations over the last decades have played a major role (Wilson, 1987). Proponents of the latter position, although they underline social and structural transformations, do not deny the harmful effects of racial segregation on the concentration of poverty (see, e.g., Jargowsky, 1997). In the US, the urban poor in major metropolitan areas are increasingly segregated into high-poverty neighborhoods, which are also increasingly divided along racial lines. A recent study shows that the number of the urban poor living in those racially segregated, high-poverty neighborhoods commonly labeled as ghettos (predominantly African American), barrios (predominantly Hispanic) and slums (mixed or white), almost doubled in recent decades, from 4.1 million in the 1970s to 8 million in 1990 (Jargowsky, 1997).

For the UK, the Joseph Rowntree Foundation reported:

> The proportion of 'poor' families in each ethnic group: 16% of white households had a low income ... All minority groups had a higher percentage, but the gap was quite small for Caribbeans (20%) and Indians (22%). The extent of poverty was more serious for Chinese (28%) and Africans (31%), though in the case of Chinese people, there were also more well-off households than in other groups. The new, more detailed, data confirm the previous survey's estimate that Pakistani and Bangladeshi households were four times as likely to be 'poor' as white households. Pakistanis and Bangladeshis were much, much more likely to be poor than any other ethnic group. Not surprisingly, low incomes were rare among working households; more common among pensioner households; and more common again among non-working households below pensionable age. This was true in every ethnic group. But the difference *between* groups is emphasized by the fact that poverty was more common in Pakistani and Bangladeshi *working* households (50%), than in white *non-working, non-pensioner* households (43%). (Joseph Rowntree Foundation, 1998)

Urban racial minorities are vulnerable to structural changes in the urban economy taking place under the pressure of the global economy. In the process of deindustrialization and reindustrialization, the urban labor market has been increasingly polarized into low-skilled and rising high-skilled sectors. Deindustrialization, including plant closing and the relocation of manufacturing, has destroyed low-skilled, blue collar jobs which were traditionally the main sources of livelihood for urban racial minorities; by contrast, the growth of high-tech, knowledge-based industries in major cities has created job opportunities for skilled workers with educational credentials. As a result of changes in the urban economic base, urban minorities have turned increasingly to the low-wage service sector.

In addition, economic restructuring has accompanied changes in the spatial organization of work. In the US, the restructuring of settlement space since the 1950s is characterized by the general process of deconcentration (see entry on *Multi-Centered Metropolitan Regions*; Gottdiener and Hutchison, 2000: chapter 5). Deconcentration is a ubiquitous leveling of industries, jobs and the labor force across space. Driven by the two distinct socio-spatial forces of decentralization and recentralization, deconcentration has produced spatial differentiation and fragmentation. Whereas command and control functions, finance and other specialized producer services tend to remain in major urban centers (due in part to the advantages of agglomeration economies), production, commercial activities and other business functions have dispersed across space. The suburbanization of jobs – that is, the movement of jobs from the cities to the suburbs – is part of this broader process of deconcentration. This spatial redistribution of employment opportunities generates a growing mismatch between the suburban location of employment and minorities' residences in the inner city. If, as is the case in most US cities, public transportation is limited in scope and service, then the inner city poor are isolated from these suburban job opportunities. Poor regional public transportation in combination with the deconcentration of employment reduces the probability of finding jobs for urban minorities living in impoverished inner-city neighborhoods.

All European cities have undergone similar processes of economic and social flight to the suburbs related to rising incomes and wealth, but also growing inequality. However, the European situation is more complex because Europe is not a single socio-economic or political entity and its countries possess differing degrees of urban reconcentration. This reconcentration is also a function of inequality, with young professionals and baby boomers appropriating the best housing in newly gentrifying urban areas in some cities (Joseph Rowntree Foundation, 1998). The socio-demographic transformation of the inner city is another important structural factor involved in the concentration of poverty in major US cities. Whereas deindustrialization and deconcentration have shaped contours of urban labor markets and employment opportunities, socio-demographic transformations have brought about changes in the urban class structure. The flight of whites to suburbia is clearly an important phase in this changing class structure and the crystallization of residential segregation. What is of more importance is the large-scale migration of high-income blacks and other racial minorities out of the inner-city neighborhoods. Gone with this selective out-migration are the social buffers and role models for the less affluent. Residents remaining in the impoverished inner-city neighborhoods are 'the truly disadvantaged' (Wilson, 1987), increasingly isolated from the mainstream.

Many studies have documented the devastating effects of living in an overwhelmingly impoverished neighborhood (for a review, see Small and Newman, 2001). The harmful 'neighborhood effects' or 'concentration effects' are manifold and far-reaching, including lack of quality schools, deprivation of conventional role models, inability to access jobs and job networks, and a high risk of crime and victimization. Without doubt, racial segregation is combined with the growing concentration of poverty. In parallel with growing neighborhood poverty and social isolation, these neighborhood effects on life chances grow more severe over time in many US cities (Massey and Denton, 1993).

THE POOR AND HOUSEHOLD COPING STRATEGIES

This phenomenon is closely tied to the *Informal Economy* (see next entry).

Some urbanists argue that it is the household group rather than the individual that should be the basic unit of social analysis. Often people belonging to households of two or more persons behave in ways that promote the general economic well-being of the group rather than individual advancement. For example, this is the argument that Roberts (1991) makes and he also claims that research on the household division of labor suggests that the group is the basic unit of urban analysis for places everywhere, not just in the third world where this argument is most obviously persuasive. Research has discovered that not all the members of a household are immediate family. Households may contain distant relatives and even friends. The collective pooling of resources does not preclude differences among members, such as conflicts between men and women.

In regard to the study of poverty, household coping strategies show that the poor do not accept their situation passively. They innovate and find ways of supporting themselves. They may engage in 'self-provisioning' which includes domestic processing or production of food, making clothes, undertaking repairs, building illegal housing or add-ons. Coping strategies are closely tied to the informal economy and may include the sex trade, drugs and begging (see next entry). Household coping as a means of meeting poverty conditions in urban areas is a better way of understanding such responses than the usual emphasis on individuals alone (Williams and Windebank, 1995).

REFERENCES

Bobo, L., J. Johnson, M. Oliver, R. Farley, B. Bluestone, I. Browne, S. Danziger, G. Green, H. Holzer, M. Krysan, M. Massagli and C. Zubrinsky Charles, 2000. 'Multi-City Study of Urban Inequality, 1992–1994 [Atlanta, Boston, Detroit, Los Angeles]' Inter-University Consortium for Political and Social Research, Ann Arbor, MI.

Body-Gendrot, S. 2000. 'Marginalisation and Political Responses in the French Context' in P. Hamel, H. Lustiger-Thaler and M. Mayer (eds) *Urban Movements in a Globalizing World*, London: Routledge. pp. 59–78.

Buck, N. 1991. 'Social Polarisation, Economic Re-structuring and Labour Market Change in London and New York' in M. Cross and G. Payne (eds) *Social Inequality and the Enterprise Culture*, London: The Falmer Press. pp. 79–101.

Davey-Smith, G., D. Dorling, R. Mitchel et al. 2002. 'Health Inequalities in Britain: Continuing Increases up to the End of the 20th Century', *Journal of Epidemiology and Community Health*, 56: 434–5.

Department for Work and Pensions 2002. *Households Below Average Income 1994/95 to 2000/01*, Corporate Document Services, London: Stationery Office.

Dorling, D. 2004. 'Housing Wealth and Community Health: Explanations for the Spatial Polarisation of Life Chances in Britain'. Available at: http://www.lancaster.ac.uk/fass/projects/hvp/projects/dorling.htm (accessed 15 June 2004).

Gottdiener, M. and R. Hutchison 2000. *The New Urban Sociology, 2nd Edition*, New York: McGraw-Hill.

'Housing Problems' 2003. Available at www.rural.home.org (accessed 25 June 2003).

Jargowsky, P. 1997. *Poverty and Place: Ghettos, Barrios and the American City*, New York: Russell Sage Foundation.

Joseph Rowntree Foundation 1998. 'The Incomes of Ethnic Minorities', *Findings* (November), London: Joseph Rowntree Foundation. Available at: http://www.jrf.org.uk/knowledge/findings/socialpolicy/pdf/sprn48.pdf (accessed 15 June 2004).

Massey, D. and N. Denton 1993. *American Apartheid*, Cambridge, MA: Harvard University Press.

Roberts, B. 1991. 'Household Coping Strategies and Urban Poverty in Comparative Perspective' in M. Gottdiener and C. Pickvance (eds) *Urban Life in Transition*, Newbury Park, CA: Sage Publications. pp. 135–68.

Sassen, S. 1991. *Global Cities*, Princeton, NJ: Princeton University Press.

Small, M. and K. Newman 2001. 'Urban Poverty after the Truly Disadvantaged', *Annual Review of Sociology*, 27: 23–45.

United Nations 2000. *Human Development Report 2000*, New York: UNDP.

Williams, C. and J. Windebank 1995. 'Social Polarization of Households in Contemporary Britain', *Regional Studies*, 29(8): 727–32.

Wilson, W. 1987. *The Truly Disadvantaged: The Inner City, the Underclass, and Public Policy*, Chicago: University of Chicago Press.

World Bank 2000. *World Development Report 1999/2000*, New York: Oxford University Press.

The Informal Economy

The informal economy is defined as the combination of workers within urbanized areas that are 'off the books', goods produced in unregulated factories with non-unionized and undocumented laborers, goods and services produced and exchanged for barter (i.e. not cash, but in kind) and goods and services sold without regulation on the streets. In some countries the informal economy is so large as to rival the money exchanged in the formal sector.

Only recently has the presence of an informal economy in urbanized places been recognized as an important subject for analysis in its own right. Prior to that reconception, people viewing poor and ghettoized areas conceived of them in terms of economic deprivation alone. Now we understand that, in many cases, residents of areas excluded from the formal opportunities of society nevertheless engage in income earning endeavors that can, in some instances, result in considerable cash rewards. Perhaps the most graphic example of the informal economy is the drug trade which amounts to billions of dollars a year in illegal, but financially lucrative transactions. Other examples extending to quasi-legal acts include the practice by legitimate businesses of paying some people for work that is off the books, such as domestic servants and/or babysitters, that are not employed with formal insurance or social security records, or the practice of using undocumented workers in otherwise legitimate businesses, such as restaurants or factories.

The issue of the informal economy is an especially important focus of third world urbanization research. As global restructuring expands in less developed countries bringing highly paid professional services, poor people drawn to the big cities find informal or casual employment as shoe-shiners, messengers, delivery persons and domestic helpers, in addition to the burgeoning demand for restaurant and other commercial laborers. In some of the newly developing countries, like Malaysia, illegal factories manufacture faux designer fashion items, such as fake Gucci or Louis Vuitton merchandise; others make imitation Rolexes and other watches that are expensive when bought in a legitimate way. Most of the time these jobs have no security and no insurance, but they provide people with the incentive to leave their homes in the rural areas and move to the large cities of the third world.

Although participants in the informal sector are not subsumed under capitalist relations of production and exchange, they are closely linked to the formal economy on a national or global scale (Portes and Schauffler, 1993). In both developed and developing countries, the informal sector is connected to the formal sector of the national and global economy through subcontracting networks and commodity chains. For instance, street vendors sell goods such as cigarettes and other branded products obtained from the formal sector; garbage collectors and recyclers are linked to the formal economy through an infrastructure that buys trash; and illegal prostitution is often one of the paramount features of a tourist economy. Around the world, formal sector firms cut labor costs by using home workers, sweatshops, and others in the informal sector who are without the benefits or safeguards of formal employment.

Engaging in the informal sector is a survival strategy of the urban poor in response to insufficient job creation. In this sense, whether we are discussing developed or undeveloped countries, the informal sector is a 'refuge from destitution' (Portes and Sassen-Koob, 1987: 36). It is undeniable that many participants in the urban informal sector are marginal in their economic status. However, as in the case of off the books or illegal manufacturing enterprises, the informal economy represents much more than a mere survival mechanism of the poor. Entrepreneurs in this sector are adaptive and resilient enough to front businesses that can grow to have considerable size and scope. In general the informal economy is a very significant, if only quasi-legal, component of national economies for several reasons: it provides goods and services at a low price; it plays the role of a reservoir of the industrial reserve army that holds down wages for the formal sector of the urban economy; and finally, the informal sector provides migrants and indigenous city residents with channels of social mobility and opportunities for the accumulation of wealth. Consequently, there is no simple relationship between working in the informal sector and being poor, nor between the presence of such a sector and the relative wealth or level of development of the country. So many functions are provided to society by this sector that it is found everywhere. For the most part, however, we can say that the informal economy is located in the large cities and is, therefore, an 'urban' phenomenon, although not exclusively so.

The exact magnitude of the informal sector is difficult to estimate due to its elusive nature. Nevertheless, there is general agreement that the informal sector represents a growing proportion of economic activity, particularly in less developed countries. There are significant variations in the level of informal employment between and within regions. It ranges from more than 50% of the labor force in urban areas of sub-Saharan Africa, to 30% in Latin America and the Caribbean. Within sub-Saharan Africa, the informal sector employment as a percentage of total employment represents 17% in South Africa and over 80% in Zambia (ILO, 2002: 241).

One study of nine different cities in developing countries estimated that at least 40% of the labor force was engaged in this economy. In the developed countries the figures are lower, but only slightly so in many cases. According to a World Bank study in 2002, the proportion of workers working informally was over 30% and their productivity was comparable to laborers in the official economy. Furthermore, in the developed countries of Europe, the World Bank study found that those with the most labor regulations and the highest taxes also had the most informal workers. Even in advanced economies, there are widely ranging estimates of the size of the informal economy: from 5–10% of national income in the UK and US, to 30% in Italy and 50% Russia (*The Economist*, 2004). Recently, the EU and Europe's statistical bureaus have included estimates of some informal activities, such as prostitution and illegal drugs, in the official counting of Gross National Income (GNI), which is used as the basis of member states' contribution to the EU budget (Abramsky and Drew, 2014).

The fall of communism in Central and Eastern Europe and the accession of many of these countries into the European Union, along with the geo-political fall-out in the Balkans, the Middle East and Africa, have all combined to produce an unprecedented influx of migrants, both legal and illegal into the UK and other Western European countries. Many of these people wind up working in the informal economy. In the UK, refugees tend to concentrate in London and the south-east of England. Indeed, there is a rise of business services employment in the London economy (Buck et al., 2002). The demand for formal business services brings in its wake greater demand for the cheap and often illegal labor that underpins this sector. Furthermore, in many cities of Europe, a vigorous construction boom has emerged over the last several decades. Construction is always a reliable sector for informal employment, and is especially prone to using immigrant labor. Immigrants and illegal refugees are also consistently found working in agriculture. Therefore, the estimates of 'off the books' workers in Western Europe seem low.

The informal sector is generally a larger source of employment for women than for men in the developing world. Studies suggest that a majority of economically active women in developing countries are working in the informal sector. Official statistics tend to underestimate the size of the female labor force in the informal sector because much of women's paid work – let alone unpaid housework – is invisible and thus not counted in official statistics.

The informal sector also absorbs a number of child workers. The number of child workers between the ages of 5 and 14 living in the developing countries is estimated to be at least 250 million (UNICEF, 2001). Most of them labor in the informal sector, carrying out a variety of work in the plantations, sweatshops, affluent households or streets. They are vulnerable to exploitation and abuse. The exploitation of children working under miserable working conditions in overcrowded cities is a global concern. Street children who work and live on the street, in particular, are the most visible manifestation of urban poverty.

The proliferation of the informal sector in major cities is attributed to the excess supply of labor created by: rural-to-urban migration; excessive regulation of the economy; and the structural transformation of the economy, including changes in the organization of production (Portes and Schauffler, 1993). In the US, for example, the process of economic restructuring in the wake of increasing global competition has been accompanied by the proliferation of the informal sector, especially in large cities. The dismantling of the welfare state, the privatization of state-run enterprises, and the decline in organized labor power have facilitated the transformation of labor markets and labor practices in the US, the UK and other countries of Europe. Researchers of this worldwide phenomenon claim that the incentives to use off the books and unregulated labor remain quite attractive in cities throughout the world. These incentives often condemn itinerant workers, new immigrants and marginal populations to a lifetime of drudgery, as affluent households buy low-paid personal services, cleaning and child-minding from work-poor households. In most cities in Europe, these work-poor households are characterized by one-parent families, ethnicity, below average or substandard housing and limited educational opportunities. The working poor are also locked into an informal debt culture in which unscrupulous lenders offer loans with exorbitant interest rate payments they cannot afford. The famous former Lord Mayor of London, Dick Whittington, came to London to make his fortune in the city whose streets were 'paved with gold'. Over the centuries many have followed in his footsteps to find themselves limited to the opportunities of the informal economy, but with no means to break out of its bonds. These restraints include being exploited by criminal gangs, often drawn from their own communities.

One of the ways the informal economy is organized at the level of daily life is by households. Rather than consisting of a sector of individuals, this part of the economy is better understood as comprised of families that work together to pool their resources in a highly restricted environment. In developing countries the limitations placed on people may be the result of labor and immigrant regulation or racial discrimination, while in the developing part of the world rural to urban migrants are faced with the daunting task of acquiring enough resources to survive their transition. In all cases these 'household coping strategies' are a significant phenomenon of urban life. Studying the household rather than individuals also gives researchers a better picture of how people cope with limited life chances. For more information on household coping strategies see the entry on *Inequality and Poverty*.

THE SOCIAL PROBLEM OF AN UNDERGROUND ECONOMY

The informal economy may involve activities that are not only illegal because they use undocumented workers or are off the books, they may also involve criminal acts in their own right. Illegal activities in the informal economy include drug trafficking, people smuggling, money laundering, gambling and prostitution. For this reason, the presence of an underground sector may constitute a serious social problem that jeopardizes the well-being of the larger society. When criminal acts are present, their effects are widespread and disturbing to others. Hence societies are faced with a number of strong incentives to monitor and even intervene in the informal economy. At the same time, because the service and construction industries rely so heavily on immigrant labor, both legal and illegal, to fill the low-wage slots, the informal economy thrives in the developed countries of Western Europe and the US.

REFERENCES

Abramsky, J. and S. Drew 2014. *Changes to National Accounts: Inclusion of Illegal Drugs and Prostitution in the UK National Accounts*, Office for National Statistics. Available at: www.ons.gov.uk (accessed 10 April 2014).

Buck, N., I. Gordon, P. Hall, M. Harloe and M. Kelinma 2002. *Working Capital: Life and Labour in Contemporary London*, London: Routledge.

Fainstein, S.S., I. Gordon and M. Harloe (eds) (1992) *Divided Cities: New York and London in the Contemporary World*, Oxford: Blackwell.

International Labour Office (ILO) 2002. *Key Indicators of the Labour Market 2001–2002*, New York: Routledge.

Portes, A. and S. Sassen-Koob 1987. 'Making it Underground: Comparative Material on the Informal Sector in Western Market Economies', *American Journal of Sociology*, 93: 30–61.

Portes, A. and R. Schauffler 1993. 'Competing Perspectives on the Latin American Informal Sector', *Population and Development Review*, 19(1): 33–60.

UNICEF 2001. *Beyond Child Labour: Affirming Rights*, New York: UNICEF.

BURGESS MODEL – CONCENTRIC ZONES

Ernest W. Burgess developed a theory of city growth and differentiation in the 1930s based on the social Darwinist or biologically derived principles that were common in the work of Robert Park and Roderick McKenzie (see entry on *The Chicago School*). According to Burgess, the city constantly grew because of population pressures. This, in turn, triggered a dual process of central agglomeration and commercial decentralization; that is, spatial competition attracted new activities to the center of the city but also repelled other activities to the fringe area. As activities themselves located on the fringe, the fringe itself was pushed farther out from the city, and so on. Thus the area of the city continually grew outwards as activities that lost out in central business district (CBD) competition were relocated to the shifting periphery.

In Burgess' theory, the city would eventually take on the form of a highly concentrated central business district that would dominate the region and be the site for the highest competitive land prices, while the surrounding area would comprise four distinct concentric rings: a zone in transition; a zone of workingmen's houses; a residential zone; and a commuter zone.

Research shortly after Burgess unveiled his model, in the 1930s and 1940s, contradicted his theory and questioned the concentric zone hypothesis. Many people to this day still think of the city in Burgess' terms, with a large central district that dominates the surrounding area constituted as rings. This is quite remarkable when we acknowledge that shortly after Burgess published his theory it was questioned by more accurate conceptions of how urban regions grew that were based on better research. As indicated in several entries of this book, city-dominated thinking is deeply entrenched in urban studies, even if it is a fallacy (see the entry on *Multi-Centered Metropolitan Regions*).

HOMER HOYT – THE SECTOR MODEL

Published in 1933, Hoyt's model was also based on Chicago but it contradicted Burgess' work (Hoyt, 1939). His sector conception of space was derived from a study of changes in the land prices within the city of Chicago extending back 100 years. Hoyt argued that cities were carved up, not by concentric zones, but by unevenly shaped sectors within which different economic activities tended to congregate. These were produced by competition for locations within a capitalist market in real estate that translated the functional needs of business into land prices. The proximity of radial railway lines is one explaining factor of this pattern.

key concepts in urban studies

Hoyt further argued that manufacturing and retailing, in particular, had the tendency to spin off and away from the center and agglomerate in sectors that expanded outward, while leaving other economic activities behind in a more functionally specialized central business district. This conception is quite accurate today, although Hoyt's general approach is limited because it remained city-based.

CHAUNCY HARRIS AND EDWARD ULLMAN – THE MULTIPLE NUCLEI MODEL

Harris and Ullman, like Hoyt, were essentially correct in conceiving of the development of urban space as consisting of irregular sectors and centers rather than concentric zones under pressure of real estate competition among users with different needs. However, both of these alternative models assumed that the CBD, or the central core of any city, would remain dominant. They did not foresee the way the entire metro region would experience functional specialization.

Harris and Ullman (1945) argued that the spin offs of activities from the CBD would take the shape of separate centers rather than sectors radiating from the central core. These smaller centers were conceived as 'homogeneous urban districts' and they remained organized around a CBD of some kind. In their model, unlike Burgess, no regular pattern could be found where spin-off districts were located in relation to each other.

The entry on *Multi-Centered Metropolitan Regions* argues, in contrast to all city-centered approaches, that the separate centers are functionally differentiated and not linked to the larger whole. Malls are not placed around the region at random, they are located by their developers according to marketing or service areas that have nothing to do with the CBD, but are dependent, instead, on the population distribution of the entire metro region. For Burgess, Hoyt, Harris and Ullman, and I should add many urbanists today, the CBD remains an all-purpose shorthand concept for economic concentration within a city. This view of urban space is false. Multiple centers are spread throughout the metro region and are produced and sustained by regional, national and global modes of societal organization.

CENTRAL PLACE THEORY AND GROWTH POLE THEORY

European urban and regional economists and geographers have been influenced by the work of two German regional scientists, Christaller (1933) and Lösch (1945), who are credited with the invention of central place theory. At its simplest, central place theory offers an explanation for two kinds of urban phenomena: the existence of an urban hierarchy, i.e. the ranking of cities from ones with the most functions and importance to those with the least; and the spatial structure of the urban system – in other words, the relationship between different cities in a region (Evans, 1985). Originally based on a study of southern Germany that was predominantly rural, central place theory has been weak on explaining the existence of an urban hierarchy in industrialized economies. Despite criticism and reworking, central place theory in the context of other theoretical developments does offer insights into the formation of Multi-Centered Metropolitan Regions (MMRs) and the earlier variant, Polycentric Urban Regions (PURs) once used in Europe. Its other utility has been to explain the hierarchy of financial services offered within the urban system of a country (Parr and Budd, 2000).

Another of the important concepts emerging from work in Europe has been that of French theorists in advancing the concept of 'regional growth poles' and development strategies using this perspective. A growth pole is defined as:

> a set of industries capable of generating dynamic growth in the economy, and strongly interrelated to each other via input–output linkages around a leading industry (or propulsive industry) [in the original French meaning]. (Richardson, 1978: 165)

The concept of the natural growth pole (defined in abstract economic space) derives from the work of Perroux (1950). Influenced by the work on innovation by the Austrian economist Schumpeter, Perroux viewed growth within an economy as stemming from domination and disequilibrium, in other words uneven development (Parr, 1999). Following Perroux, a subsequent generation of economists developed growth pole strategies for many urban developments around the world. 'New towns' in the UK and the French equivalent, *les grandes ensembles*, are examples of growth pole schemes whose central purpose was the deconcentration of urban areas. The subsequent relative failure of this form of urban policy in a European setting is based on many causes. Part of the problem is that the original Perroux model was focused on inter-sectoral or inter-industry linkages and little or no consideration was given to the external effects of the flow of goods and people across an urban region. The latter is currently the key factor of spatial development as a consequence of globalization, along with transport and computer innovation.

In sum, central place theory, despite limitations, states that individual centers exist within a wider system and are characterized by complex interactions (as in a Multi-Centered Metropolitan Region). Growth pole theory focuses solely on the internal workings of the pole and not its external relationships within a wider region. There are limitations to the applications of central place theory, the most dominant being that it deals with spatial equilibrium at a specific point in time, while growth pole theory is concerned with dynamic change over time. There are further objections concerning the range of economic activities covered by central place theory, and the spatial-hierarchical structure implies few levels of centers. However, as Parr (1973) demonstrates, many of these objections can be overcome. In doing so, these approaches open up rich possibilities for exploring the Multi-Centered Regional – or Polycentric Urban Regional – perspectives in a European context.

REFERENCES

Burgess, E. W. 1925. 'The Growth of the City. An Introduction to a Research Project' in R. Park, E.W. Burgess, and R. McKenzie, *The City*, Chicago: The University of Chicago Press: pp. 47–62.
Christaller, W. 1933. *Die Zentralen Orte in Süddeutschland*, Jena: Fisher.

Evans, A. 1985. *Urban Economics: An Introduction*, Oxford: Blackwell.

Harris, C.D. and E. Ullman 1945. 'The Nature of Cities', *Annals of the American Academy of Political and Social Sciences*, 242: 7–17.

Hoyt, H. 1933. *One Hundred Years of Land Values in Chicago*, Chicago: The University of Chicago Press.

Hoyt, H. 1939. *The Structure and Growth of Residential Areas in American Cities*, Washington, DC: Federal Housing Administration.

Lösch, A. 1945. *Die Raumliche Ordnung der Wirtschaft*, Jena: Fischer.

Parr, J.B. 1973. 'Growth Poles, Regional Development and Central Place Theory', *Papers in Regional Science*, 31: 174–212.

Parr, J.B. 1999. 'Growth-pole Strategies in Regional Economic Planning: A Retrospective View', *Urban Studies*, 36: 1195–215 (Part 1), 1247–68 (Part 2).

Parr, J.B. and L. Budd 2000. 'Financial Services and the Urban System: An Exploration', *Urban Studies*, 37(3): 593–610.

Perroux, F. 1959. 'Economic Space: Theory and Applications', *The Quarterly Journal of Economics* (1950) 64 (1): 89–104.

Richardson, H. 1978. *Regional and Urban Economics*, Harmondsworth: Penguin.

Modern Urban Planning

The urban form of historic cities can be explained as the result of an evolutionary process where many local decisions aggregate together over time. Yet, the old civilizations, from ancient China to medieval Europe, did engage in forms of planning. Often building was carried out according to an overarching symbolic scheme based on religious beliefs. In medieval Europe and in some places in Asia, urban form was defined by planned fortifications for self-defense. Modern urban planning is linked to capitalist industrialization. During the 19th century, first in Europe, then in the United States, new conceptions of how to guide city growth emerged, replacing the rationale of religion or defense. Some of the most notable ideas in the 19th century sought to overcome the ills of pollution and public health crises, characteristic of the industrial cities under capitalism.

One important 19th-century thinker was Ebenezer Howard. He thought that the industrial city was too large and non-human in scale. Howard proposed, instead, that new development should take the form of *garden cities*, mixing factory construction with countryside living and regional connectivity by train. Exemplified by Welwyn Garden City and Letchworth in England, the garden city, then, brought together the best sides of city and country living (Howard, 1902). In the United States, garden cities in Long Island, New York, and Baldwin Hills outside Los Angeles, California, were built according to this model. Other early landmarks are

Hellerau in Dresden, Germany, and Patrick Geddes' plan for Tel Aviv in Israel. After World War II, Howard's approach gave rise to the *New Town Movement* in England, resulting in the construction of factory centers outside the large cities.

CIAM

A group of European avant-garde architects assembled in the 1920s and 1930s to critically discuss urbanization and planning. The gatherings were titled *CIAM*, the International Congresses of Modern Architecture. CIAM's *Athens Charter* is one of the foundational manifestos of modern urban planning. The Charter was conceptualized in 1933 and published as a book ten years later by the French architect Le Corbusier. It gave a general spatial interpretation to the main *functions* of the industrial society. Mass-production of goods, organized public consumption of surplus in social housing and reproduction of labor were interpreted spatially as homogenous and mutually exclusive metropolitan *land uses*. This reading led to separation between industrial areas, housing areas and green parks for leisure. Transport served as the necessary link between the three main functional zones. Commerce was not central in the modernist conceptualization of urban space, but in practice a city center was assumed to exist, serving both commercial and cultural functions.

Modern urban planning cannot be separated from *modernism*, defined as the socio-cultural articulation of technology, democracy, architecture, consumerism and city life. Emerging during the 19th-century period of capitalist industrialization and urbanization, modernism concerns both the social transformation of rural–urban migrants and the 'high culture' of the arts, opera, drama, literature, cuisine and fashion. In architecture, Le Corbusier and the German architects, Walter Gropius and Mies van der Rohe, articulated a modernist school of design known as the *International Style*. They expunged all local cultural traits and superfluous surface elements, conceiving of buildings in geometrical forms, using the most up-to-date technology in heating, lighting and building materials. These designs populated the planned segregated functional areas, with a preference for high-rise skyscrapers surrounded by open space. After World War II, the principles of modern urban planning and architecture dictated how cities were rebuilt and expanded. *Zoning*, the separation of social functions in separate land-use districts (Gallion and Eisner, 1980), became a key tool of urban planners everywhere. While living conditions were improved for many, the neglect of historical and social contexts and the destruction of existing neighborhoods sparked protests. (For planning critiques see the entries on *Planning and Public Space* and *Urban and Suburban Politics*.)

There is another aspect to the modernist legacy, however. One of the most overlooked effects of modernism is the role of the metropolis in explaining globalization. The British literary and cultural theorist Raymond Williams (1989) describes the connections between modernity, the metropolis and globalization through the agency of urbanization. The sociologist Anthony Giddens (1990) states that globalization is a radicalizing of modernity. The planning theorist Peter

Hall stresses the regional and metropolitan dimension of modern urban planning, for example the idea of a regionally distributed *Social City* as a key to Ebenezer Howard's urban vision. Indeed, in the UK there has been a recent revival of interest in building new garden cities. Similarly, the proposed eco-cities in China are redolent of Howard's vision, often working as centers of metropolitan systems with global connections.

ZONING, GROWTH AND CONTROL

Looking from the perspective of property rights, the first steps in the direction of modern city planning can be traced back to practices establishing districts within which certain rights of citizens were legally curbed. In the late European Middle Ages slaughtering places for cattle were located on the outskirts of town so that offensive odors would not permeate the city. The segregation of the storage place for gunpowder away from the city center in early 18th-century Boston was one of the first recorded acts of *zoning*. In 1876 the State of California ruled that the 'County of San Francisco could regulate the placement of slaughter houses, the keeping of swine, the curing of hides or the carrying on of any business or occupation "offensive" to the senses or prejudicial to the public health or comfort, in certain portions of the city'. Slowly, through various rulings, the power of communities to regulate land for the general welfare became established as law. According to Gallion and Eisner (1980: 185):

> One of the most important legal decisions in the history of zoning was the Euclid case [*Village of Euclid, Ohio v. Amber Realty Company*, 272 U.S. 365] in 1926. In his decision, Justice Sutherland of the US Supreme Court pointed out that each community had the right and the responsibility to determine its own character, and as long as that determination did not disturb the orderly growth of the region or the nation, it was a valid use of the police power.

This decision made it clear that communities, which were incorporated municipalities with their own powers over land, could determine the nature of development through zoning limitations.

During the 20th century the technique of zoning became increasingly more important. Modernist planning guided development into separate zones according to functions. Once planned out, the zoning scheme was then left to the private market in land to attract potential developers. In the United States planners cannot interfere with the way businesses and people utilize the land within the zoning categories. Furthermore, many jurisdictions believe they are in competition with each other in attracting new business. Consequently, public officials support growth and try to be liberal in the application of regulations.

In the US, planning documents involve the *comprehensive plan, zoning ordinances* and *subdivision codes*. There is also a coordination function in places that are growing (Gallion and Eisner, 1980: 192). After the 1950s, municipalities started to draw up *master plans*. This comprehensive approach was made necessary because cities

modern urban planning

89

could not develop without taking into account what was happening in their regions. Planners turned to the collection of concrete data on existing land uses and assessed precisely how much space was devoted to the various zoning categories, such as light manufacturing, single family residences or parks. Once the inventory was complete, a plan for future growth based upon present and anticipated needs was developed. Master plans could then be aggregated for regional development.

Despite comprehensive techniques for monitoring and predicting land-use needs, planners in the US have few powers to realize their schemes. Developers and real estate speculators are well known for being able to get around the obstacles of planning prescriptions. Furthermore, with very few exceptions, regional and comprehensive planning that fosters cooperation between cities and suburbs does not exist. In short, most places lose out to single-minded and narrowly focused developers by increments. One small exception leads to another until the basis of comprehensive planning in an area is eroded completely. Similarly in the UK, production of sustainable housing is thwarted by the power of private developers. Demands by planners that development should include a certain percentage of social housing for key public sector workers (e.g. teachers, nurses) are rarely fulfilled or, if so, only at the margins. In the over-heated private housing market, developers can undermine these demands. Moreover, they have built up large land banks, which they exploit at appropriate moments in the cycle.

Unlike in the US and UK, in many Central European, Scandinavian and Asian countries, planning has a relatively strong role in coordinating and even initiating development. There are also examples of meaningful regional planning and policy. The reasons for this comparative difference can be found in the general societal model, planning legislation and the amount of public landownership. That said, the tension between public good and private profit also demonstrates itself in multiple ways in the more strongly planned societies. For these reasons there have been a number of well thought out critiques of planning in our society. Increasingly, people concerned about the lack of coordination for growth and the problems of regional sprawl have developed alternative approaches. (See entries on *Slums and Shanty Towns, Sprawl* and *Sustainable Urbanization*).

SYSTEMS VIEW OF PLANNING

In the 1960s the focus of planning started to move away from physical design and fixed land-use zones. Rapid regional growth and interest in the 'science of cybernetics' gave rise to the *systems view of planning*. This idea entails a change in how planners understood both the object of planning and its process. Towns, cities and regions were now seen as a system of interconnected parts. Their planning was understood as a *rational process of decision making*.

Nigel Taylor (1998) links the systems and rational process views to modes of thinking and action characteristic of modernism. In 1960s, planning was practiced as science, not as art. Its aim recalled that of the European 18th-century Enlightenment: to use science and reason for human progress and well-being. Taylor (1998: 60) suggests, thus, that 'the systems and rational process theories of planning, taken together, represented a kind of high water-mark of modernist optimism in the post-war era …'. While the applicability of the scientific method in planning has been questioned and discredited since the 1970s, the contemporary interest in complexity science, algorithms, self-organization, resilience, and advanced tools of data gathering and urban modeling is a return to the thematic first addressed by the systems view of planning 50 years ago. How far this return can proceed will be discussed in the entry on *Planning and Public Space*.

REFERENCES

Gallion A. and S. Eisner 1980. *The Urban Pattern: City Planning and Design*, New York: D. Van Nostrand.

Giddens, A. 1990. *The Consequences of Modernity*, Cambridge: Polity.

Howard, E. 1902. *Garden Cities of Tomorrow*. London: S. Sonnenschein & Co. Ltd.

Le Corbusier 1973. *The Athens Charter*, New York: Grossman. [Translated by Anthony Eardley from French original published in 1943.]

Taylor, N. 1998. *Urban Planning Theory Since 1945*, London: Sage.

Williams, R. 1989. *The Politics of Modernism*, London: Verso.

Multi-Centered Metropolitan Regions

The form of settlement space known as 'the city' is about 10,000 years old. Classically, it consisted of a central area with a relatively high population density surrounded by a supportive space of agricultural production. This bounded city form remained virtually unchanged until the period of capitalist industrialization during the 19th century. At that time, the creation of two distinct classes, the workers and the capitalists, split the population with regard to wealth. Affluent families established homes away from the city in the hinterland while retaining a place in town as well. Furthermore, when the forces of profit making were extended to a capitalist market in real estate, speculators began immediately to stake out land outside the central city for sale. They encouraged prospective buyers to use whatever means of transportation were available at the time to commute to work. Crude steam-powered passenger trains, then electrical trolleys and finally the automobile itself for transportation to and from outlying areas, eventually replaced horse-drawn carriages. At each stage of urban development, the boundaries of settlement were pushed further away from the city center. Throughout this early period of 'suburbanization', however, the areas outside the urban core were always attached to it through economic dependency for money making, working-class jobs, commerce and participation in 'high' culture, i.e. art, music, fashion, and the like.

Some urbanists still claim that modern-day suburbanization is the result of the mass production of the automobile. Cities like Los Angeles are celebrated as landmark places of sprawl created by this means of transportation. Yet nothing could be further from the truth. Analysts that rely on such technological determinism, still a common misconception, are always wrong because they fail to think in terms of social organization. Political, economic and cultural, as well as mere technological forces always work together to create significant changes in society. Mass suburbanization really began in the years immediately following World War II in the United States. It was a product of powerful forces unleashed by government programs and economic prosperity that transformed ordinary workers into a 'middle class'. In the end, this profound demographic shift of people from the central cities to the outlying areas created a new form of space that is not the city. We call it the *Multi-Centered Metropolitan Region*, and it is as qualitatively different from the traditional city as was the city itself from its predecessors 10,000 years before that (see entries on *Models of Urban Growth* and *Social Production of Space*; Gottdiener, 1994; Gottdiener and Hutchison, 2000; Gottdiener and Kephart, 1991). Among its distinguishing characteristics is the way the classical downtown has spun off its many functions to other centers so that each is more functionally specialized than in the past. Our urbanized regions now possess multi-centers, some of which are dominated by the function of consumption, or white collar office operations, or manufacturing of some kind, or residential life or recreational and leisure activities. The traditional central city still exists and still remains important in its own right, but it is much more specialized as a place of business and consumption, as well as having a population that is much less representative of the society as a whole.

We can only wonder why urbanists today discuss the features of the new spatial form, such as independent industrial parks that are centers of employment in their own right, or the immense spaces of consumption, known as suburban malls, that draw people, not only from many surrounding cities, but even from other states, while retaining a discursive focus on 'the city', as if the central core still retained the same overarching importance as it did prior to the 1950s. Most urban analysis is now out of date because of this failure to recognize the transformation of settlement space into the new form of multi-centered and regional multi-functionality. We continue to see books with the word 'city' in the title – *Understanding the City*, *City Builders*, *City Culture*, *The Postmodern City*. Such a proliferation of terms containing the word 'city', makes its meaning impossible to pin down, because the word itself is no longer a spatial but a metaphorical concept. Urbanists have created a great terminological confusion by their own inability to sort out the concrete from figures of speech. They write about the global city, the dual city, the informational city, the divided city, the fragmented city, the analogue city, the digital city, the sprawling city, or the edge city. These terms are simply wrong. They apply an attribute, such as the increasing use of digital means of communication, characteristic of settlement spaces that are now regional or even national and international in scope, to some imputed center, a 'city', that just does not exist. We no longer live in a spatial form of centrality, like an edge city, but in a sprawling region of development with many separate centers, each with their own levels of functional specialization.

The multi-centered metropolitan form of space was produced in part by powerful government programs. Two, in particular, are quite deterministic and, in their own way, much more significant than the role of the automobile itself. After the depression of the 1930s, the US government launched ambitious housing programs to help both the banking and the home construction industries back to recovery. Among other aspects, the government allowed a 'home owners' interest rate deduction on taxes. It still exists today and means that people who own their own homes but who carry a mortgage of some kind can deduct the full interest on their payments from their pre-tax income. They don't pay taxes on their mortgage interest. This is a direct subsidy to anyone that can afford to buy their own home. It is also a great incentive to become an owner rather than a renter, *if you can afford to do so*. Renters that cannot, get nothing in the way of a break on their taxes. Because rentals are more characteristic of the traditional city and home ownership more characteristic of suburbia, government housing programs clearly worked to disperse or deconcentrate the population and to promote living in a single family, suburban home.

A second program does involve the automobile, but makes it the means of suburbanization, rather than the cause, in opposition to the claims of technological determinists. During the 1950s, the US government decided to build a crisscrossing web of 'interstate' highways allegedly to facilitate military transportation should we ever be attacked. This National Defense System of Highways Act, passed in 1956, led immediately to the carving up of the nation's hinterland by the asphalt and road construction industries and created the opportunities for speculators to rush in and develop real estate. Massive and sprawling single family home construction on land that was once only valued for agriculture, linked by newly minted high-speed highways, soon followed. Industry, commerce and even cultural or leisure activities, along with once compact urban population, dispersed on a mass basis throughout the expanding metropolitan region, and then re-coalesced into separate and more specialized centers. Gas-powered vehicles became the means by which locations were connected across this ever expanding sprawl of settlement space.

In Europe, there has been a revival of interest in Polycentric Urban Regions (PURs). The distinction compared to Multi-Centered Metropolitan Regions is that the former consists of 'a set of neighbouring but spatially separate regions' (Parr, 2004: 231), whereas the latter is not as spatially separate because of improvements in transportation and communications. Although some British researchers claim that PURs are a variant of Multi-Centered Metropolitan Regions (Champion, 2001), post-war urban policies sought to contain the coalescence of Multi-Centered Metropolitan Regions. In the UK, Birmingham conforms to the latter, but like Greater Boston in the US, developed from the former. There are numerous examples of PURs in the rest of Europe, including the Randstaat in the Netherlands and the Ruhr in Germany (Champion, 2001). Given the density of populations in most European areas, there are strong attempts to spatially separate different urban areas. Also, planning restrictions tend to apply where ribbon developments along rail links would tend to produce spatial coalescence between urban areas. The European Commission is actively seeking to encourage the growth of PURs as the policy solution to regional development (European Commission, 1999). However, as Davoudi notes, 'Instead of being used to describe an existing or emerging reality, the concept is coming to determine that reality (Davoudi, 2002: 117).

The growth of the Multi-Centered Metropolitan Region took place through the twin processes of *decentralization* and *recentralization*. The same processes can be said to underlie the development of PURs. The questions for European policy-makers is the degree to which these processes may be contained to avoid PURs becoming Multi-Centered Metropolitan Regions.

Decentralization means the overall and absolute reduction in the numbers of people and activities from the traditional city. It involves a dispersal not simply of actions but of social organization. With decentralization comes a different way of connecting people through social as well as technological means. The general leveling of population density itself is referred to as deconcentration.

At the same time that decentralization took place, the linked process of *recentralization* also occurred. By the latter is meant the reformation of activities and people in relatively more concentrated spaces with an attendant mode of connection that reflects closer proximity. Thus, both decentralization and recentralization have their own distinct features of social organization. The building up of population centers after dispersal is referred to as *reconcentration*.

One important reason why more urbanists do not take the multi-centered metropolitan region as their basic unit of settlement space instead of the central city is because the US census has yet to abandon its city-centered terms for urban forms. Yet, there has already been considerable evidence from the census itself over the years to suggest that we have passed over to another type of settlement space. By the 1970s, for example, the census revealed that more Americans were living in suburban regions outside the central city than in the city itself. Other data confirmed that economic functions were also dispersing. Between 1948 and 1982, for instance, the census used a category, the Major Retail Center (MRC), to capture 'large concentrations of retail stores within metropolitan areas'. These were centers in both cities and suburban regions. For the latter, they were invariably malls of some kind. The emphasis on centers within the metro region was important, but the census discontinued collecting data with this designation 'because of the high costs of defining the areas' (US Census Bureau, 2003).

At present, the main census category that includes the regional basis of settlement space is the Metropolitan Statistical Area, which does not really convey the complexity of that space and also still retains an emphasis on the traditional central city that is no longer deserved. Metropolitan Statistical Areas for the 2000 census together include about 93% of the US population – about 83% in metropolitan statistical areas and about 10% in micropolitan statistical areas. (In the previous census, 1990, the same classification only included 80% of the total population.) Of the 3142 counties in the US, 1000 are in the 362 metro stat areas and 674 are in micro stat areas; 1378 remain outside the classification.

In the US, the regions of Houston, TX, Phoenix, AZ and Las Vegas, NV are good examples of the new form of space. Elsewhere, in Europe, for example, London, England, Amsterdam, the Netherlands and Paris, France are also good illustrations, as are São Paulo, Brazil and Hong Kong. Houston, for instance, has a downtown, but it is functionally specialized in financial and business services. It is virtually deserted at night. Commerce takes place at several large shopping malls dispersed throughout the region and the same is true for light industry and manufacturing, which can be found in industrial parks or similar districts. Even places like New York also illustrate the new form of space, although that form is harder to see in this case. To be sure, Manhattan represents a traditional city center that still functions much like the core districts of the past. Yet, even so, it is only one place of highly concentrated activity. The New York City region is home to over 20 million people and encompasses parts of the states of New Jersey and Connecticut, as well as New York. People in many areas of this region, such as Northern New Jersey or Long Island, live their lives without ever necessarily having to visit Manhattan. If they do, it is for the kind of special occasion that resembles tourism. They can shop, work and engage in leisure activities close to their homes and in specialized centers spread out within this immense region. The same can be said for residents of Chicago, Atlanta, Los Angeles and other large population concentrations in the US. To speak of these agglomerations as 'cities', the way many urbanists still do, is to ignore the basic reality on the ground, one that consists of a new form of settlement space with many centers that are functionally specialized and tied together by a variety of communication and transportation modes.

In the entry on *Classifications and Definitions of Places* there is a discussion of the relationship between MMRs and PURs in respect of the plan to double the official population of Shanghai by 2020. The planning authorities are adopting a combination of central place theory and growth pole theory to create a Multi-Centered Metropolitan Region, structured hierarchically. In this view, creating this kind of region is the only way to make this plan sustainable. However, the tendency for regional nodes to begin to merge with each other, either as travel to work areas or functional economic regions, suggest that MMRs are part of regional growth strategy but not necessarily a final outcome. Similarly, mega-city regions should not be seen as the ultimate metropolitan form, as this relates to a population count across a particular geography with urban characteristics. For many economies large regional nodes based upon an urban center (for example Istanbul and Ankara in Turkey) will tend to display polycentric characteristics. But, if immanent development trends lead to greater suburbanization in these kinds of countries, the MMR may come to be a dominant form associated with this kind of intentional development. It does, however, point to the problem of applying conceptual templates to complex urban and regional systems.

multi-centered metropolitan regions

REFERENCES

Champion, A.G. 2001. 'A Changing Demographic Regime and Evolving Polycentric Urban Regions: Consequences for the Size, Composition and Distribution of City Populations', *Urban Studies*, 38(4): 657–77.

Davoudi, S. 2002. 'Polycentricity – Modelling or Determining Reality?', *Town and Country Planning*, 114–17.

European Commission 1999. *Sixth Periodic Report on the Social and Economic Situation and Development of Regions in the European Union*. Brussels: European Commission.

Gottdiener, M. 1994. *The Social Production of Urban Space, 2nd Edition*, Austin, TX: University of Texas Press.

Gottdiener, M. and R. Hutchison 2000. *The New Urban Sociology, 2nd Edition*, New York: McGraw-Hill.

Gottdiener, M. and G. Kephart 1991. 'The Multinucleated Metropolitan Region: A Comparative Analysis' in R. Kling, S. Olin and M. Poster (eds) *Postsuburban California: The Transformation of Orange County Since World War II*, Berkeley: University of California Press. pp. 31–54.

Parr, J.B. 2004. 'The Polycentric Urban Region: A Closer Inspection', *Regional Studies*, 38(3): 231–40.

US Census Bureau 2003. *Metropolitan and Micropolitan Statistical Areas Main*, Washington, DC: US Census Bureau.

Neighborhood

Perhaps more than any other concept, with the exception of community, that of neighborhood is interpreted according to diverse ideological conceptions and/or agendas of planning. As in the case of *community*, these interpretations have little to do with actually existing places (see the entry on *Community Development Programs*).

The apostles of the *New Urbanism*, Duany and Plater-Zyberg, for example, invoke the organicist ideology of the Chicago School regarding 'natural areas' (see the entries on *The Chicago School* and *Planning and Public Space*):

> Like the habitat of any species, the neighborhood possesses a natural logic that can be described in physical terms. The following are the principles of an ideal neighborhood design: (1) the neighborhood has a center and an edge; (2) the optimal size of a neighborhood is a quarter mile from center to edge; (3) the neighborhood has a balanced mix of activities – dwelling, shopping, working, schooling, worshipping and recreating; (4) the neighborhood structures building sites and traffic on a fine network of interconnecting streets; (5) the neighborhood gives priority to public space and to the appropriate location of civic buildings. (LeGates and Stout, 2003: 208)

Patently, this is not a neighborhood that we can recognize as existing, but one that some planners wish realized through intervention. Yet the concept of 'natural area' as conceived by the Chicago School was based on research of that city at the time – the 1920s. It referred to a neighborhood that was culturally homogeneous or where one ethnic/racial group clearly dominated, such as Chinatown, Little Italy or Hunkey Town. This concept was closely tied to another, the 'ethnic enclave' or a neighborhood with a large population of residents that share the same ethnic/religious background, usually resulting from a high level of foreign immigration. US cities of the period prior to the 1960s were characterized by neighborhoods very much like these. Since that time, however, forces operating to disperse and mix populations throughout the multi-centered metropolitan region, as well as a drastic falling off in mass immigration, have created sections of urban areas that are ethnically and socio-economically diverse or mixed, if not racially so. (For a discussion of the persistence of racial segregation in US and UK cities, see the entry on *Segregation and Hypersegregation.*)

Perhaps the most influential thinker in regard to the concept of the 'neighborhood' as a distinct feature of the larger regional array, was Jane Jacobs (1961). When she wrote her classic book, *The Death and Life of Great American Cities*, urban planners and architects were laboring under the spell of the International Style (see entry on *Modern Urban Planning*) and replacing large sections of cities with dense, high-rise developments. Jacobs decried this development and claimed it would actually destroy the modern city, not revive it. History has, in some measure, borne her out. According to one observer:

[Jacobs] celebrates the seemingly small things that make a city work well for its residents: the presence of people on the street deters crime; a mix of shops and housing makes a neighborhood both convenient and lively ... cities are ecosystems that can be smothered by rigid, authoritarian planning; ... busy, lively sidewalks help cities thrive as safe, healthy places ... good urban design mixes work, housing and recreation. (Walljasper, 2002)

Many contemporary architects and planners remain influenced by Jacobs' idea that city vitality is based on a healthy neighborhood street life (see the entry on *Urbanization and Urbanism*). Neighborhood vitality, according to the New Urbanist approach, requires a balanced mix of functions – housing, shopping, civic institutions and open space. Pedestrian circulation (the necessary 'human scale' that is sought for in this approach) is encouraged through a mix of streets and open space with conveniently located service centers.

The problem with understanding the *imagined* neighborhood of balance and centrality envisioned by urban planners is the same as that of idealized conceptions of community. Some researchers now argue that neither term captures the social ties of contemporary urban residents because today people possess networks that are less dependent on any particular space. This situation is considerably different than at the time Jane Jacobs was writing. Cyber-tech means of staying in touch were not yet invented. Now social contact no longer requires neighborhood proximity or physical communion. This concept of 'community without propinquity' was discussed in the entry on *Community Development Programs*. Although the claimed effects on society of ICT, i.e. digital information and communications technology, by contemporary academic avatars of change are clearly overrated. Today the cell phone and the Internet, along with the ubiquitous use of the automobile as opposed to public transportation, allow people to remain in close contact with a network of friends and family that are spread out across metro regions (Graham, 2004).

Neither the New Urbanists nor the network researchers, however, deal with the need of a localized space that is used as a resource for people marginalized by our society. New Urbanists profess ideas that only the relatively well-off can afford. Networkers and social scientists that extol the alleged power of ICT to change our lives also focus on the behavior of people with sufficient resources to 'network' across the regional realm and who can afford computers. Both approaches are also biased in favor of males and professional people. Marginalized segments of the society, in contrast, need neighborhood and community relations more. This is especially true of mothers and children. 'Children's environment is not restricted to home, home yard or playground; the whole neighborhood acts as a stage that either affords or restricts children's activities' (Kyttä, 1997: 41).

Children are actually among the largest consumers of public outdoor environments. Yet, their needs are often ignored by planners and developers:

> In western Europe the possibilities of children to move around freely have narrowed down during the last decades. In a large survey carried out in England, a dramatic decrease of the freedom of children to move around was found between 1971 and 1990. The researchers of the study have been worried about the so-called 'battery children', overprotected children who are not active and independent in their environments. If the contacts with the environment are regulated by adults, how does that affect the emotional and cognitive level of children's relationships in the environment? (Kyttä, 1997: 42)

According to comparative studies, children have fewest daily journeys outside the home when they live in cities, compared to rural or small-town areas.

Another group of people that need fully functioning neighborhoods are those that are restricted either financially or because of age or disability. Minority people that are poor and cannot afford cars need neighborhoods and close-in access to services. So, too, do the elderly, if they cannot drive. New Urbanists seem to go too far when they prescribe balanced and fully functioning enclaves for all people in the metro region, especially in the face of so much evidence from network researchers that points to a 'spaceless' neighboring style; yet, their conception is quite appropriate for less powerful segments of our society. In this sense, vital neighborhoods are important for everyone because they play an important role in the life cycle.

REFERENCES

Kyttä, M. 1997. 'Children's Independent Mobility in Urban, Small Town, and Rural Environments' in R. Camstra (ed.) *Growing Up in a Changing Urban Landscape*, Netherlands: Van Gorcum and Co. pp. 41–51.

Graham, S. (ed.) 2004. *The Cybercities Reader*, London: Routledge.

Jacobs, J. 1961. *The Death and Life of Great American Cities*, New York: Random House.

LeGates, R. and F. Stout (eds) 2003. *The City Reader, 3rd Edition*, London: Routledge.

Walljasper, J. 2002. 'Jane Jacobs: Defender of the Urban Neighborhood', *Conscious Choice*. Available at: www.consciouschoice.com (accessed 25 June 2003).

Nightscapes and Urban Escapades

Night activities are one of the key ways central cities can be differentiated from suburbia and rural areas. *Night as Frontier* (Melbin, 1987) was the first book to examine systematically the colonization of the night-time by urban dwellers. There are several factors behind the process. Electrification illuminated the built environment, chasing away the darkness and marking an extended period of urban activity that contrasted with rural life. Agriculture was bound by the day/night rhythm. When electric lights became ubiquitous, urban social activities were able to transcend nature.

Illuminated night-time in urban areas signified socializing and consumption. People visited each other in their homes or went out to purchase food and drink. Restaurants and bars were open until the local authorities declared a closing time. Throughout the industrialized countries, the hometown hour when bars were supposed to close varies considerably to this day. In London, for example, the last call in most public houses is at 11:00 pm, but new legislation in 2002 allowed some variation, while in the city of Buffalo, New York, closing time is 4:00 am. Consumption activities have expanded so effectively in advanced industrial societies that we can now speak of '24-hour' cities – the extended zone of space and time dedicated to unrestricted availability of consuming experiences. While many cities talk about this feature as an aspect of proposed redevelopment schemes, it is really only the Las Vegas region that can truly be called a 24-hour place.

Illumination also affected production. Factories could run all the time, if necessary. In fact, the 24-hour cycle is completely compliant with current union demands for an eight-hour work shift. Las Vegas casinos, which are heavily unionized, discovered that it was much preferable to keep open all the time and accommodate three shifts of workers, rather than extending two shifts by having to pay overtime wages. It is said that the bars in Buffalo, New York remained open until four in the morning precisely because that was the end of the night-time shift at the steel plants. Work started up again at 6:00 am and the bars could have a respite until that shift ended in the afternoon. In short, production and consumption, which are always related, were tied together by the colonization of the night-time.

These work and leisure activities gave urban areas an ambiance completely lacking in areas more tied to the rhythms of agriculturally oriented or suburban life. The film *Taxi Driver* is an excellent visual representation of that late night feeling experienced only in a big city that has expropriated the daily cycle.

Chatterton and Hollands (2003) extend this analysis of the night-time further by arguing that the central city, or downtown, in particular, has increasingly become a late-night place of consumption, play and hedonism for young adults. Increasingly too, new consumption venues are constructed that facilitate these activities. These spaces where people meet to drink, dance and socialize are called 'nightscapes', and they are now common features of large cities. Both cash-starved urban governments and profit-hungry global corporations have discovered that there is an immense critical mass of young adults eager to party at night. Increasingly, alcoholic products further differentiated from ordinary beer or wine, such as hard lemonade or coolers, are produced for this market, and 'chic' venues are constructed that sell them. Both the products and the spaces are manufactured by global corporations that franchise these operations.

So successful has been this new market of young adult consumption, that cities now consider catering to it as part of a general redevelopment scheme for depressed urban areas. In some places, the production of nightscapes, which includes permissive regulation by local authorities, marks one of the few successes of campaigns to bring people with money to spend back to the city center. Many urban places now have these relatively unique, youth-oriented, ludic districts of drink, dance and sexually oriented leisure. In fact, after several years of advertising itself as a 'family destination', Las Vegas ad campaigns in 2003 were strictly designed to dispel that orientation and to proclaim that the area is a place of play for young adults. The ads state quite boldly that 'What happens here, stays here'. Giant discos have been constructed by many of the casinos that cater to the all-night young adult market, including such names as 'Studio 54'. Currently, and in keeping with the Las Vegas style, these new nightscapes compete with each other through theming and environmental design.

The relatively recent transformation of the night-time terrain to a place of communion and consumption is quite remarkable. Once bars were characterized as seedy and, quite frankly, 'deviant', if not 'subcultural'. Mainstream and middle-class people never ventured downtown after hours to 'hang out', unless they were looking for activities outside the normative. Today, many downtown districts of large urban areas remain relatively deserted, except for these 'down and out' places. However, in locations where there has been a revitalization of the city center, nightscapes catering to young adult consumers have led the way. Using the techniques of branding products and theming environments, corporations have transformed these spaces to accommodate an expanding market of active consumers that seem to be up all night. Rather than a place on the margin, or a space of deviance, the nightscapes are now ordinary, mainstream locations where the business of buying and selling goes on as elsewhere and urban dwellers can talk with some pride about a '24-hour' city.

Exactly how this transformation from seediness to trendiness occurred is instructive because it illuminates the interplay of capital and space. In the early 1990s a dance club, the Ministry of Sound, opened in London. Now it is the largest global dance record label in the world. Through the use of theming, branding and franchising, global corporations create environments that tie in activities such as dancing with the consumption of alcohol, fashion, and the commodification of 'cool'. The Ministry of Sound, like other operations, is no longer just a place to dance, it is a global brand that sells many different kinds of merchandise. A second logic of corporate merchandising is the segmentation of markets. All young people are not alike in their musical preferences, fashions or tastes for drink. Global corporations segment these markets or follow the rifts in consumer practices to design different products for actually existing subcultural segments. Alcoholic beverages are a good example. One company, Anheiser-Busch, the largest beer producer in the world, makes several different brands and markets them in different ways. Advertising is the key to creating this virtual product diversity. In reality, all market segments are serviced by the same manufacturer. Only the brand names differ. Companies that create nightscape venues also construct places that seem to differ from each other in appearance. In this way, franchising the night-time does not always mean that businesses are in competition with each other. They may all belong to the same corporation and are merely appealing to different market segments.

The result of all this profit-making activity is a proliferation of consumer places downtown and an explosion of the night-time population, something that depressed cities collectively thought impossible just a decade ago. As elsewhere, with regard to the effects of globalization, it has been the local, independently owned venues that have suffered from this juggernaut. Yet, Chatterton and Hollands (2003) make an excellent point in their analysis of the phenomenon. By applying a Gramscian cultural studies framework, we become attuned to the fact that there is a *mainstream* that is corporately controlled, but there are also *residual* and *alternative* spaces in the locational array. Antonio Gramsci argued that any society undergoing change does not simply shift from one state to another. There are elements of the old regime that remain and these are the *residual* aspects of society. In the case of clubbing, not all original venues shut down simply because new, flashy locations were built. Nightscapes contain a mix of the new with the old; consumers can still find, in most places, those residual and locally owned spaces that have 'character', as long as seediness, for example, isn't picked up by one of the global corporations and marketed as a theme, that is.

Along with the mainstream and residual dimensions, Gramsci argued that there are always forces of opposition appearing in any society undergoing change. In fact, according to the Gramscian perspective, it is precisely the oppositional activities that often lead to change itself. In the case of clubbing, market segmentation by giant corporations can never hem in alternatives. Youth subcultures are much too robust and original for that outcome because those subcultures are authentic expressions of identity issues. Consequently, nightscapes are also populated by places that cater to lifestyles or modes of symbolic expression that see themselves as alternatives to mainstream patterns of consumption. These locations are also added to the mix of the nightscape. In sum, within any of the areas that have a viable night-time, there are places of corporate control, franchising and market segmentation, and there are also places that are locally owned and those that cater to alternative lifestyles. As with other aspects of culture, this mix of diversity means that consumer practices and symbolic definitions will always be in a state of flux, much of it being quite healthy and innovative. As long as city administrations nurture these nightscapes and prevent powerful corporations from obtaining complete control, the central city will remain attractive to a wide variety of people. In some cases, however, such as the transformation of 42nd Street in Manhattan, the mix of venues was obliterated in favor of a mini-version of Disneyworld and for the sake of the tourist industry alone. In that case, it is understandable when observers lament the passing of 'authentic' city life.

REFERENCES

Chatterton, P. and R. Hollands 2003. *Urban Nightscapes: Youth Cultures, Pleasure Spaces and Corporate Power*, London: Routledge.
Melbin, M. 1987. *Night as Frontier*, New York: The Free Press.

Planning and Public Space

Because of its origin as a corrective to the problems of industrial cities, the founders of modern urban planning never took seriously the positive dimensions of dense, historic settlements and vibrant urban life. The big city was seen as evil. Planners overlooked key spatial, social and political characteristics of existing urban settlements. Public urban space was neglected, and the urban street was rendered anachronistic and inefficient. Also, the underlying socio-economic material relations in the production of the built environment were understood rather naively.

PLANNING CRITIQUES

Already in the 1960s, the conceptual foundations, practices and results of planning were heavily criticized. Jane Jacobs' *The Death and Life of Great American Cities* (1961) focused attention on the positive values of urbanity, defending neighborhoods that were wrongly labeled as 'slums'. In Europe, seminal critiques were Aldo Rossi's *L'architettura della città* (1966), which discussed historic urban form, and Henri Lefebvre's *Le Droit à la ville* (1968), which underlined the political significance of public urban space, the 'right to the city' (see Harvey (2012) for a recent discussion). Urban conflicts and protests helped citizens to realize that planners' activities were neither neutral nor rational. A new understanding of *planning as political process*, and later as *communicative action*, started to surface.

In tune with Jane Jacobs' ideas, William H. Whyte (1988) argued for the critical importance of pedestrian life for city culture. Whyte did film studies of people on the streets of Manhattan. He documented how the sidewalks were a kind of public space. Most pedestrians simply used them to get from one destination to another, but Whyte noticed how some people met acquaintances on the street and stopped to chat with them. This 'schmoozing', as Whyte called it, using the Yiddish expression, was an important interactive dimension of city life. In a sense, schmoozing is a basic form of social interaction. It reinforces friendship ties, enables people to catch up on news about acquaintances and binds together individuals that know each other in some way. It is as essential to urban life as is meeting other inhabitants at more formal places like restaurants and bars. With the discovery that schmoozing was a frequent and obviously important mode of interaction, Whyte established that the city street was a crucial public space in its own right and also one that was very typically 'urban'.

In the 1980s, Anthony Downs published a series of planning critiques based on the positive aspects of an idealized Western European town. According to him, the suburban norms of living in single family homes and relying on the private automobile had to be abandoned. Furthermore, he called for a regional government that would integrate the needs of the city and the suburb. To replace the current arrangements of living and working, he turned to the European urban model:

> It featured high-density residential settlements, high-density workplaces, tightly circumscribed land use patterns that prevent peripheral sprawl, and massive use of heavily subsidized public transit systems for movement. These traits are only possible under a governance system that centralizes power over the land use patterns in each metropolitan area in a single governing body with authority over the entire area. (Downs, 1989: 256)

Downs' prescriptions, when addressing the case of the United States, led immediately to a well-known dilemma. With very few exceptions, local governments historically refused to surrender any power to make room for regional governance. This is especially true for control over land-use regulation, because it is precisely that power which provides local governments with revenue. In the UK, full-blown regional government and appropriate revenue-raising powers did not fully develop under the devolution program of the last Labour government (1997–2010), despite local authorities' power being reduced since the late 1970s. The following coalition government of the Conservative and Liberal Democrat parties espoused new localism through its 'Big Society' initiative, which constitutes a further weakening of local government. (See the entry on *Community Development Programs*.)

Elsewhere in Europe, there continue to be pressures for moving to a more 'American style' of privately led development in order to be economically competitive. These pressures are countered by a sustainability agenda that stresses the benefits of dense built structures, mixed use, good public space and poly-nucleated regional systems with limits of sprawl (see the entries on *Sprawl* and *Sustainable Urbanization*). To take an example, the US economist Robert Gordon cites the differences in the productivity performance of the US compared to European economies in wholesale, retail and financial services. He states that if planning were looser in Europe the benefits of allowing the building of lots of Wal-Marts in suburban shopping malls would increase productivity. The fact that European societies may not like to choose this option appears to have passed Gordon by. Furthermore, there is a growing European consensus that unregulated and sprawling growth patterns are also economically inefficient. In favor are *Poly-Centric Urban Regions* (PURs) or *'city-regions'* – a planning term with essentially the same meaning.

NEW URBANISM

Another source of planning critiques emerged in the 1990s with the appearance of the New Urbanists. Above all other considerations they were opposed to the pattern of regional sprawl and sought to return dwelling spaces to a more human scale. Architects Peter Calthorpe and William Fulton outlined a program that provides an alternative to sprawl. They argue that every element of the planned environment interacts with every other. Planners embracing the New Urbanist conception should follow a holistic and ecological approach that harmonizes the intimate scale of the neighborhood with the big scale of the region (Calthorpe and Fulton, 2001). Thus, their ideas are complementary to the conception of settlement space as a multi-centered metropolitan region. In fact, they have called for residential developments within the region to be built at higher densities than at present and surrounded by greenbelts. These mini-centers would resemble garden cities with a mix of service and light manufacturing functions, and would enable people to use alternative means of transportation. In this regard, Calthorpe and Fulton claim they oppose modernist principles of planning such as zoning codes. They no longer see the need for strict separation of social functions, arguing instead that contemporary, 'post-industrial' society possesses cleaner and less obtrusive modes of production, which can be located close to residencies.

As in the case of Down's proposals, New Urbanists' vision of mixed use regional development requires massive state control of local areas: 'The idea that a region can be "designed" is central to the Regional City'. They call for 'an active role on the part of central governments, especially in the provision of transit systems, open-space, and development financing' (Calthorpe and Fulton, 2001). But here they conceive of 'regions' as reifications. This is a monolithic view that fails to understand how multi-centeredness means flexibility and functional differentiation. They assume that different centers can be easily aggregated and that all regional functions can be objectified. This conception hints that the authors cannot see beyond the fallacy of thinking in *physicalist* terms alone.

Calthorpe and Fulton conceive of the landscape as resulting from existing planning codes. They critique the present forms of planning by insisting that these are out of date and based on modernism. They fail to account for both how the market in real estate and how government programs have produced regional sprawl. They are so enamored with the power of the planning profession, even in the light of its immense failure, that they cannot see how plans and codes have been constantly circumvented by developers and how suburbanization looks the way it does because for generations the federal government subsidized home ownership and highway construction. (See the entry on *Multi-Centered Metropolitan Regions.*)

PROCESS AND FORM

Can planners really do anything when capitalist political and economic institutions are so strong? The failure of planning in the US is not just about the strength of the real estate market. It is also about the immense investment of suburban and urban governments in retaining their control over land. Planners have no power because local governments will not let them have it. They are retained solely in an advisory capacity. This is supposed to be a reflection of democracy because it implies that experts should not have the final say regarding what our landscape should look like. But, in practice, this arrangement leaves an opening for special interests that they enjoy and take advantage of with immense relish. Even the advisory role of planners is thus subverted. The European position is similar, as noted by one British planning writer:

> Yet the local planning process is no level playing field, allowing all the participants an equal chance of success. Rather it is a highly political activity controlled by various policy processes, each of which may suit particular interests better than others. (Adams, 1994: 177)

Andeas Faludi, the Dutch planning theorist, in the early 1970s made a distinction between *substantive* and *procedural* planning theories. This distinction has survived the test of time, so that even today we analyze planning both in terms of its substantive aims and in terms of the process. Recognizing the difficulties of both theoretical positions – participation and physicalism – Susan Fainstein proposes a synoptic of three contemporary planning approaches:

> (1) the communicative model; (2) the new urbanism; and (3) the just city. In my conclusion I defend the continued use of the just city model and a modified form of the political-economy mode of analysis that underlies it. ... Within a formulation of the just city, democracy is not simply a procedural norm but rather has a substantive content. (Fainstein 2000: 461)

In the best cases planners can address both process and form in novel ways. The notion of a *just city* refers to a forward-looking vision where increased economic wealth is combined with equal access to resources. Public urban space takes a double role as the political arena of debate and decision making and as a desirable result facilitating a livable city and a good urban life (Knierbein et al., 2014).

To conclude, the apparently most dynamic economies in the world are still infused with a planning approach to the challenges of urbanization. For example, the BRIC countries of Brazil, Russia, India and China still plan, in spite of different political provenances and trajectories. In China, urban planning has evolved over time as an explicit activity arising out of economic planning whose driver has been rapid urbanization. Although there is hierarchical division of planning responsibilities, from master plan to urban design and land parcel development, which was the outcome of 2008 reforms, the top-down perspective still pervades planning decisions. In Russia, the single-industry towns, *monograds*, are giving way to a plan to concentrate Russia's population in 20 large urban centers. This appears to be a throwback to Soviet-style planning. The *Urban Planning Code of the Russian Federation* was adopted in 2004, devolving the General Plans to local administrations. The legacy of the previous era lives on, however, in the form of the relationship between the state and the oligarchs. It is apparent that the ability of planning systems to negotiate and manage significant urbanization in economies that are growing rapidly will be limited. Many of these economies are not fully functioning market economies, nor are there administrative arrangements subject to contractual disciplines underpinned by legal statute. It is perhaps ironic that for the dominant market ideology, the developed economies resist the concept of planning to help make sense of a chaotic capitalist system, despite the hard experience of recent crises.

This state of affairs does not mean that no planning takes place in the US and elsewhere in the West. Considerable design and adherence to zoning codes occurs on a daily basis. Planning agencies work constantly to control growth as best they can by monitoring it and by providing local government with advice and recommendations. Zoning itself remains a powerful tool that often does reduce the negative effects of environmental nuisances. Planning critiques provide people with ideas about how to make the process better. Both New Urbanists and *advocacy planners* seek the stimulation of local citizen participation (see entry on *Urban and Suburban Politics*). The basic idea is that an informed populace will opt for better planning and put pressure on government to improve the environment and defend the public realm. This is an end that planning can realize, if we let it.

REFERENCES

Adams, D. 1994. *Urban Planning and the Development Process*, Abingdon: Routledge.

Calthorpe, P. and W. Fulton 2001. *The Regional City: Planning for the End of Sprawl*, Washington, DC: Island Press.

Downs, A. 1989. 'The Need for a Vision for the Development of U.S. Large Metropolitan Areas', reproduced in R. Legates and F. Stout (eds) 2007. *The City Reader*, 4th Edition, New York: Routledge. pp. 245–55.

Fainstein, S. 2000. 'New Directions in Planning Theory', *Urban Affairs Review*, 35(4): 451–78.

Harvey, D. 2012. *Rebel Cities*. London: Verso.

Jacobs, J. 1961. *The Death and Life of Great American Cities*, New York: Random House.

Knierbein, S., A. Madanipour and A. Degros 2014. '(Re)Framing Public Policies, (Re)Shaping Public Spaces' in A. Madanipour, S. Knierbein and A. Degros (eds) *Public Space and the Challenges of Urban Transformation in Europe*, New York: Routledge. pp. 23–37.

Le Febvre, H. 1968. *Le Droit à la ville, 2nd edition*, Paris: Anthropos (2nd ed.); Paris: Ed. du Seuil, Collection "Points".

Rossi A.M.I. 1966. *L'architettura della città* (*The architecture of the city*), Padua: Marsilio.

Whyte, W.H. 1988. *City. Rediscovering the Centre*. New York: Doubleday.

Preservation and Conservation

The issue of preservation has become increasingly important for cities and for developing countries that are experiencing globalization. It encompasses a variety of different circumstances that have in common the desire to protect the built environment, because of its historical/cultural importance, from deterioration, demolition, redevelopment, social upheavals and simple neglect.

PRESERVATION IN URBAN SETTINGS

The built environment of metropolitan regions is also a historical repository of architectural constructs that represent an irreplaceable cultural heritage. Often cities develop and recondition themselves in order to attract new investment, especially after disturbing periods of decline, by removing 'old' buildings in order to offer open land for new projects. This 'creative destruction' is one aspect of real estate under capitalist land market conditions (see the entry on *Real Estate*). In some cities, older buildings that are under-utilized are removed simply to provide parking spaces in the hope of attracting suburban residents to visit downtown. Buffalo, New York tore down the Frederick Larkin office building, one week in 1960, in just such an effort. It happened to be designed by Frank Lloyd Wright, the most famous and most influential American architect. The Larkin was the only office building of Wright's ever built. Once it was removed, it was gone forever. It is precisely because of such retrospective knowledge, and a growing appreciation for past architectural projects as social heritage, that the issue of preservation within cities has become so important.

According to Anthony Tung:

> The universal factor which causes cities to erase their own patrimony is the allure of
> a better future. With industrialization, an extraordinary global phenomenon occurred:
> during the twentieth century, cities across the world, at different stages of development,
> of different historic cultural characteristics, were seduced by the appeal of modernization

and in the name of a somewhat illusionary future embarked upon what we might today describe as a global wave of eradication of architectural patrimony. International experts estimate that something on the order of 50% of humankind's historic architectural heritage was erased in 100 years. (Tung, 2003: 1)

Experts on preservation, like Tung, who calls 20th-century urban development a 'culture of destruction', fail to see how the logic of capitalist real estate operates to undercut the social value attributed to landmark buildings. He is a critic of modernist ideology (see the entry on *Modern Urban Planning*), but he is not a critic of capitalist real estate markets. As he argues:

> Can we conceive of an urban environment that is pluralistic but not fractured and schizophrenic? Can we invent a contemporary architecture that is a true cultural expression of modern life, yet relates with respect, with civility, to the architecture of the past? I think a question of the ethic of architectural planning emerges: how do we build new life-enhancing environments without simultaneously being destructive? (Tung, 2003: 1)

Because of its confrontation with the profit motive and the recycling of urban land, preservationism requires government support, even sponsorship, and intervention in the private market. In 1966 the US Congress passed the National Historic Preservation Act (Public Law 89-665) that gave legal powers to lower levels of government and Native American tribes to preserve aspects of the environment deemed 'socially' significant. Resources were directed towards 'financial and technical assistance', providing leadership in retrieval efforts, the administration of federally owned historic sights, and guidance to non-publicly owned places of cultural value. Furthermore, under the Secretary of the Interior, a register of National Historic Places that were part of the country's heritage would be composed and regulated. Properties meeting the criteria under the act were designated 'National Historic Landmarks' and preserved with the help of public funds.

In 1996, efforts towards preservation were given a boost when the federal government issued Executive Order 13006, *Locating Federal Facilities on Historic Properties in Our Nation's Central Cities*. It directed government agencies to use landmark facilities whenever possible, thereby channeling resources into their upkeep. Promoting the renewal and use of already existing structures, rather than the demolition of the 'old' in order to build something 'new', is the essence of preservation efforts.

GLOBAL CASES

Cities around the world have a special need to preserve and sustain the built environment because in almost every case they are located in areas with a long history that is embodied in architecture. Preservation, in the face of the need for economic development, becomes important to third world nations that are being forced to modernize, but do not want to lose their cultural and historical heritage.

Preservation is also important in developed countries with a long history. Often, the primate city of the country, such as Bangkok, Thailand, or Helsinki, Finland, is also a concentrated depository of the nation's heritage. The challenge for these places, as it is in the US, is to identify those structures most worthy of preservation, while also fostering the construction of new and distinctive projects. This task is somewhat easier for the US, because of its relatively recent founding, than it is for areas of the world that have been settled for millennia.

Preservation is usually accomplished through municipal planning once the power to preserve is accorded to local government. Those structures worthy of attention must be identified in a democratic manner so that citizen involvement, as well as the participation of local historians and planners, is important. As material from the plan of Copenhagen, Denmark, states:

> The interest in urban preservation does not only focus on individual buildings, but increasingly on whole urban environments and city-scapes. This may involve overall developments that form an entity with a characteristic building pattern and joint features. Or it may be concentrations of individual buildings of high preservation value. It may also be buildings that together form distinctive features. ('Urban Preservation')

Expanding the definition of historical preservation, Dolores Hayden's work (1995) advocates broadening the concept of heritage to include public art, spatial struggles, the inclusion of diverse perspectives, especially from minority and gendered community representatives, and the relationship between landscape and public memory. To the principal question of 'what buildings to preserve?' Hayden adds 'whose history should be preserved?', thereby advocating diversity in the historical preservation movement. From this perspective, the participation of citizen groups in the process of sustaining the urban environment becomes a critical factor.

Hayden's work, however, is trivial compared to the global issues raised by the efforts of UNESCO to determine 'world heritage' sites. These are not only places designated for preservation within countries, but also cities themselves under the more recent program of designating 'cultural capitals'. The alleged positive aspects of allowing political issues to be part of the preservation/heritage equation trumpeted by Hayden, turn into mixed benefits when viewing the politicization of world heritage issues from UNESCO. One of the key issues involves the globalization of values assigned to places that determine the worthiness of obtaining heritage designation. In practice, these judgments most often represent the interests of politically powerful actors belonging to the United Nations, including those from less developed countries such as Saudi Arabia as well as the hegemonic Western nations. Local and weak perspectives are not acknowledged by the UN's activities most often because UNESCO ignores them. Furthermore, the 'cultural capital' program of UNESCO has been co-opted by city boosterism and promotes consumerism and tourism at the expense of local culture itself, where the past is reconditioned as a form of nostalgia that is then commodified (Munasinghe, 1998). The commodification of nostalgia and a themed version of the past also characterize those sites that are 'representations' of historical places, such as Williamsburg, VA.

The key issue raised by the preservationist movement is in regard to the articulation of values that then determine which sites are worthy. In the main, there is a failure to acknowledge diverse norms and differences of value that, if recognized, would empower less advantaged, more localized cultural interests. According to Tunbridge and Ashworth (1995) this problem involves the 'dissonance of heritage'. In many cases, these values express the norms of hegemonic Western cultures. They also have been co-opted by consumerism and the promotion of place to the extent that one observer refers to the preservationist movement as a 'heritage industry' (Hewison, 1987). Among other things, the commodification of heritage can be seen in the mechanical reproduction of 'old fashioned' house furnishings and architectural components, such as doors or windows under the sign of *nostalgia*.

One of the earliest and perhaps the best illustration of the value dilemma embodied by global preservationist efforts is the Venice Charter of 1964 and its effects. Meant to provide protection for historical sites in European cities that were facing renovation and redevelopment, it privileged the kind of building characteristic of Western civilization, namely, monumental structures that were architecturally significant from the perspective of European aesthetics. City spaces and, in particular, historically significant areas within the city and the active neighborhood culture of the street itself were all ignored in favor of a focus on individual buildings (Appleyard, 1979). Subsequent 'charters' drafted in global meetings in different parts of the West broadened the definition of cultural worth, but retained the Eurocentric perspective on aesthetic values that so-called peripheral countries, like Sri Lanka and Cambodia, now struggle against. The fact that local preservation interests in these areas must fight against UN as well as first world designs, makes this effort very difficult. Despite such international control, fanatical Muslims in Afghanistan, for example, were able to destroy millennia-old giant rock carvings of the Buddha in the 1990s, while UNESCO remained active in that part of the world. Once destroyed, such totally priceless manifestations of a world-class culture cannot be retrieved.

REFERENCES

Appleyard, D. (ed.) 1979. *The Conservation of European Cities*, Cambridge: MIT Press.

Hayden, D. 1995. *The Power of Place*, Cambridge: MIT Press.

Hewison, R. 1987. *The Heritage Industry*, London: Methuen.

Munasinghe, H. 1998. *Urban Conservation and City Life*, Oulu, Finland: Oulu University Press.

Tunbridge, J. and G. Ashworth 1995. *Dissonant Heritage: The Management of Past as a Resource in Conflict*, New York and London: J. Wiley & Sons.

Tung, A. 2003. 'In the Cause of Architecture: Interview with Anthony Tung'. Available at: www.archrecord.com (accessed 7 July 2003).

'Urban Preservation'. Available at: www.urbanpreservation.org (accessed 20 July 2003).

Venice Charter: International Charter for the Conservation and Restoration of Monuments and Sites (1964). International Council on Monuments and Sites (ICOMOS). http://www.icomos.org/charters/venice_e.pdf (accessed 11 October 2015).

A country's leading city is always disproportionately large and exceptionally expressive of national capacity and feeling. The primate city is commonly at least twice as large as the next largest city and more than twice as significant. (Jefferson, 1939: 227)

So wrote the US geographer Mark Jefferson in 1939. He created the law of the primate city to explain how the large metropolises account for a large proportion of a country's population as well as its economic activity. The law states that the primate city is twice the size, in terms of population, compared to the next biggest city. The obvious examples are London and Paris in Europe, Los Angeles and Mexico City in the Americas, Bangkok in Asia and Accra in Africa. Indeed, in his original paper Jefferson points to the conditions that make London the primate city of the United Kingdom:

The finest wares are always to be found there, the rarest articles, the greatest talents, the most skilled workers in every science and art. Thither flows an unending stream of the young and ambitious in search of fame and fortune, and there fame and fortune are found. London is the kingdom's market for all the superlative in intellectual and material productions. Its super eminence as a market runs parallel in size. (Jefferson, 1939: 226)

Notice that size runs parallel to eminence, which in the mega-city account is the main determinant of the primate city. Moreover, it gives a lie to the claim that we now live in an informational age in which the creative classes sustain the eminence of cities. In respect of urban areas in emerging economies, Jefferson's perspective is relevant to the age-old problem of the rural–urban shift.

Jefferson's law relates to the development of urban hierarchies. Predecessors and contemporaries wrote equally influential papers presenting the view that the size distribution of most US cities and a few European cities followed a rank-size rule (see Auerbach, 1913; Goodrich, 1925; Singer, 1936). That is, the distribution of the size of cities follows regular ranking from largest to smallest, at an initially rapid rate of difference that then slows down. So a city with a rank of three would contain a third of the population of the largest city. We can see some of this evidence in the size distribution of Chinese cities, developed in response to regional growth poles strategies and trickle-down economics, especially in the coastal regions.

What appear to be the drivers of primate cities and an indication that this 'law' could be renamed the 'law of capitals', is a combination of economic, demographic and geographical factors. But political history is also a powerful determinant. In many places political power has always been located in capital cities that are the seat of government. This appears to be the case in Latin America, large parts of the wider Europe and Asia. Like Multi-Centered Metropolitan Regions (MMRs), the law of the primate city has conceptual and analytical appeal because it depends on the strength of economic, political, geographical and demographic factors. It is not universal, describes the world on a pragmatic basis and does not fall into the tautological category of the 'information city', for example.

The issue of whether primate cities are parasitic on national economic and political systems never really goes away. In Bruce London's account of Bangkok, it dominates political decision-making. He states:

> It is just a short step from contrasting those highly developed primate cities with their underdeveloped hinterlands to assuming and asserting that the primate city actually acts as an obstruction to hinterland economic growth. In addition, we should emphasize that in the case of the primate city the 'hinterland' is the entire nation. (London, 1977: 50)

Although taking an ecological system approach to the primate city debates, London connects parasitism and the primate city to capitalism and underdevelopment. There is an implicit discussion of this phenomenon in Andre Gunder Frank's thesis of 'the dialectic relationship' between capitalism and underdevelopment, which places the primate city in an international rather than solely a national setting. Hence he relates a city's parasitic effect on its hinterland to its dependent ties to the larger, world capitalist system. The primate city is no longer the dominant city, but the intermediary – at once exploiter and exploited. In Frank's terms:

> These metropolis-satellite relations are not limited to the imperial or international level but penetrate and structure the very economic, political, and social life of [dependent] colonies and countries. Just as the colonial and national capital and its export sector become the satellite of the ... metropoles of the world economic system, this satellite immediately becomes a colonial and then a national metropolis with respect to the productive sectors and population of the interior. Furthermore, the provincial capitals ... are themselves satellites of the national metropolis – and through the latter of the world metropolis ... we find that each of the satellites ... serves as an instrument to suck capital or economic surplus out of its own satellites and to channel part of this surplus to the world metropolis of which all are satellites. (Frank, 1969: 6)

The issue of parasitism has arisen again in regard to London versus the rest of the UK. London appears to be taking on the appearance of a playground for the global nouveau riche who are buying up real estate on a large scale and sustaining a speculative boom in top-end commercial and residential markets. This has led to London being termed Borisstan, after the Mayor of London Boris Johnson, who appears to be determined to turn London into a kind of European Dubai. One could argue that this is the capital city problem which has always been with us. One finds a similar trajectory in Paris, whose inhabitants have long been called 'salopards de Parigot' (Parisian bastards) by inhabitants in other regions. Essentially, many city and urban boosterists implicitly support the primate city model, but do not take account of the complex interaction between the capitalist development and the metropolitan region as being central to its ecology.

REFERENCES

Auerbach, F. 1913. 'Das Gesetz der Bevölkerungskonzentration', *Petermanns Geographische Mitteilungen*, 59: 74–6.

Frank, A.G. 1969. *Latin America: Underdevelopment or Revolution*, New York: Monthly Review Press.

Goodrich, E.P. 1925. 'The Statistical Relationship between Population and the City Plan' in R. Burgess (ed.) *The Urban Community*, Chicago: University of Chicago Press. pp. 144–50.

Jefferson, M. 1939. 'The Law of the Primate City', *Geographical Review*, 29(April): 226–32.

London, B. 1977. 'Is the Primate City Parasitic? The Regional Implications of National Decision Making in Thailand', *The Journal of Developing Areas*, 12(1): 49–68.

Singer, H.W. 1936. 'The "Courbe des Populations." A Parallel to Pareto's Law', *The Economic Journal*, 46(182): 254–63.

Real Estate

The buying and selling of land, whether it is developed or not, is a major force in the production of space (Gottdiener, 1994; Lefebvre, 1991). Capitalism extended its relations of profit-making to the ownership of land and its market turned that asset into 'real estate'. Agricultural land is a natural resource and its value depends on how fruitful the location is for the production of useful products. The value of urban land, in contrast, is entirely contained in its attributes of location. It has little intrinsic value, unlike farmland, except for its potential as a place where societal activities can occur. Consequently, urban land acquires its value, in part, through society. Its worth depends on the collectivity. For example, it is possible to buy a piece of property within a city or suburb, just hold it while other pieces of property are developed, and then sell it at a higher price without making any improvements at all. The greater price obtained is the product of collective societal activities in the adjacent area. Real estate is only one of a few select commodities with this characteristic that has been made possible by the extension of capitalist relations to the market for land. Gold and diamonds are similar; they increase in value without any apparent effort on the part of the owner, although, like land, they can also lose value if the market declines.

When an individual buys a suburban home, for example, the value of the property is primarily in the house not in the land, although the latter can be priced at a significant fraction of the overall cost, depending on circumstances. Yet, the value of this one property depends considerably on how well the neighbors maintain

real estate

113

theirs. If the houses in the surrounding area decline or become unattractive, for whatever reason, all properties in the suburban development are affected. When an individual buys a condominium (apartment) in the central city, he/she is not purchasing the land exclusively at all, only the commodified shelter of the condo (apartment block). The land is owned collectively by all the condominium residents and they are all equally responsible for its maintenance. In sum, even developed real estate, not just land itself, contains within its valuation, under capitalist conditions of a free market in property, a proportion that is directly tied to the collective actions of others.

The collective component of metropolitan real estate's value is privately expropriated in a capitalist society. This is a basic contradiction of capitalism. Some of that value, of course, is recovered for the collective good by our system of municipal taxation. Property tax is the key way many school systems in capitalist societies are financed. Taxes on real estate also help support metropolitan services. Taxing the value of land, however, is quite limited as a measure of public finance precisely because there is so much resistance to the idea in a capitalist society. Even single family home owners seek to make a profit from the ownership of their houses when the time comes to sell. Consequently, the private expropriation of the collective value of metropolitan real estate results in a perpetual fiscal crisis of local government because the latter does not have powerful enough fiscal tools to make people pay for the maintenance of the collective environment (see entry on *Financial and Fiscal Crises*). In capitalist societies there is always considerable tension between property owners and local government. The former seek to retain as much of the increase in the value of their real estate as they can, while the latter seek to tax that increased value in order to advance the public good by maintaining and improving the environment. While it makes objective sense for all citizens to support the public sphere in this regard, it is precisely a contradiction of capitalism that private interests tied to profit-making in property overpower these obvious collective considerations. Individual real estate owners hate property taxes.

Forms of agency are also important in understanding real estate markets and their spatial effects. There are at least six different types of actors in the production of property:

Speculators – they purchase land hoping it will increase in value without improving it. Due to the collective nature of urban land's value, as discussed above, all other categories of agency also include the component of speculation in them.

Developers – they buy real estate and then construct aspects of the built environment for sale, such as houses, factories, office buildings, retail shops, mini-malls and giant malls. Sometimes developers also retain ownership and rent out property, as in the case of malls, but, most often they simply sell off their projects and move on to another vacant piece of metropolitan land that is ripe for speculation or development.

Homeowners – they acquire shelter, either through single family, multiple family or condominium home purchases that are also held for future gain on property value.

Local politicians – they may not own local property, but they are very active in its development because city finances depend so heavily on the real estate tax. Unfortunately, campaign contributions from land developers are also the primary way local politicians acquire money to run for or stay in office.

Large corporations – these are the least connected to local individuals but are often the most powerful forms of agency. Corporations may decide to invest in a location and spend money to finance the development of land for factories, marketing centers, office buildings, or any one of the various forms of consumer outlets, such as big box department stores. They may work closely with local developers or may have in-house people that specialize in land development and construction. In any case, their actions to invest or to disinvest, such as by closing down a factory, have a great impact on local areas. In the UK the large food retailers bought development sites in the 1990s in order to build ex-suburban malls. Private construction companies have also engaged in this process, known as 'land-banking', in which land is only released into production when prices are high enough. Assisted by the accounting treatment of capital gains as a cost rather than a revenue stream (thereby reducing corporate tax liabilities), the speculative use of land becomes just as financially important as selling groceries or building homes.

Banks and other financial conduits – this last category is as important as the one before it. The private market in real estate depends for its lifeblood on the channels that allow money to flow into and out of it as investments and/ or purchases. In many advanced capitalist societies the financial sector is so developed that there are numerous ways to invest in land. This fragmentation of conduits for profit-making is typical of capitalism and its regulation is quite difficult. There are mortgage companies, real estate trusts, holding companies, bonds, secondary mortgage lending, commercial loans, savings loans, and more. People can work in the area of real estate investment full-time or part-time. In the aggregate, the sector of finance capital involves both many jobs and considerable profit under capitalism, while investment in land is one of its principal activities, along with the flow of money into the primary circuit.

CRITIQUE OF THE 'GROWTH MACHINE' METAPHOR

One fallacy that was widely spread among urbanists derives from the writings of Logan and Molotch (1987) who maintained that there was a special class of people with interests in real estate, called the *rentiers*.

According to this approach, rentiers formed a 'growth machine' that worked full-time to promote the development of land. This is a false way of viewing the phenomenon of real estate under capitalism. We have seen how many different ways there are to invest in property, how attractive that investment is and how many types of people are involved in the second circuit. To be sure, pressures for 'growth' are always strong under capitalism. But it is clearly a mistake to attribute those pressures as originating from a select group or collectivity linked together by a single purpose. The second circuit of capital is fragmented both structurally and with regard to agency. Many different types of people invest in land in order to make money. Often they conflict with each other and there is always competition. This makes profit-making in the second circuit of capital a complicated and often contentious affair. The metaphor of a 'machine' completely misses the mark.

Financial innovations on a global scale, discussed above, further undermine this contention. In fact, the growth machine perspective seems particularly ignorant of the field of financial economics in general, and, more curiously, as it relates to real estate investment in particular. Even within particular city regimes that advocate growth, it is wrong to assume the monolithic view that only a single rentier class is in control. The city booster movement in the UK, seen, for example, in the pressure groups promoting cities like Manchester as the new northern powerhouse and Liverpool as a European City of Culture in 2008, is heavily represented by real estate interests. They seek to exploit returns from developing derelict downtown sites, through building apartments, offices and shops close to the new sporting and cultural sites. However, the flow of finance into these kinds of development come from manifold sources and are not just part of some specific mode of social agency called a 'machine'.

Countries like the US have never had a rentier class to begin with and advanced capitalism did away with such a specialized group in most countries a long time ago. There is no singular elite present in metropolitan areas, because that concept is a simplistic fiction, but there is always pressure for investment in land, and the actions taken under that pressure by those forms of agency that temporarily wield power are not always helpful to the public good. A study of the long history of land ownership and its relation to capitalist development in the UK reinforces this point:

> The evidence presented in the preceding chapters – in terms of theoretical, economic analysis, of the empirical study of the economic relations of landownership, and the ideologies and political struggles with which the different group of landowners were associated – indicate that there is no single group, based on landownership by capital, which can be said to be a distinct and coherent fraction. (Massey and Catalano, 1978: 186)

We have a built environment that constantly changes, grows as well as declines, and there is little the public sector can do to control it. Development is always a contentious affair. Understanding metropolitan growth requires attention to both the factions involved and the way capital ebbs and flows through the fragmented institutions of the second circuit which currently are increasingly more complex in their opportunities for capital investment. In the US the 'growth machine' perspective remains popular, but, echoing the observation of Massey and Catalano above, it is probably because of its simplicity rather than its truth.

SECOND CIRCUIT OF CAPITAL AND CRISES

Real estate under capitalism has both a structural force and forms of agency that combine to make it the most powerful factor influencing the shape of metropolitan regions. Aspects of agency, such as the behavior of real estate agents, are easy for most people to see and understand, but the dimension of structure is also clearly important, as it is for all other aspects of advanced capitalism, and it is a great deal more difficult to comprehend. The French philosopher, Henri Lefebvre (1991), has written the most important works for understanding the significance of real estate as a component of social structure in advanced capitalism. Our economic system is dependent on investment flows that have their ups and downs. *Crises* develop at both ends of this cycle leading to social and personal problems. According to Lefebvre, investment in land is a separate structure from that of investment in industry and commerce. Its behavior differs, thereby leading to a separate investment cycle of prosperity and decline. Most investment is in the industrial sector, or what Lefebvre calls the 'primary circuit of capital'. When people seek other means of making money, they invest in real estate, or the 'second circuit of capital'. Lefebvre argued that, because these two circuits are slightly out of sync, money-flows into real estate are significant because it represents the development of land, which is not easily convertible into liquid assets.

This second circuit affects capitalism in two distinct ways. First, during periods of first circuit decline, money shifts to the second circuit. This appears as excessive development of land and speculation that is detrimental to the environment. Second, when the first circuit is about to recover, it cannot do so quickly because the money invested in the built environment is not easily converted back to cash. Eventually, when this does occur, real estate values plummet and, by connection, so too do municipal and metropolitan revenues dependent on property taxes. In short, the *structural* aspects of real estate investment are significant for understanding the uneven development and problems of the built environment under capitalism. These processes include the way in which land is both a form of fixed capital, which gives rise to the production of the built environment, and circulating capital, which gives rise to a set of financial flows that stem from rents and changes in the capital values of the built environment. Land is, thus, a peculiar and multi-faceted part of capital, in that its use and exploitation includes many residual elements from feudal times. In the contemporary context, we find that the majority of personal wealth holding in the UK and US is in housing and that over 95% of the wealth in both countries is accounted for by real estate.

Changes in the nature of finance, such as disintermediation (direct access to finance rather than through the intermediary of a bank) and securitization (creating financial instruments to be bought and sold on the basis of changes in the value of an underlying asset such as an office block), on a global scale now exacerbate the real estate cycle as a whole range of financial investors enter and leave the market. Most of the proximate causes of the East Asian Crisis in 1997, for example, were not just global capital flows, but, more specifically, over-investment in speculative real estate in the case of Thailand and over-production of other parts

real estate

of the built environment (factories, warehouse and infrastructure) by international financial capital (Berry et al., 2001).

The financial crisis of 2007 was rooted in real estate, as well. The causes of the initial credit crunch, subsequent crisis and ensuing recession lay in the sub-prime part of the housing market in the United States. Novel financial 'tools', such as Collateralized Debt Obligations (CDOs) and other Special Investment Vehicles (SIVs), were used to create assets which packaged mortgages and mortgage payment to poorer individuals in cities like Detroit in the US, and then resell them as triple A rated securities to investment banks. The $9.5bn bailout of Dubai World, the major development company in Dubai, in late 2009 by some of the United Arab Emirates governments due to real estate speculation on a massive scale, is another manifestation (*The Times of India*, 2009). In the run-up to the 2007 crisis, real estate speculative booms in Europe turned to crises, with the consequent economics and politics of austerity. The EU, IMF and European Central Bank (ECB) attempted to resolve the consequent fiscal crises in Portugal, Ireland, Greece and Spain. The basis of the continuing crisis in the Eurozone is the role of banks in the largest economies in real estate lending to the periphery. But real estate bubbles are not just a condition of developed economies or of the United States and Europe. Commodity economies, from Australia to Kazakhstan to South Africa, are experiencing real estate bubbles as an effect of the recent boom in global commodities prices. For example, in Sydney house prices rose by 23% in 2014. In China, authorities have tightened monetary policy to deflate a potential financial bubble, caused by over-urbanization and speculation, that underpins the rise in the total debt to GDP ratio to 245%: the world's largest. The balance sheets of Chinese financial institutions are opaque, but there is enough qualitative and increasing quantitative evidence to suggest that they are carrying toxic real estate assets, related to the significant scale and increase in urban development.

It can then be argued that all financial crises are rooted in the role of real estate in capitalist societies, of which the Florida Real Estate Bubble to the 2007 crisis are just two examples (Budd and Parr, 2008; Krugman, 2003; Roach, 2009).

REFERENCES

Berry, J., S. McGreal, L. Budd and P. Scholes 2001. 'Relationships between Financial and Property Markets in the Asia-Pacific Area', *Pacific Asia Property Review*, 7(2): 113–25.

Budd, L. and Parr, J.B. 2008. 'Neglected Aspects of the East Asian Financial Crisis', *21st Century Society*, 3(1): 31–48.

Case, K.E. and R.J. Schiiler 1988. 'The Behaviour of Home Buyers in Boom and Post-Boom Markets', *New England Economic Review*, 83–92.

Gottdiener, M. 1994. *The Social Production of Urban Space, 2nd Edition*, Austin, TX: University of Texas Press.

Krugman, P. 2003. *The Great Unravelling*, London: Penguin.

Lefebvre, H. 1991. *The Production of Space*, Oxford: Blackwell.

Logan, J. and H. Molotch 1987. *Urban Fortunes*, Berkeley: University of California Press.

Massey, D. and A. Catalano 1978. *Capital and Land*, London: Arnold.

Roach, S.S. 2009. *The Next Asia: Opportunities and Challenges for a New Globalization*, Hoboken, NJ: Wiley.

The Times of India 2009. Dubai World to get $9.5bn bailout package 25 March. Mumbai: Times of India.

Segregation and Hypersegregation

A ghetto is an area of a city or suburb occupied exclusively, and relatively involuntarily, by members of predominantly one social group. The term today connotes an urban area of poverty, unemployment and substandard housing.

In 1970, nine of the 10 largest metro central city areas in the US had white majorities, ranging from 55% (Detroit) to 82% (Boston). Twenty years later, only Philadelphia (51%) and Boston (58%) were predominantly white. The rest of the city cores had populations that were mixed, with whites as a single group being a distinct minority. Where did the white people go? To the suburbs. Since 1950 they have been leaving the city in vast numbers. Beginning with the opening up of employment opportunities during World War II, large numbers of African Americans left the South and migrated to cities of the Northeast and Northcentral states. The record numbers involved in this population shift of whites to the suburbs and blacks to the inner city, combined with overt racial discrimination in housing, led to the segregation patterns that have prevailed since that time. Declining economic prospects and shifts in the labor requirements of new jobs have left these emergent ghetto areas of the cities in distress. By 1970, the majority of Americans lived in suburbs, not cities. Because blacks could not suburbanize as rapidly or in as large numbers due to racial discrimination and poverty, inner city areas with African Americans increased their concentration of blacks. Ghettos became more extreme.

According to Cutler, Glaeser and Vigdor (1999), racial segregation in the US remains at a very high level. On average, 60% of blacks would have to move in order for blacks and whites to be equally distributed in US cities. Cutler, Glaeser and Vigdor examined segregation in US cities over the century from 1890 to 1990. From 1890 to 1940 blacks migrated to urban areas and located almost exclusively in ghettos. Between 1940 and 1970, black ghettos expanded. Since 1970 though, urban segregation has declined, especially for more educated African Americans.

Cutler, Glaeser and Vigdor suggest and evaluate three different explanations for urban segregation. The most important factor is the involuntary segregation of ghettoization, whereby whites took collective action either through informal or formal means to segregate blacks in particular areas. Cutler, Glaeser and Vigdor call this 'collective action racism', and it includes restrictive covenants, racial zoning, policy instruments and threats of violence. These factors were widespread before 1960 but became illegal after that as a consequence of fair housing laws and civil rights legislation. However, racial practices such as screening and loan biases still exist.

Another factor is lifestyle, especially for African Americans that move north from the South. These people, like other immigrants, sought areas of the northern cities that had the cultural resources they needed, such as black churches. According to Cutler et al., African American migrants from the South are 10% more likely to belong to an all-black church than native northern blacks and 24% more likely to prefer a segregated neighborhood.

The third factor is 'white flight' where inner city white residents pay more to live in all white suburban communities: 'the data seem to support this explanation today as a contributing factor for the persistence of segregation decades after equal housing laws were enacted'. Simply put, most inner city blacks cannot afford suburbia and those whites that can, move away to live in segregated suburban areas, thus perpetuating the involuntary segregation of blacks within the city.

Cutler, Glaeser and Vigdor find that, despite gains in integrated metro areas, 'there are more completely black areas in our cities than there have been in the past'. Furthermore, although blacks on average pay less than whites for urban housing, they pay relatively more for rental housing.

Over the years, urbanists have developed demographic means of measuring segregation. Until recently, two key measures have been used: the 'index of dissimilarity' and the 'index of isolation'. Massey and Denton (1993) have defined these as follows:

(a) *Dissimilarity* – If blacks disproportionately reside in some areas of a city relative to whites, we say that dissimilarity between the two races is high. The index of dissimilarity measures the proportion of whites that would have to move to black areas in order for the two races to be evenly distributed. The highest level of dissimilarity is 1 or 100% of whites would have to move. A level of 0.3 is considered low, between 0.3 and 0.6 is considered moderate, and above 0.6 is considered high.

But, dissimilarity alone does not make a ghetto:

(b) *Isolation* – In measuring the *isolation* of blacks from whites, we want to know how much interaction there is between the races. An index of greater than 0.3 using the authors' index of isolation is considered isolation. According to Massey and Denton, 'a city possesses ghettoization if the index of dissimilarity is greater than 0.6 and the index of isolation is greater than 0.3' (1993: 74–5).

Massey and Denton (1993: 74–7) introduce three other measures of segregation: *clustering, concentration* and *centralization*. Cutler et al. (1997) found that these latter three are highly correlated to the first two and thus use only dissimilarity and isolation in their study. But Massey and Denton use the five measures as separate dimensions to identify a phenomenon they call 'hypersegregation':

Not only are blacks more segregated than other groups on any single dimension of segregation, but they are also more segregated on all dimensions simultaneously; and in an important subset of US metro areas, they are highly segregated on at least four of the five dimensions at once, a pattern that we call *hypersegregation*. (Massey and Denton, 1993: 77)

Massey and Denton find that nearly one-third of the black population in the US continues to live under conditions of extreme segregation:

> Typical inhabitants of these ghettos are not only unlikely to come into contact with whites within the particular neighborhoods where they live; even if they traveled to the adjacent neighborhood they would still be unlikely to see a white face; and if they went to the next neighborhood, no whites would be there either ... No other group in contemporary United States comes close to this level of isolation within urban society. (1993: 77)

Despite this grim evidence of both segregation and hypersegregation, data since the 1970s also reveal that there have been 'modest' declines in the level of segregation within US metro areas. According to Cutler et al. (1997), after 1970 substantial waves of Hispanic immigrants came to the US and they often mixed with blacks in low income neighborhoods. In addition, there have been some positive effects following the fair housing laws passed since the 1960s to combat racial segregation in real estate. Educated African Americans have particularly benefited from legal powers that allow them to purchase homes in formerly restricted areas of the metro region.

Racial segregation is not a problem exclusive to the US. With a significant influx of black people from the Caribbean and Africa, the UK has recently exhibited its own problems in this area of concern, which had not been experienced since the riots in the inner London suburb of Brixton in 1981. Still there are differences between the two nations. In the UK, racial composition is less diverse than in the US. In addition, racial minorities constitute only a small proportion of the total population. It is estimated that about 4 million racial minorities live in the UK, representing about 7% of the population, and about half of them live in London (Katwala, 2001). Major minorities include: Indian, Pakistani, black Caribbean, black African, Bangladeshi and Chinese. Racial minorities are disproportionately concentrated in major cities and large metropolitan areas. Within a city, racial minorities tend to be segregated into impoverished neighborhoods or areas of low-quality housing due in part to discriminatory practices in housing markets and economic marginalization.

Notwithstanding spatial concentration and segregation, the majority of racial minorities live in mixed areas (Daley, 1998). As in US cities however, racial segregation and racial tensions are by no means trivial in UK cities. Inexorable racial segregation, combined with relentless social exclusion and deprivation, leads to racial conflict and racially motivated riots. During the summer of 2001, for example, clashes between white and South Asian youths swept through the northern towns and cities of England, including Bradford, Burnley and Oldham. These towns, once celebrated as examples of Victorian industrial affluence and pride, have been in economic decline for decades. The disappearance of large-scale employment from traditional industries and the consequent flight to the suburbs bordering on the countryside, have created employment exclusion for Asian and Caribbean youths. This heady brew has thrown the remaining urban white population into the arms of atavistic racism and its political proponents.

There is a distinct division of ghettoization in the UK, however, that reflects the regional imbalance. In London, racial concentration tends to occur in large public housing estates (projects), or where there is a dominance of owner occupation, in particular suburban areas (Southall and Wembley) that have large Asian populations. These areas co-exist alongside high levels of cosmopolitanism, underpinned by the affluence of urban professionals. The contrasts are stark. Affluent finance professionals in the Isle of Dogs (part of the old Docklands close to the financial district of the City of London) live in up-scale, gated communities while surrounded by large post-World War I housing estates that are predominantly populated by working poor Bangladeshis. The latter came in large numbers to London to occupy the bottom of the international division of labor in the garment industry in the East End of London. A UK government report of the late 1980s, at the time when the City of London was gaining global finance status, stated that Bangladeshis had poor levels of health and educational achievement and were likely to be the occupiers of the poorest public housing (Rhodes and Nabi, 1992).

Now with the increasing effects of globalization and trans-national migration patterns, often occasioned by unstable geo-politics, other countries in Europe are increasingly experiencing both the influx of racially and ethnically diverse groups and their subsequent segregation in specific areas of the metro region. Existing third generations from Algeria and Morocco, born and bred in European cities, find themselves more and more marginalized and identified closely with the problems of newer immigrants. The recent banning in France of the *hijab*, the headscarf worn by Muslim women, is symptomatic of these tensions, but also points to the long history of France's relationship with its former colonies in North Africa. The problems that have emerged, such as the high level of youth-related crimes among Muslim immigrants in the public housing estates of the outer Paris region, are remarkably similar to the US experience – a record of racial segregation that was once considered unique.

REFERENCES

Cutler, D., E. Glaeser and J. Vigdor 1999. 'The Rise and Decline of the American Ghetto', *The Journal of Political Economy*, 107: 455–506.

Daley, P. 1998. 'Black Africans in Great Britain: Spatial Concentration and Segregation', *Urban Studies*, 35: 1703–24.

Katwala, S. 2001. 'The Truth of Multicultural Britain', *The Observer*, 25 November. Available at: http://www.theguardian.com/uk/2001/nov/25/race.world4 (accessed 10 May 2003).

Massey, D. and N. Denton 1993. *American Apartheid*, Cambridge, MA: Harvard University Press.

Rhodes, C. and N. Nabi 1992. 'Brick Lane: A Village Economy in the Shadow of the City?' in L. Budd and S. Whimster (eds) *Global Finance and Urban Living: A Study of Metropolitan Change*, London: Routledge.

key concepts in urban studies

Slums and Shanty Towns

A slum is a concentrated, densely settled area where housing is inadequate, residents are poor and community functions are lacking.

Although the emphasis is usually placed on the presence of deteriorated housing, because that is the most visible element, slums are afflicted by inadequate public services, poor medical and educational care, and a general neglect of its population by the larger society. Consequently, a slum is an area of inadequate housing *plus* inadequate community services, private sector stores, professional offices such as doctors, and the like. Slum populations are invariably racially and economically deprived. Generally health problems are compounded by overcrowding and the lack of both cheap and fresh food and professional medical assistance in the area.

Slum settlements represent over 30% of the urban population in all developing countries. In some cases, the Middle East and Africa, the share is as high as 60% (see Table 4).

Table 4   Slums and squatter settlements as a percentage of the urban population

City	% of city population
Latin America	
Bogotá, Columbia	60
Mexico City, Mexico	46
Caracas, Venezuela	54
Rio de Janeiro, Brazil	20
Middle East and Africa	
Addis Ababa, Ethiopia	79
Casablanca, Morocco	70
Ankara, Turkey	60
Cairo, Egypt	60
Asia	
Calcutta, India	67
Karachi, Pakistan	44
Manila, Philippines	35
Jakarta, Indonesia	26

Source: 'World Population Growth and Global Security' (1983).

Since this information was published, the rapid increase in urbanization has progressed on a global scale alongside the rise of emerging economies. The same city-level information is not available but Table 5 gives a regional breakdown for developing regions. We can see that although the proportion of urban populations living in slums has decreased the growth of cities has shifted slums and shanty towns beyond city limits.

Table 5 Slum incidence by region

Region	Slum population as % of urban population				
	1990	1995	2000	2005	2010
Northern Africa	46.1	42.8	39.3	35.7	32.7
Sub-Saharan Africa	34.4	28.3	20.3	13.4	13.3
Latin America & the Caribbean	70.0	67.6	65.0	63.0	61.7
Eastern Asia	33.7	31.5	29.2	25.5	23.5
Southern Asia	43.7	40.6	37.4	33.0	28.2
South-eastern Asia	57.2	51.6	45.8	40.0	35.0
Western Asia	49.5	21.6	20.6	25.8	24.6

Source: UN Habitat (2011).

SHANTY TOWNS – INFORMAL HOUSING

Shanty towns can be slums, but they are also different. They are sections of the city into which people have moved 'unofficially', i.e. the people are squatters, and have constructed housing using informal means and found materials.

The shortage of affordable housing for low-income urban households in the developing countries, coupled with the massive rural to urban migration, has resulted in a proliferation of these squatter settlements (UNCHS, 1999). Often the sheer number of urban migrants in the developing countries is too great for either the private or public sector to provide adequate housing or shelter, and thus many families end up in squatter settlements. Shanty towns have many names all over the world – *favelas* (Brazil), *bustees* (India), *barriadas* (Mexico), *poblaciones* (Chile), *villas miserias* (Argentina), *bidonvilles* (Africa), *kampungs* (South Asia). Despite different names, these squatter settlements have many features in common, including frequent public health crises, crime, crushing poverty, and no future for the next generation because few countries provide them with schools.

There is also another face of shanty towns. Despite inadequate housing, many of the residents have jobs, including a large number that are either part-time and/or in the informal economy. Not all the housing is put up by the family that lives there. Many of the individuals who build these settlements are real estate entrepreneurs. The majority of shanty town dwellers live in rental housing (Datta, 1990). The urban poor find cheap rental accommodation in shanty towns despite impoverished living conditions. Shanty towns are often the only places where the working class can find affordable housing. Informal settlements with predominantly rental accommodation are common in many cities of Latin America where the demand for cheap rental accommodation far exceeds the supply and where controls on the quality of housing are negligible (UNCHS, 1996: 218). In general, shanty towns continue to grow because they are where the increasing numbers of poorly paid urban workers and rural migrants to the city can obtain shelter. It is precisely within these squatter settlements that socio-spatial networks flourish and provide new arrivals to the urban region with access to jobs and other personal assistance.

Visual images of informal settlements are bleak and observers may assume that these are defeated, disorganized neighborhoods. Although social problems, such as limited urban services and infrastructure, persist in most informal settlements, case studies show that these are vital and viable communities. Many shanty towns possess a robust social order (Aina, 1990). A common conception is that life in these places is totally peripheral to the vibrancy of the urban economy. The marginality of shanty town inhabitants, however, is largely a myth (Perlman, 1976). Many shanty towns support robust economies in themselves including areas of real estate investment. They often are the location for small-business enterprises started by urban migrants. Shanty towns may also be sites for small and medium-sized factories. In addition, recent penetration of multi-national corporations as part of the restructuring of the global economy has brought the support of subcontracting in the developing countries (Safa, 1987). This phenomenon of vertical disintegration creates new manufacturing jobs and helps local entrepreneurs while integrating shanty towns into the global economy.

In fact, the development literature contains a debate among researchers with regard to what features of shanty town life are positive or negative. Janice Perlman (1976) for example, lists at least six positive functions of these areas. Shanty towns provide: (1) free housing; (2) reception centers for migrants; (3) employment in family and cottage industries; (4) mobility within the city so people can locate closer to their jobs; (5) a sense of community and social support during times of difficulties; and (6) rewards for small-scale entrepreneurs that invest in building shanties for real estate speculation.

> Despite their visual disarray and clear spatial distinction from the rest of the urban grid, squatter settlements are both highly organized within themselves and highly integrated into the rest of the housing system. There is tremendous diversity within shanty towns with regard to income, education, occupation, and material and size of dwelling units. (Perlman, 1976: 18)

DEVELOPING SLUMS, THE CASE OF INDIA

Yet not all researchers accentuate the positive aspects of these places. In the past many developing countries have viewed shanty towns as unsightly and dysfunctional. Now we know that shanty towns do serve positive functions, but they also have many problems and the best policy is simply to improve them as much as can be done. According to Sarosh Anklesaria (2002: 1):

> One fourth of the urban population of India today lives in slums, under inhumane conditions. These shanty towns, common to many cities of the developing world, are characterized by low-quality housing and lack of physical infrastructure. With little access to clean drinking water and sanitation, the inhabitants face a constant threat of

disease. In a typical slum, houses are built of mud and plastic sheets. Streets and alleys are often no more than seven feet wide and double as open sewers. Despite these conditions, the slum population of India doubles every ten years.

Many of the slum dwellers are employed but they do not invest in their housing because the settlements are considered illegal and can be demolished at any time. They live there because they cannot find any other affordable alternatives. The official response to these slums used to be demolition and eviction of squatters. But, this simply resulted in the slum relocating elsewhere because the need for cheap housing in India remained.

> Then relocation schemes attempted to move the illegal squatters temporarily to make-shift camps while five to six storey apartments could be built. But this proved to be both capital intensive and socially inappropriate. The residents could not adapt to these dwellings and simply resold their flats and moved back to the slum. Such projects failed to help those who needed the housing most. (Anklesaria, 2002)

The latest approach in India uses a community asset-based plan. The idea is to improve shanty town districts, rather than replace them, so that living conditions there become adequate. Working with the existing community infrastructure, services are improved. Most importantly, government programs in India construct underground sewers because these are probably the one improvement that the dwellers need. Another policy feature allows squatters to buy the land where they are living. This provides the economic incentive for improvement of housing. Finally, improvements in transportation infrastructure that service the shanty towns enable the workers to continue to hold down jobs in the formal economy. In short, policies that improve shanty towns have replaced those that sought to tear them down.

REFERENCES

Aina, T. 1990. 'Shanty Town Economy: The Case of Lagos, Nigeria' in S. Datta (ed.) *Third World Urbanization*, Stockholm, Sweden: HSFR. pp. 133–48.

Anklesaria, S. 2002. 'Improving Urban Shanty Towns', *Architecture Week*, 21 August.

Datta, S. (ed.) 1990. *Third World Urbanization*, Stockholm, Sweden: HSFR.

Perlman, J. 1976. *The Myth of Marginality: Urban Poverty and Politics in Rio de Janeiro*. Berkeley, CA: University of California Press.

Safa, H. 1987. 'Urbanization, the Informal Economy and State Policy in Latin America' in M. Smith and J. Feagin (eds) *The Capitalist City*, Oxford: Blackwell. pp. 252–74.

United Nations 2008. *World Population Policies 2007*, New York: United Nations, Department of Economic and Social Affairs/Population Division.

United Nations Center for Human Settlements (UNCHS) 1996. *An Urbanizing World*, Oxford: Oxford University Press.

United Nations Center for Human Settlements (UNCHS) 1999. *Basic Facts on Urbanization*, Nairobi, Kenya: UNCHS Habitat.

UN Habitat 2011. *State of the World's Cities 2010/11*, Washington, DC: United Nations.

'World Population Growth and Global Security' 1983. Washington, DC: Population Crisis Commission.

Social Production of Space

Henri Lefebvre's *La Production de l'espace* (1974, English translation 1991) famously brought together a new vision about historical and socially produced space that reflects the conditions of its production and simultaneously provides seeds for change. Space is a very peculiar product. It is simultaneously the end result of production and the context of production, setting its conditions. This double aspect is grasped by Marx's (and Hegel's) concept of concrete abstraction. The *logical form* – in distinction to 'substance' or 'reality' – of social space is 'encounter, assembly, simultaneity' (Lefebvre, 1991: 101). This idea opens up a way to understand Lefebvre's project of 'spatializing the dialectic'. He continues:

> But what assembles, or what is assembled? The answer is: everything that there is *in space*, everything that is produced either by nature or by society, either through their co-operation or through their conflicts. Everything: living beings, things, objects, works, signs, and symbols. (Lefebvre, 1991 [1974]: 101)

When developing the idea of social production of space, Lefebvre constantly works against any simplistic reading of urban situations. Space is complex, and there is always deep-seated *otherness* in space (Lefebvre, 1991 [1974]: 28–9). The only possible way to conceive is dialectical, a movement or change (cf. Gottdiener, 1994 [1985]: 128). Lefebvre's key idea is to propose a *synchronic dialectic*, a dialectic of the present. He spatializes Marx's (and Hegel's) dialectic, which is usually conceived of as a temporal movement from one stage to the next (Lefebvre, 1991 [1974]: 65–7). In Lefebvre's mature thinking, the dialectic consists of a continual movement between three terms, for example those of conceived, perceived and lived space (Elden, 2004: 36). That is the discourse 'of' space, instead of scientific-representing discourse 'on' space (Lehtovuori, 2012: 74–5).

Lefebvre's analytic framework is not descriptive, but rather hints at action and societal change. For Lefebvre, urban space is the ground of 'urban revolution'. Christian Schmid (2005: 110) suggests that for Lefebvre the core of the dialectical problem of form and content is in an effort to understand action. Criticizing Hegel's abstract thought, Lefebvre foregrounds social practices through Marx and individual poetic creativity through Nietzsche (*ibid.*: 111). A painter, for example, could not develop his skills and awareness without actually painting. Painting is not a pretext or an arbitrary manifestation of an inner, pre-existing talent, but its source. Similarly, space can only be understood *in its production*. The terms of a spatial dialectic influence each other, co-producing space in a dialectical movement. Different elements come together in a moment of production. Space can be understood as the possibility of simultaneous existence of differences, but those differences are not necessarily on the same plane of analysis. As Massey (2005: 9) formulates, space is a 'coexisting heterogeneity' (Lehtovuori, 2012: 76).

UNEVEN DEVELOPMENT

In *The Social Production of Urban Space*, Mark Gottdiener operationalizes Lefebvre's ideas to contemporary urban studies. Gottdiener views urban process through a Giddensian lens of social structuration, so that the structures, institutions and agency are mutually interdependent (Gottdiener, 1994 [1985]). The real estate sector receives important agency in the production of urban space. *Uneven development* is caused under capitalism by the differential way investment chases the highest rate of return under conditions of a free market in land, which leads to the spatial effect of poverty adjacent to wealth.

Urban and suburban settlement spaces flow and develop because of capital investment. The concept of uneven development can also be applied to entire societies, not just their spatial patterns. This more general way of viewing the concept is characteristic of the Marxist analysis of capitalism. According to Marx, 'a major contradiction of capitalism is the simultaneous emergence of concentrations of wealth and capital, on the one hand, and poverty and oppression, on the other. This "general law of capitalist accumulation" as Marx termed it, highlights the capital-labor conflict' (Bond, 1999).

For Henri Lefebvre, the unevenness in accumulation and ownership is expressed spatially in terms of inequalities in the residential pattern and in the provision of urban services. Lefebvre's interpretation is responsible for the perspective of the 'socio-spatial' approach to urban studies.

THE SOCIO-SPATIAL APPROACH TO URBAN STUDIES

The socio-spatial approach to urban analysis is the consequence of a paradigm shift that took place from the late 1960s (Lefebvre, 1991 [1974]). Prior to that time, the dominant view of urban processes among sociologists and geographers was called 'human ecology' (see Gottdiener, 1994 [1985]; Gottdiener and Hutchison, 2000). Ideologically biased, human ecology grounded the relationship between social and spatial processes in a biologically based metaphor borrowed from the plant and animal kingdoms. Urban patterns of population dispersal and development were viewed as an *adjustment* process to the environment that is organic and adaptive rather than being the product of class-, race- and gender-based social relations stemming from a complex mode of social organization. Human ecology therefore, with its emphasis on adaptation, was particularly inadequate to the understanding of urban conflict during the 1960s and the long period of deindustrialization that has occurred since that time as a consequence of changes in the world capitalist system.

The key concept of the new paradigm in urban studies is that the form of settlement space is related to the mode of organization of the economy. This does not mean that clearly defined stages of urban growth are directly correlated to exact stages of economic development. It does mean that important spatial patterns, which define the *spatial* organization of society, are associated with specific aspects of the cultural, political, social and economic features of the correlated mode of *societal* organization. According to this socio-spatial approach, the stages of urban development are related to changes in the *political economy* of society. In the case of the US, urban forms emerged and became modified because of phases in the development of capitalism. Table 6 summarizes these trends.

Table 6 Stages of capitalism and urbanization

Stages of capitalism	Stages of urbanization – for the US
Mercantile-colonial period (1630–1812)	Colonial waterfront city – Boston, New York, Philadelphia, New Orleans, San Francisco
Industrialization period (1812–1920)	Industrial city – Chicago, Akron, Cleveland, Pittsburgh, Detroit, Atlanta, St Louis, LA
Monopoly capitalism (1920–1960)	Metropolitan city and suburbs – Manhattan, Chicago, Denver, Minneapolis, Boston
Global capitalism (1960–present)	Multi-Centered Metropolitan Region – NYC, LA region, Las Vegas region, Phoenix, Minneapolis – St Paul, Dallas – Fort Worth

Most histories of this development, prior to the paradigm shift, make the claim that land-use pattern changes were the result of changes in transportation technology. For example, the suburbanization of contemporary US land-use patterns is commonly blamed on the mass introduction of the automobile. This is an old and outdated view. More accurate is the understanding that real estate is developed constantly, especially in the US, as investment is attracted there from other possibilities. With a free market operating in land, developers and speculators use whatever technological means are available to pursue growth. Thus, suburbanization was already quite evident in the 1800s and cities have always spun off other centers, whether transportation was dominated by horse-drawn carriages or the steam locomotive.

The socio-spatial approach argues that development patterns in the US involved two different but related shifts of population and economic activities that were massive and historically unprecedented in scale. The first was a shift to the suburbs that accelerated on a mass basis after the 1940s. The second was the shift to the sun belt that accelerated after the 1960s. In both cases, the war efforts since World War II had a great deal to do with providing both the infrastructure and the economic resources for these transformations to occur. According to the socio-spatial perspective, land-use development is as much a product of the interventionist state and state policies as it is of economic investments and resource development. This is what is meant by a 'political economic' approach to urban growth.

Another aspect of the socio-spatial approach is the explicit recognition that social life is comprised of classes and of other social divisions that are important, such as those of race and gender. For Karl Marx and Friedrich Engels, the industrial cities of the 1800s, especially those found in England, such as Manchester, were the best places to study the *extended relations* of the capitalist system, just as the factory was the best place to study the organization of capitalist production itself. Engels (1973) interpreted city life, not as a species adaptation to the environment, but as a class adaptation, specifically as the way the different social logics of entrepreneurs and workers played themselves out in a space dominated by the private real estate market. Everything was determined by cash. All values, ideas, beliefs and preferences were translated by the marketplace itself into consumption choices that were limited by budgets. Those who could afford more, got more. Those who had little, had little choice about bettering their quality of life.

According to this socio-spatial approach, urban life was not an adaptation by a species to an environment, but the *production* of forces and choices, of structure and agency. Now we understand that the spatial arrangements of urban areas are also the product of racism and, in many places, such as suburbia, they have embedded within them relations of gender domination as well (see the entries on *Gendered Spaces* and *Segregation and Hypersegregation*).

Within the urban environment produced by the capitalism of the 1800s, Friedrich Engels (1973) observed the many social problems resulting from social inequalities and the uneven distribution of wealth. Families that could ill-afford all their children, abandoned some of them to the street where they had to fend for themselves. It was not uncommon to see urban 'waifs' selling matches or shining shoes and living without families in the squalid areas of the industrial towns. There was also terrible pollution from the factories and large areas of substandard housing. Public health crises were common and, because of inadequate or non-existent medical care, the infant mortality rate among the urban working class was quite high. Today urban areas still have to deal with the negative effects of an unequal distribution of wealth through various public programs, such as subsidized housing. These *public policies* are restricted by the current *fiscal crisis* of the state, which is an ongoing condition in societies organized around private enterprise (see the entry on *Financial and Fiscal Crises*).

The socio-spatial perspective pays particular attention to real estate as the 'leading edge' of growth. According to Henri Lefebvre (1991), it is this aspect of the economy that results in the production of space. The real estate sector of society constitutes a separate circuit of capital where money can be made, not in the manufacture of things for sale, but in the ownership of land that can then be sold as is, or developed and sold at some later time when the social wealth of the surrounding area has made that investment more valuable. This quality of wealth creation in the second circuit of real estate is quite different from the way capitalist investment returns a profit in the primary sector of manufacturing. We owe to Lefebvre the insights that have enabled the socio-spatial perspective to advance the argument that space itself is an important factor in metropolitan development and one that is governed by a logic of profit-making at some variance from the way capitalists in the primary circuit make money (see the entry on *Real Estate*).

Accordingly, the socio-spatial perspective has the following aspects:

1. It is possible to use standard categories of political economic analysis, such as profit, investment, rent, class exploitation and the like, in the analysis of urban development.
2. The second circuit of capital – investment in real estate – follows a cyclical pattern of growth and decline that is somewhat at variance with the primary circuit of industrial production. Consequently, analyzing the development trends of society requires specific attention to both circuits and the relationship between them. These aspects of analysis are much more complex than the simplistic approach of urban ecology or other forms of urban sociology, like the Chicago School.
3. All social activities are also about space. Space is an integral factor in everything we do. Understanding this idea means that, when we explore built environments, we must pay as much attention to the way space helps define our behavior as other variables of a social or interactive kind. Attention to the spatial aspects of human life means that design and architecture play an important role in the way people interact. Cities are different, for example, in part because of differences in their spaces.
4. Spatial environments contain signs and symbols. They are represented in peoples' minds, as mental maps, and in the conception of the city by politicians, police and ordinary residents. This space has a meaning, therefore, to everyone that lives in it. Sometimes the representation of space is commonly accepted by diverse individuals; at other times, people conflict over the meanings of space and the definitions of what is acceptable behavior in particular places. These aspects are an important part of metropolitan culture. They can be present in both cities and suburbs. In the past, the representational aspects of space have been ignored by urban analysts. For the socio-spatial approach, in contrast, the symbolic and cultural dimension is extremely important.
5. Finally, the approach highlights the important role government plays in space. Politics defines metropolitan boundaries. Conflicts about these lines in abstract space often lead to serious political problems, if not war, when they occur on a national scale. Governments also transfer wealth across spatial boundaries. This kind of public investment is important to the general well-being of places. When a government channels money from one region under its jurisdiction to another, we say this is a transfer of value in space. This mechanism is behind the production of uneven development when it is perpetrated by the private sector. When the public sector is involved, it is also uneven development, but the presence of government policies also means that there may be some genuine injustices at work. For these reasons, the role of the state in space is an important aspect of the socio-spatial approach.

REFERENCES

Elden, S. 2004. *Understanding Henri Lefebvre: Theory and the Possible*, London: Continuum.
Engels, F. 1973. *The Condition of the Working Class in England*, Moscow: Progress Publishers.

Gottdiener, M. 1994 [1985]. *The Social Production of Urban Space*, Austin: University of Texas Press.

Gottdiener, M. and R. Hutchison 2000. *The New Urban Sociology, 2nd Edition*, New York: McGraw-Hill.

Lefebvre, H. 1991 [1974]. *The Production of Space*, Oxford: Blackwell.

Lehtovuori, P. 2012. 'Towards Experiential Urbanism', *Critical Sociology*, 38(1): 71–87.

Massey, D. 2005. *For Space*, London: Sage.

Schmid, C. 2005. *Stadt, Raum und Gesellschaft: Henri Lefebvre und die Theorie der Produktion des Raumes*, München: Frank Steiner Verlag.

Sprawl

Ever since suburbanization became a mass phenomenon in the 1950s, urbanists have lamented the pattern of sprawl characteristic of that growth in places like the US and Canada. Sprawl is usually defined as 'haphazard growth' of relative low density over an extended region, with residential units dominated by single family homes. It implies a lack of planning and often results in the duplication of public services, such as policing, firefighting and elementary education. This condition is curious because local administrations invariably possess planning staffs that engage in drafting comprehensive schemes for the direction of growth. In at least one study, this contradiction was explained as a social problem because of the way both local politicians and developers circumvent guidelines, with regional sprawl as the result (Gottdiener, 1977). Sprawl is planned because it is, in part, the direct result of federal government subsidies that encourage this kind of growth – the tax subsidy on single family homes; the subsidy of highway building (see entry on the *Suburbs and Suburbanization*).

The attack on sprawl by critics over the years, however, is also an attack on suburbia – especially the pattern of single family homes on separate plots. Critiques of sprawl never link the two except in negative ways, but the popularity of the pattern of settlement in suburbia counters whatever undesirable effects are imputed to sprawl. Despite the collective costs of regional development, an overwhelming majority of suburbanites prefer their way of life over central city living. The issue raised by the sprawl pattern of growth is one of private satisfaction versus its social, collective costs.

Despite the frequent attacks on sprawl, negative and haphazard growth in distinction to comparatively orderly but low-density development is hard to distinguish. According to one significant study, Los Angeles, which is often cited as the epitome of a sprawling metropolis, actually has less of it than does Portland, Oregon, which is often cited for its tough anti-growth laws. The city with the worst sprawl is Nashville, Tennessee, a place that is rarely cited as an example of anything except as a center for country music (El-Nasser and Overberg, 2001).

key concepts in urban studies

Consequently, there is much confusion about this term, especially among those urbanists that assert critical points in order to advance a kind of analysis condemning current patterns of growth. Some Los Angeles geographers, for example, point to the pattern within their region of single family homes stretching for many miles as uniquely representing sprawl. But, in actual fact, the LA area is quite dense because almost all the houses are on small lots. By contrast, in the Northeast and Midwest, houses tend to be on much larger lots and, therefore, their densities are much lower. Yet, the Midwest, in particular, is rarely cited as an offending region when it comes to this phenomenon.

Much of the problem of sprawl is the consequence of rapid growth within our largest metropolitan regions. A projection from the Maryland Office of Planning stated that from 1995 to 2020 more land will be converted to housing in the region surrounding the Chesapeake Bay than in the past three and a half centuries. In greater Chicago, in the two decades from 1970 to 1990, the consumption of residential land grew an amazing 11 times faster than the region's population. In greater Cleveland land consumption has been growing even while the population has been declining. Since 1970, the regional population has declined by 11%, while the amount of urbanized land has grown by 33%. In the sun belt the situation is the same, even though these cities have a net increase in population. Phoenix is reported to be developing open land at the rate of 1.2 acres per hour. Indeed, the geographic reach of Phoenix is said to be equivalent in size to Delaware. Atlanta has grown in population at a rate of 2.9% since 1950. Almost all of this growth has been in the suburbs.

In 2001 a comprehensive study of metro regions in the US measured the extent to which there was excessive and spread-out low-density development. This feature was taken as an indicator of sprawl, although the actual failures in planning for more dense and serviceable growth were not studied (El-Nasser and Overberg, 2001). Using an empirical index for the measurement of sprawl, the study uncovered the fact that a boom in population doesn't necessarily trigger sprawl. In fact, sprawl can occur when the population in a metro area is shrinking, as for example, in the Buffalo, New York region since 1970.

Topographic and environmental features limit sprawl. Los Angeles is hemmed in by the ocean and the high mountain range to the north. Las Vegas' development is restricted by access to water. The Southeast, in contrast, has few such physical limitations. So, for example, 'Unrelenting sprawl along interstates 85 and 20 is creating a "string city" that stretches 600 miles between Raleigh, NC and Birmingham, AL' (El-Nasser and Overberg, 2001).

Contrary to the common perception of the west as having the most egregious examples of sprawl, 16 of the most sprawling metro regions are east of the Mississippi River. Four of the top five are in the Southeast: Nashville, Charlotte, Greensboro and Atlanta. In the south-west, growth is more orderly than the east because development in the former is tethered to water lines. In the east, builders can go just about anywhere in a metro region and find a water supply. At the same time, the easy availability of cheap land in the south-west has enabled many smaller metro areas to expand and increase the sprawl.

Turning to the case of the UK, despite the planning system, and, in particular, through the green belt policy in London and the south-east of England to contain outward metropolitan growth, sprawl has turned the Greater London area into a Multi-Centered Metropolitan Region. Even with a commitment to build only on brownfield sites, the pressure for speculators to develop greenfield areas held in their land banks is intense, particularly as housing prices in this part of the UK continue to grow at unprecedented rates (at the time of writing). Cheshire and Sheppard (1989) estimated that, if all planning restrictions were scrapped, the urbanized area of the south-east would expand from 19% to 28% of the region. Yet, at the same time, house prices would only fall by some 3–5% as plot sizes increased. Thus, before speculative development gets out of hand in the UK, a more considered perspective, that would engage the socialization of gains with the management of any consequent tendency to sprawl, would have to form part of the policy to scrap the green belt around London (Edwards, 2000).

In the US lack of regional government and the fragmentation of regions into many local governments can abet the sprawl pattern. Many European countries have highly developed systems of regional government. Yet, even with dedicated systems of planning in place, possessed of wide-ranging powers, the imperatives for sprawl still exist because many of these are non-spatial (Marcuse and van Kempen, 2000). In the EU, Brussels and Helsinki belong to the most sprawling metropolitan regions. The fact that such different regions in terms of their planning and governance are characterized by sprawl confirms Marcuse and van Kempen's findings as well as Gottdiener's notion that sprawl is planned, even though in an indirect manner.

FIGHTING SPRAWL

According to a US national survey, sprawl is perceived as a major problem. When voters were asked to name the most important problems in their community, sprawl and traffic were named most often, on a par with crime and violence. Each was cited by 18% of those surveyed. Issues such as education, health and medicine trailed far behind (El-Nasser and Overberg, 2001). For over a century people have been fleeing the central city in search of lower density and a more 'suburban' lifestyle. Now people living in these same areas of the metro region are calling on government to prevent the very sprawl that their moves created. This distinction is the most trenchant contradiction of metropolitan growth patterns today (Duany et al., 2000).

Sprawl is implicated in the following social problems:

- social isolation and obesity – people driving everywhere;
- asthma and global warming – automobile emissions;
- flooding and erosion – too much pavement;
- the demise of small farms – real estate speculation and regional development;
- the extinction of wildlife and the unbalancing of nature.

With regional, low-density development producing increasing costs to local residents throughout metropolitan areas, residents have begun to fight against sprawl. 'Since 1997, 22 states have enacted some type of land-use law designed to rein in sprawl. In 1999 alone, law-makers introduced 1,000 bills in state legislatures, and they passed more than 200' (El-Nasser and Overberg, 2001). The political issue of controlling sprawl is now known as 'smart growth' rather than the previous term of 'growth control' (see the entries on *Sustainable Urbanization* and *Planning and Public Space*). Some commentators are opposed to smart growth and controlling sprawl because they see it as a device to control the housing market. According to El-Nasser and Overberg, people nevertheless agree on one thing: municipalities must plan better.

While people at large still do value the suburban lifestyle, in many European metropolitan regions a trend away from sprawl has recently become visible. Increasingly, individuals and families choose to live in city centers and inner-city areas with good public transport and services in walking or biking distance. This trend is new and statistical evidence is not reliable. Sporadic evidence from Germany shows that while successful urban centers grow and maintain relatively high prices for apartments and houses, suburban house prices go down. In extreme cases, German banks do not offer mortgages for suburban house-buyers (see redlining in the entry on *Housing*). Young people do not want to have driving licenses anymore, and in developed countries car-ownership is stable or in modest decline.

THE EXAMPLE OF PORTLAND, OREGON

Claimed as the best example of the positive effects of growth control and anti-sprawl, the truth of Portland, Oregon is much different and the area has experienced only limited success. According to El-Nasser and Overberg (2001):

> In 1973, Portland established an urban growth boundary to stop development and preserve open space beyond a certain line. The boundary encouraged denser development inside it ... However, Portland's sprawl index puts it roughly in the middle of the list of big metros. One reason: Growth is escaping the control of the Portland Metropolitan Council, a regional board of three counties and 24 cities that set up the boundary. Growth is occurring to the south in Salem, OR, and to the north across the state line in Vancouver, Wash. Both cities are part of the Portland metro area, as defined by the Census Bureau, and are within easy commuting distance of Portland.

(See the entry on *Sustainable Urbanization* for more discussion.)

WHITE FLIGHT

According to the 2001 study, most of the cities in the Midwest score high both on the level of racial segregation in the metro area and on the level of sprawl. It is the decline of the core and its racial problems that contributes to sprawl at the periphery.

Many medium-sized cities of the Northeast have a similar problem of a declining and racially segregated core surrounded by a growing suburban region.

> By many measures, the Midwest has both the highest racial segregation and the most concentrated poverty at the cores. That centrifugal push makes it possible for developers to offer ever-more distant alternatives to urban problems. (El-Nasser and Overberg, 2001)

The same can be said for cities that have declining populations but which are located in sprawling metro regions, such as those in the Northeast.

White flight is a more complex issue in the UK (see the entry on *Housing*). In the declining northern cities this is manifested in the spatial segregation of housing and employment opportunities as the white middle class moves to the rural edge of these cities. In London, the most cosmopolitan place in Europe, the patchwork of the spatial distribution of ethnicity does not preclude white flight, but segregation is less complete as urban professionals occupy gentrifying areas that still are characterized by a mixture of classes. However, as Malcolm Cross notes: '"Race" is therefore integral to the crisis of London ... it is coming increasingly to define the urban underclass marooned in crumbling estates and weighed down by poverty, joblessness and despair' (Cross, 1992: 116).

As proof, by 2002, Operation Trident had been launched by the Metropolitan Police to combat black on black crime. In areas where this was rife, it had been accompanied by professional and white flight, leaving behind poorer families who suffer the socio-economic and cultural consequences of remaining in these areas.

LOSS OF FARMLAND AND LANDSCAPES

Historically the best farmland was located near cities. When suburbanization occurred, it consumed these farms. From 1982 to 1992, the US lost, to urban and suburban development, an average of 400,000 acres per year of 'prime' farmland, the land with the best soil and climate for growing crops. During that same period an additional 26,600 acres per year of 'unique' farmland, used for growing rare and specialty crops, was lost.

The lands most suitable for growing crops also tend to be most suitable for growing houses. This is because inland urban settlements in the US have tended to be situated in river valleys and other fertile areas that are also highly productive for farming. These same areas are valued as beautiful and culturally significant landscapes.

ECONOMIC LOSS

Over 130 million Americans enjoy observing, photographing and catching wildlife and fish, thus supporting a nature-oriented tourist industry worth in excess of $14 billion annually. This industry is threatened by the disappearance of open space. Similarly, Europeans are having to travel ever greater distances to escape the embrace of an increasingly suburban sprawl. In the south-east of England, the most densely populated part of Europe, the sound of the motor vehicle is never far from earshot.

UNHEALTHY AIR

Current development patterns also bring substantial air pollution, largely because of the increased automobile dependence that is associated with sprawl. Motor vehicle use in the US doubled from 1 to 2 trillion miles per year between 1970 and 1990. In the 1980s, vehicle miles traveled grew more than four times faster than the driving-age population and many times faster than the population at large. This translates directly into growing emissions of greenhouse gases and the continued inability of our metropolitan areas to cleanse themselves naturally of unhealthy air. According to a US government report: 'Despite considerable progress, the overall goal of clean and healthy air continues to elude much of the country. Unhealthy air pollution levels still plague virtually every major city in the US' (El-Nasser and Overberg, 2001).

A similar situation reigns in most UK urbanized regions. Recently, an asthma epidemic, particularly among the young, has emerged. According to the Department of Health, there is a one in two chance of children in the UK developing asthma symptoms. The causes are related to modern lifestyles and, in metropolitan regions, increased car ownership and usage.

RUNOFF

Haphazard sprawl development also brings runoff water pollution to more and more watersheds, degrading streams, lakes and estuaries. It is now thoroughly documented that, as the amount of impervious pavement and rooftops increases in a watershed, the velocity and volume of surface runoff increases; flooding, erosion and pollutant loads in receiving waters increase; groundwater recharge and water tables decline; stream beds and flows are altered; and aquatic habitat is impaired. (Benfield et al., 1999: 80)

Typical suburban sprawl completely destroys water habitats for all species. In many areas of the country, pollution from suburban runoff now exceeds that produced by industry. Floods that were once decades apart now occur regularly. Runoff pollution is now the nation's leading threat to water quality, affecting about 40% of the US's surveyed rivers, lakes and estuaries.

CONCLUSION

Since the 1950s, the metropolitan areas of the US have been inexorably developing towards a new form of settlement space, one that mixes low-density residential areas with increasingly specialized, functional centers. This new form of space is discussed in the entry on the *Multi-Centered Metropolitan Regions*. It is quite possible, therefore, that what many see as an aberration of growth that is irrational,

sprawl

may, in fact, be a mode of settlement space that has its own powerful and functional logic while transcending the older model of city-centered urban life. Both processes of decentralization and recentralization are at work bringing a kind of order to the alleged chaos of sprawl. Now, the Internet and cell phone technology make low-density living arrangements even more feasible than in the past. In short, the current push to consider sprawl as a critical social problem may not be misguided, because there are very serious public policy issues that must be addressed, but that same effort must also take the time to truly understand the new form of space – the multi-centered metro region and all its implications.

REFERENCES

Benfield, F. et al. 1999. *Once There Were Greenfields: How Urban Sprawl is Undermining America's Environment, Economy and Social Fabric*, New York: National Resources Defense Council.

Cheshire, P. and S. Sheppard 1989. 'British Planning Policy and Access to Housing: Some Empirical Evidence', *Urban Studies*, 6: 469–85.

Cross, M. 1992. 'Race and Ethnicity' in A. Thornlet (ed.) *The Crisis of London*, London: Routledge. pp. 103–18.

Duany, A., E. Playter-Zyberk and J. Speck 2000. *Suburban Nation: The Rise of Sprawl and the Decline of the American Dream*, New York: North Point Press.

Edwards, M. 2000. 'Sacred Cow or Sacrificial Lamb? Will London's Green Belt have to Go?', *City*, 4(1)(April): 106–12.

El-Nasser, H. and P. Overberg 2001. 'A Comprehensive Look at Sprawl in America', *USA Today*, 22 February. Available at: http://usatoday30.usatoday.com/news/sprawl/main.htm (accessed 20 July 2003).

Gottdiener, M. 1977. *Planned Sprawl*, Newbury Park, CA: Sage Publications.

Kunstler, J. 1996. *Home from Nowhere: Remaking Our Everyday World for the 21st Century*, New York: Simon and Schuster.

Leo, C. et al. 1998. 'Is Urban Sprawl Back on the Political Agenda?', *Urban Affairs Review*, 34: 179–211.

Lopez, R. and H. Hynes 2003. 'Sprawl in the 1990s: Measurement, Distribution and Trends', *Urban Affairs Review*, 38(3)(January): 325–55.

Marcuse, P. and R. van Kempen 2000. *Globalizing Cities*, Oxford: Blackwell.

Suburbs and Suburbanization

Suburbs represent a physical form of settlement, neither urban nor rural but something in-between. The field of urban studies has always had a problem defining what is meant by 'urban'. These days the concept of 'suburb' is even more problematic. In fact, the US Census Bureau does not officially use the term 'suburb' at all. Instead, areas lying outside large cities are defined together with those cities as Metropolitan Statistical Areas or MSAs. It is commonly understood that a suburb is a residential area outside the large central city, with less population density than the city but higher than the adjacent rural area. Early conceptions considered these places as dependent on the city. That is a fallacy, as is the belief that these areas are dominated by residences alone. Historically, for instance, some suburbs started out as cities but were then absorbed by urban growth. Harlem and Brooklyn in New York, Old Irving Park in Chicago and Country Club Plaza in Kansas City are some examples (Gilfoyle, 1998).

Now, if we understand that the form of settlement space is the Multi-Centered Metropolitan Region, we can see that areas usually called suburbs are, in fact, quite diverse, multi-functional and connected to cities in different ways. Many white-collar and high-tech companies prefer to locate in areas adjacent to but outside the central city. Manufacturing takes place in suburbs. Most of the retailing in metro regions also occurs there. Across the US, sports stadiums and recreational complexes are often also situated in suburban locations. When a diverse and large population is added to this mix, it becomes clearer that these areas are merely a lower density variant of the multi-functional array of activities that comprise developed cities themselves. By the 1980s, in fact, there were already over 20 counties in the US with a large workforce and population and a diverse functional profile that could characterize them as 'fully urbanized', even though none possessed a single large city (Gottdiener and Kephart, 1991).

Because of the free market in land and abundant space, early in US history people already exhibited a strong preference for living outside the city in single family buildings with large lots and for tolerating a long journey to work. US suburbs have also been distinctive because of their political independence. In comparison to Europe, incorporated suburbs thwarted movements toward metropolitan governance. Suburbs from Brookline, MA, and Evanston, IL, to Beverly Hills, CA, fought annexation and evolved as municipalities (Gilfoyle, 1998). This political power contributed to the emergence of the fragmented, multi-centered metropolis that we possess today.

According to Fichman and Fowler (2003), one way that suburbanization differed markedly from the process of city formation was its racially exclusive nature. For decades in the US, the mass residential developments outside the city were dominated by whites. Even though there is considerably more diversity today, suburban regions remain comparatively more white and more affluent than inner-city areas. They also hold the bulk of the US population. In 1998, 51% of the total population was suburban as compared to 29% of the population that resided in the inner cities of the nation, according to the US Census. Across the US, as suburbanization proceeded, inner cities lost as much as 50% of their populations. Places such as Baltimore, Philadelphia, Chicago, Boston, Detroit, St Louis, Buffalo and Cleveland have fewer people than their surrounding regions. Among the few cities that have grown since the period of mass suburbanization beginning with the 1950s are Dallas, Houston, Phoenix and San Diego, but they have done so largely because they possessed the ability to annex outlying territory. Without such powers in the rest of the country, traditional cities were overwhelmed by the shift of population to adjacent areas in the regional array.

In addition to racial and class exclusion, the vast areas of suburban growth in our society are the result of government programs that favored this pattern of development by promoting family desires for single home ownership. Two programs in particular are critical for an understanding of how suburbanization became so popular and so vast a land-use transformation in the US – the homeowner tax subsidy, passed in the 1930s to revive a depression-era housing industry, and the 1950s' National Defense System of Highways Act, which established the means by which the intricate web of interstate highways were constructed across the country. Both policies operated openly to produce massive suburban development outside our central cities and they are responsible for the emergence of regional growth. (See the entry on *Multi-Centered Metropolitan Regions* for an extended discussion of these forces.)

In other entries (*The City, Sprawl, Sustainable Urbanization*) critiques of suburban living are discussed. Among the first to lament this pattern of growth was Lewis Mumford. As he most often did, Mumford emphasized the superior benefits of clustered development in the manner of Ebenezer Howard. This critique, however, was directed less against suburbanization, per se, than at the sprawl pattern it assumed. Since Mumford's time, suburban life has often been vilified by critics with a city bias. But these constant attacks have neither prevented the pace of suburbanization from proceeding nor convinced government leaders that the suburban alternative was wrong. Instead, our society has been split between a relatively small group of architects, planners and urbanists who continued to attack the development of suburbs, and a large majority that went to live there.

To be sure, the pattern of sprawl presents many problems that have to be faced by our society. Yet, critiques of sprawl often miss their mark because they are mixed together with attacks against the suburban way of life itself. From the European perspective, however, some writers have questioned this critique by pointing to the fact that the high-tech, information economy, which provides the US with its global comparative advantage, is located more consistently in suburban rather than inner-city places.

According to *The Economist* (2000), for example:

> The film *American Beauty* recycles a view of the suburbs, that they are vortexes of tedium and alienation – which has been a staple of artistic contempt at least since John Cheever. This view has probably never been very accurate. But it is getting less accurate by the day, as the suburbs mutate in all sorts of extraordinary ways. If the complaints about the suburbs are doomed to remain forever the same, the suburbs themselves are changing beyond all recognition.
>
> The most obvious change is that the suburbs are the smithies of almost everything that is new and innovative in the American economy. Microsoft sits in a suburb of Seattle. Silicon Valley is an unappetizing sprawl of modest (though costly) bungalows and strip malls. The new economy and the new suburbs are really the same thing.

This article went on to say that, in agreement with the socio-spatial approach, the current information and high-tech-oriented economy is helping to sustain multi-centered regional development in much the same way that the 18th-century manufacturing system of capitalism produced the factory town. Also noted in the article is the increasing diversity of the areas outside the inner city with regard to both class and race:

> The suburbs are also becoming ever less monolithic and bourgeois. Suburbs can be blue-collar or ultra-liberal. Increasingly though, some are a social jumble within themselves. Nor are the suburbs the all-white enclaves that metropolitan sophisticates imagine. Atlanta, Chicago and Washington, DC, all have thriving black suburbs. In Southern California the new Chinatowns and little Saigons are in the suburbs rather than downtown. Many of the most ethnically diverse places in the US are now suburbs. (*The Economist*, 2000)

The key issue raised by the dominance of suburbanization seems to be not to do away with the suburb, as New Urbanists argue, but to do something about its negative aspects, especially its sprawl. For this reason, political movements such as 'sustainable urbanism' and other holistic approaches are important. In fact, both urban and suburban areas are the sites for significant social movements that attempt to address key issues of daily living in our society.

Lastly, it is a mistake to view the vast suburban areas of countries like the US as devoid of social problems. The issue of sprawl and its negative consequences has already been noted. Suburban regions lack public space and rely too exclusively on the automobile. They lose out to the advantages that higher density, clustered development might provide (see the entry on *Sprawl*).

REFERENCES

Fichman, M. and E.P. Fowler 2003. 'The Science and Politics of Sprawl: From Suburbia to Creative Citybuilding', unpublished paper, York University.

Gilfoyle, T. 1998. 'White Cities, Linguistic Turns and Disneylands: The New Paradigms of Urban History', *Reviews in American History*, 26: 175–204.

Gottdiener, M. and G. Kephart 1991. 'The Multi-Nucleated Metropolitan Region: A Comparative Analysis' in R. Kling, S. Olin and M. Poster (eds) *Postsuburban California*, Berkeley, CA: University of California Press.

The Economist 2000. 'When Life is More Interesting than Art', 24 March.

Sustainable Urbanization

The basic idea of *sustainability* is elegant: to ensure that humanity meets the needs of the present without compromising the ability of future generations to meet their own needs (United Nations, 1987). To this end, Earth's *natural resources* should be preserved and the *resilience* of natural systems, i.e. nature's capacity to respond and adjust to changes, should be maintained.

Globally, the idea of *sustainable development* emerged in the 1970s as a guiding principle in the formulation of policies about the relationships between population, environment and industrial development (Marquette, n.d.). The early debate was shaped by the Club of Rome's first report on the depletion of natural resources (Meadows et al., 1972) and the shock of the first and second oil crises (1973–75). In 1987, the UN established the World Commission on Environment and Development to institutionalize sustainable development among member states. The Commission report, *Our Common Future*, is also known as the Brundtland Report after its Norwegian chair. It defined five principles of sustainable development for policy-makers:

1. Changing current patterns of economic growth, technology and management that may have negative impacts on the environment and population;
2. Ensuring employment, food, energy, safe water, and sanitary services for all populations;
3. Controlling global population growth;
4. Protecting natural resources for future generations;
5. Integrating economic, environmental and population considerations in policy, decision making and planning.

The Brundtland Report also noted that the lifestyle enjoyed by the citizens of the North, and that includes the way in which the cities are built, is not environmentally sustainable (United Nations, 1987). This was the central message that inspired Rio de Janeiro's 'Earth Summit' in 1992 and resulted in the signing of the Agenda 21 as the basis for turning around the development process towards sustainability. The implementation of Agenda 21 was intended to involve action at all levels from international to local. The local authority programs are known as 'Local Agenda 21'. An important actor in this process is ICLEI – Local Governments for Sustainability, which organizes action in more than 1000 cities, towns and counties worldwide.

The Brundtland Report's lasting legacy is the subdivision of sustainability in three components: environmental, socio-cultural and economic sustainability. Sustainable development, thus, can be described as the intersection between the three goals. Adriana Allen (2009) succinctly states that:

> the most pressing problem with this model is that it offers relatively little understanding of the inherent trade-offs found in the simultaneous pursuit of these goals. Coupled with this, the picture it provides is too abstract to appreciate how sustainable development unfolds at the urban level but also to acknowledge the political dimension of the process.

Indeed, after several decades of research and development, the definitions of *sustainable urbanization* and *sustainable city* are disputed. In the UK, to take an example, sustainable cities are central to urban policy, but what constitutes a sustainable city for British policy-makers is not fully clear. In China, the government promotes 'eco-cities' but the results on ground are often just standard urban developments. However, neither the difficulties of exactly defining sustainable urbanization nor the lack of fully convincing practical results should discourage us from improving our built environment and finding better solutions step-by-step. The reason is simple: while the world's population growth is slowing down, the rapid growth of urban populations still continues. Especially in the developing countries, cities and metropolitan regions will grow massively in the coming decades. It is estimated that 70% of the world's population will be urban by 2050 (United Nations, 2012; see the entries on *Immigration, Migration and Demography* and *Urbanization and Urbanism*). Urban areas are the prime engines of population movements and economic performance. Simultaneously, they are central in solving social and environmental problems of a global scale.

URBANIZATION AND CLIMATE CHANGE

Cities and metropolitan regions are never sustainable in the sense of being self-contained. On the contrary, urban dwellers and economic activities depend on environmental resources and services from outside their built-up area (Allen, 2009). *Ecological footprint* refers to the scale and extent of this dependency. A key aim in making cities more sustainable is to reduce their material and energy use and thus their ecological footprint.

In the EU, the recent debate has focused on climate change, specifically to the reduction of CO_2 emissions. In 2007, the Union set a '20-20-20' target: to reduce greenhouse gas emissions by 20% from 1990 levels; to raise the share of renewable sources in energy consumption to 20%; and to improve the EU's energy efficiency by 20% (http://ec.europa.eu/clima/policies/package/index_en.htm). Currently, more demanding targets are already being discussed. The emission and energy targets touch urban areas a lot, because globally, the built environment directly accounts for 40–50% of natural resource use and about a third of CO_2 emissions (UK Green Building Council). These emissions come from the construction industry, from heating, cooling and lighting buildings and from urban transport. In developed countries that have 'exported emissions' of industrial production to newly industrialized countries the role of built environment is much larger, typically over 50% of CO_2 emissions. Regarding the climate targets, in developed countries the built environment, thus, is more important than industrial production or agriculture and other extensive land-uses. In the developing world, the sheer scale of urbanization calls for a rethink on how to achieve more sustainable patterns than historically has been the case in the US and Europe.

The carbon emissions should be addressed across all scales from city-region to city, district, urban block and individual house. Peter Hall (1997) discusses historic ideas and examples, such as Ebenezer Howard's 'Social City' (see the entry on *Modern Urban Planning*), British new towns, and Copenhagen and Stockholm's progressive post-war regional plans, bringing the debate round to more recent data and observations. Referring to the geographer Susan Owens, Hall states that:

Sustainable urban form would have the following features. First, at a regional scale, it would contain many relatively small settlements; but some of these would cluster, to form larger settlements of 200,000 and more people. Second, at a sub-regional scale, it would feature compact settlements … with employment and commercial opportunities dispersed to give a 'heterogeneous', i.e. mixed, land use pattern. Third, at the local scale, it would consist of sub-units developed at pedestrian/bicycle scale; at a medium to high residential density, possibly with high linear density, and with local employment, commercial and service opportunities clustered to permit multi-purpose trips. [Owen's] work strongly suggests that a cluster of small settlements may be more energy-efficient than one large one; the optimum upper limit would be 150,000–250,000; that linear or at least rectangular forms will be the most efficient; and that though densities should be moderately high, say 25 dwellings or 40 people per hectare, they need not be very high to be energy-efficient. (1997: 173)

While Hall's references are Euro-centric and his measures have to be recalibrated to fit East Asian, South American or African urbanization, the basic idea of an integrated approach across scales and a partial self-sufficiency of networked urban settlements is relevant. While cities cannot be viewed as 'islands of reform' (Allen 2009), much needs to be done in them to achieve sustainability. Currently, several countries, urban regions and cities show promising results in changing their land-use and mobility patterns. The Dutch VINEX policy in 1990s and early 2000s did shorten commutes and reduce sprawl of housing nation-wide. In Nordic city-regions, a continuous urban planning since 1950s has facilitated relatively well-organized regional form of living and working, with clear incentives to walk, bike and use public transport on a daily basis. In Scandinavia, Australia and Canada, many cities and regions have achieved large gains in *ecological efficiency* through the integration of urban infrastructures, and have thus reduced CO_2 emissions and the use of natural resources per inhabitant or per unit of economic output. The integration may involve municipal central heating and cooling, combined production of heat and power (CHP), heat pumps that gain energy from waste-water, clever management of material flows of industry, or green roofs and other green infrastructure to contain storm water and balance the urban microclimate.

SOCIO-CULTURAL DIMENSIONS AND GOVERNANCE

Equal opportunity and equal access to resources independent of income, gender and race are the clearest socio-cultural dimensions of sustainability. Sustainable urbanization, thus, fights segregation and promotes socially mixed neighborhoods, good public space and accessible service provision (see the entry on *Planning and Public Space*). Freiburg in Germany is often cited as an exemplary sustainable city, while in the developing world the equitable transport planning of Bogotá in Colombia under Mayor Peñalosa has become a cherished benchmark.

An important dimension of sustainable urbanization is the role of local action in improving urban life. Several cities both in developed and developing countries have active movements to promote sustainability, requiring a revival of civic associations and activism (see the entries on *Community Development Programs* and *Urban and Suburban Politics*). Such movements have addressed renewable energy, transport, local food production, waste recycling, green infrastructure and women's rights, among other themes.

The notions of sustainability, sustainable development and sustainable urbanization link several dimensions of human activity. What brings these elements together is an increasing global population accommodated by significant growth in urbanization, especially in the developing countries. Allen (2009: 2–3) summarizes the different forms of urban sustainability as follows (quote edited by the authors):

> *Economic sustainability* entails putting local and regional resources to productive use for the long-term benefit of the community, without damaging or depleting the natural resources on which it depends and without increasing the settlement's ecological footprint. The full impact of the production cycle should be considered.

> *Social sustainability* refers to the fairness, inclusiveness and cultural adequacy of an intervention to promote equal rights over the natural, physical and economic capital that supports the livelihoods of local communities, with particular emphasis on the poor and marginalised groups. Cultural adequacy is here defined as the extent to which a practice respects cultural heritage and diversity.

> *Ecological sustainability* (environmental sustainability) concerns how production and consumption in the urban centre impact on the environment and citizens' wellbeing. Resources shouldn't be depleted and nature's carrying capacity should be kept. How the state manages the demands on environmental resources is central to this form of sustainability.

> The *sustainability of the built environment* concerns the capacity of an intervention to enhance the liveability of buildings and urban infrastructures for 'all' city dwellers without damaging or disrupting the urban region environment. It also includes a concern for the efficiency of the built environment to support the local economy.

> *Political sustainability* is concerned with the quality of governance systems guiding the relationship and actions of different actors among the previous four dimensions. Thereby, it implies the democratisation and participation of local civil society in all areas of decision-making.

For the UN, a democratic and goal-oriented work towards sustainable urbanization requires multi-level governance. Such work recognizes linkages, promotes flows beyond official urban boundaries and accepts the participation of different actors. It concedes to the need for an overall governance architecture, accommodating different interests and solving conflicts (United Nations, 2012).

SUSTAINABILITY INDICATORS

To set targets, measure progress and compare cities and regions, policy-makers often utilize indicators of varying kinds. Because sustainable urbanization is a holistic and contextual concept, clear indicators are hard to establish. The global consultancy company McKinsey has, nevertheless, constructed the *Urban Sustainability Index* for China. It ranks 112 Chinese cities based on investment in social welfare, economic development, air quality, waste management, built environment and resource utilization (McKinsey & Co, 2011). Although useful, it produces a league table of sustainability, which like any performance management indicator creates unintended consequences and non-relevant outcomes. Indices hardly ever tell the whole truth, and analysis should look broadly at the economic and social forces at work in each country and metropolitan region. Studying a selection of US cities in the early 2000s, Portney (2003) notes that sustainability is a way of doing *strategic planning* where the goals of growth are made explicit and where there are well-defined indicators that show whether or not goals are being achieved. In this context, *smart growth* refers to an idea that growth itself should be tied to the quality of life. Smart growth should not be confused with the more recent and contested notion of the *smart city*, which is understood as a technologically advanced, networked and responsive environment, ideally facilitating optimal use of natural, technical and social resources.

To conclude, Wulf Daseking, the long-term planning director of the city of Freiburg in Germany, has given the following guidelines for urban sustainability:

- Compact – a 'city of short paths';
- Meticulous integration of urban structure (land-uses) and public transport system;
- Typological and morphological variation of built structure that supports social mix;
- Integration of workplaces, public spaces and private services;
- Preservation of valuable natural areas and an identifiable park network that reaches from inner city to open nature and water bodies.

Like Peter Hall's discussion on regional form, Daseking's points need to be contextualized. Nevertheless, Freiburg's experience from the 1970s until today is useful in showing the linkages of different forms of sustainability and the need of long-term, dedicated policy and planning to achieve a systemic change towards sustainability.

REFERENCES

Allen, A.E. 2009. 'Sustainable Cities or Sustainable Urbanisation?', *Palette UCL Journal of Sustainable Cities*, London: University College London.

Daesking, W. 2011. 'Universal Principles for a Sustainable City paper presented to Academy of Urbanism Congress IX *Towards a Greener Urbanism*, Urbanism 22–24 May 2014, Bristol, UK.

Hall, P. 1997. 'The First Megacities Lecture', February 1997, Rotterdam, Megacities, World Cities and Global Cities (lecture transcript).

Hall, P. and C. Ward. 2014. *Sociable Cities. The 21st-Century Reinvention of the Garden City, 2nd Edition*, Abingdon: Routledge. [First Published 1998].

Meadows, D.H., D.L. Meadows, J. Randers, and William W. Behrens III. 1972. *Limits to Growth*, New York: New American Library.

Marquette, C. n.d. 'Population and Environment in Industrialised Regions', International Union for the Scientific Study of Population, Policy and Research, Paper #8.

McKinsey & Co 2011. *2011 Urban Sustainability Index*, Urban China Initiative, New York: McKinsey & Co.

Portney, K. 2003. *Taking Sustainable Cities Seriously*, Cambridge, MA: MIT Press.

UK Green Building Council. http://www.ukgbc.org/content/new-build.

United Nations 1987. *Report of the World Commission on Environment and Development: Our Common Future* [the Brundtland Report] Oxford: Oxford University Press.

United Nations 2012. *Sustainable Urbanization: Thematic Think Piece*, UN Habitat, UN System Task Team on the Post-2015 UN Development Agenda, Washington, DC: United Nations.

Temporary Uses and Adaptive Urbanism

In recent years, temporary uses have received attention as a novel planning and policy approach from both urban scholars and practitioners. While popular and inviting, the notion is often used without fully understanding the complex role temporary uses play in the social production of urban space today.

The term temporary use refers to 'temporary activation of vacant or underused land or buildings with no immediate development demand. In principle, any action that uses a place for other than its common use for a period of time is temporary use' (Lehtovuori and Ruoppila, 2012: 30). Temporary uses can be transient, recurring or migrant. The relatively short usage time (typically from some months to some years) should not be used as their only defining factor, however. In the academic discourse, we can distinguish two main ideas regarding the role of temporary uses in urban process. Firstly, the concept of temporary use may refer to those uses that carry a *development orientation*, i.e. capacity and goal to explore the potentials of the places they are located in. Hence, they are seen to form an analytic category between momentary events and permanent (re)development (Lehtovuori and Ruoppila, 2012). Secondly, *the critical character* of temporary use should be emphasized. Discussing temporary uses in Vienna, Austria, Florian Haydn and Robert Temel (2006) link them to activism and the do-it-yourself-mentality of city residents. Haydn and Temel claim that in contrast to the pragmatic and economic North American use of the term 'interim use', in Europe 'temporary use' should be seen as an approach to ensure diversity and alternative space provision. Temporary uses are, thus, seen in the context of popular and critical appropriation of the city space.

A famous example of temporary use is the Paris Plage, the series of annually recurring temporary beaches at the Seine river front and La Villette. The beach project was initiated in 2002 by the socialist mayor Bertrand Delanoë to introduce an amenity for those Parisians who cannot afford to escape the city in summertime. Another exemplary case is the temporary cultural re-use of the NDSM wharf in Amsterdam. The project was supported by City of Amsterdam's Breeding Places

Fund. Since 2000, NDSM has played a central role in initiating a large-scale regeneration of the whole Amsterdam North, an industrial and harbor zone.

Recently, the success of the NDSM wharf as a development tool has made explicit the conflict between cultural users and real estate developers. NDSM's cultural re-use was pioneered by a group from Amsterdam's counter-cultural squatting movement. After less than ten years, the unique large-scale cultural center created through temporary use had attracted so much new development to the area that the alternative character of NDSM was hard to sustain and many original users could not stay anymore. Because of economic pressures, NDSM started to shift from an alternative and experimental 'free zone' towards a commercially run space for cultural entrepreneurs and other businesses. This shift caused tensions between users and between NDSM, the City and developers. The question is whether temporary uses are just an instrumental tool to facilitate economic real estate development processes in unusual locations, or a novel approach to create social settings and urban spaces with inherent value. The transition from temporary to permanent was not part of the plan in NDSM and has now to be solved in retrospect.

Does the notion of 'culture-led gentrification' (see the entry on *Gentrification and Urban Redevelopment*) apply to NDSM and similar cases? Yes and no. Many inner city working-class and industrial neighborhoods in Europe and North America, and even some slums in Rio de Janeiro, have in recent decades witnessed ostensibly similar processes as NDSM, characterized by a spiral of increasing attention, increasing flow of people with purchasing power and increasing rents and real estate values. Finally, the higher prices and expensive conversions start to push out the artists and other cultural producers, the group that originally recognized an attractive combination of low rents and environmental qualities.

The users of NDSM seem to face a similar situation, with the well-known conflict between low-income or precarious users/residents and profit-seeking real estate developers. However, NDSM and other cases where temporary uses are involved, reveal a unique dimension of this process. Unlike in the case of gentrification of existing neighborhoods, temporary uses often take place in abandoned areas and buildings that are completely out of the normal real estate cycle and where there is no perspective of a new renter or owner at all. (Demolition might be an option, but is either impossible because of heritage protection or too expensive in itself.) Temporary uses, thus, do not represent a case of one tenant pushing another out, but a case of opening closed or abandoned areas for public use, a case of novelty and creation of a context. Sometimes these new kinds of location might be called *spatial innovations*. The unique, place-based processes of social, cultural and economic hybridization may be nearly impossible to repeat in another location. In these pioneering cases, temporary users take private risks for common good. This specific dimension of pioneering use and spatial innovation is currently falling out of the policy-makers' picture. A clear conceptualization of the shared value of alternative urban spaces, and a public intervention to support them, would be required. NDSM in Amsterdam is a case in point.

FROM TEMPORARY TO ADAPTIVE URBANISM

In their book *The Temporary City* Peter Bishop and Lesley Williams argue that temporary, interim or intermittent uses form a powerful new trend – 'temporary urbanism' – by which they mean intensification of temporary uses and their conscious use in urban planning and management. Confirming their adherence to the development orientation, the authors write:

> Urban planners need to recognize that this enthusiasm is not incidental but represents an appreciation of experimentation and a willingness to 'see what happens' that is perhaps the spirit of our time. When planners and policy makers start to experiment as well, this could represent a powerful mechanism to retune our cities for whatever lies ahead. (Bishop and Williams, 2012: 35)

Indeed, temporary uses may have a role in developing a wide variety of locations, not only in the most difficult and abandoned places discussed above. Emphasizing the variety of temporary uses' developmental roles, Lehtovuori and Ruoppila (2012) provide the synoptic typology set out in Table 7.

Table 7 Types of usage in development

	Urban central areas	Currently underused areas	Areas losing significance
Use, function	Defined	Not defined, loose	Defined, but weakening
Attention and flux of people	High	None	Some, could be better
Apprehension, meaning	Fashionable, classic, elitist	Edgy, daring, promising	Out of fashion, low-brow
Development perspectives	Stable, lack of new ones	Open (risky)	Redevelopment optional
Goal of temporary uses	Intensification	Introduction, initiation	Redefinition, diversification

There is a structural economic dimension to the current interest in temporary uses. Quentin Stevens and Mhairi Ambler (2010) link temporary uses to the post-Fordist urban economy, characterized by recurring economic crises, unclear development perspectives, weak public finances and lack of public investment, as well as private actors' increasing appetite for short-term profits and flexible projects where light investment can be combined with rapid turn over (see entry on *Financial and Fiscal Crises*).

Looking at the broad picture of urban change in different contexts, 'temporary urbanism' seems, however, a non-ideal term to describe the landscape of experimental, flexible and multi-actor approaches to planning and development. Recently, some authors have started to use the term '*adaptive urbanism*' instead. Adaptive urbanism is a conceptualization of planning and urban process that aims to link the case-driven apprehension of experimentation through temporary uses to a theoretical reading of cities and urban regions as complex, adaptive and self-regulating systems. As an example of the adaptive urbanism discourse, Manuel Fernandez (2013) scrutinizes the effects of the recent financial crisis and real estate bubble in Spain as follows:

> Rigid planning and formal regulations give narrow chances to face this unexpected situation [of a bursting real-estate bubble]. ... From an adaptive approach, cities should avoid keeping [the unfinished boom-time projects] out of work and expelling any alternative use to the one they were planned for. ... Cities need to manage this exceptional 'meanwhile' time because it will be the new normal for some decades. ... [They] must keep offering solutions using flexible formulas and transitional planning, and give importance to social, collaborative and grass root processes now that big investment cannot be part of the agenda. It will be time for the imagination. It will be time for limited resources but more creative action, time for case-by-case solutions instead of pretentious long-term planning.

In discussing alternative planning and policies, the term 'tactical urbanism' is also much used. Tactical urbanism is inspired by architect-mayor Jaime Lerner's innovative urban interventions in Curitiba, Brazil, in the early 1990s. Talking about 'urban acupuncture', Lerner initiated experimental, low-cost and open-ended urban transformations that worked because they brought human resources cleverly together, thus overcoming the relative poverty of Curitiba.

After the global financial crisis and slowed economic growth, wealthier cities in the US and Europe are also looking for alternative planning and urban design methods. Lydon et al. (2012: 2–3) discuss recession, revived interest in inner-city living and the power of the Internet in organizing a novel 'civic economy' as the main drivers of tactical urbanism, characterized by rapid realization, low risk and a promise to improve the social capital and organizing capacity between citizens and other urban actors. Cherished examples of tactical urbanism include guerrilla gardening, pop-up shops and the temporary occupation of parking places for public use. Michel de Certeau's famous distinction between strategy and tactics is helpful in distinguishing between long-term, strategic planning for urban space and tactical planning for interim uses of space. Squatter housing is an example of temporary space meeting people's needs (Vasudevan, 2014). Haydn and Temel (2006) see in tactical urbanism a promise to challenge the character of the capitalist city as a product. According to them, tactical urbanism, instead, would open the way for democratic action and human expression, helping to shape urban space as a collective work, an *oeuvre* (Lefebvre 1991 [1974]). Finally, the notion of tactical urbanism is used for a radical rethinking of urbanization in developing countries. Instead of perceiving slums (which house at least one billion people globally) as a problem to be cleared away, tactical urbanism could provide tools for people to improve their conditions on site, gradually leading to more dense and developed 'vertical slums' (Flint, 2014; see also the entry on *Slums and Shanty Towns*).

REFERENCES

Bishop, P. and L. Williams 2012. *The Temporary City*, London: Routledge.

Fernandez, M. 2013. 'Adaptive Urbanism: Creative Solutions when Long Term Planning Doesn't Work'. (Interview by Sanny Wensveen). Available at: http://www.eukn.eu/e-library/project/bericht/eventDetail/adaptive-urbanism-creative-solutions-when-long-term-planning-doesna-post-work-by-manu-fernandez/ (Accessed 30 June 2015).

Flint, A. 2014. 'At MoMA, How "Tactical Urbanism" Can Preserve the Future of Cities', *City Lab (The Atlantic)*, 9 December. Available at: http://www.citylab.com/design/2014/12/at-moma-how-tactical-urbanism-can-preserve-the-future-of-cities/383577/ (accessed 23 December 2014).

Haydn, F. and R. Temel (eds) 2006. *Temporary Urban Spaces: Concepts for the Use of City Spaces*, Basel: Birkhäuser.

Lefebvre, Henri 1991 [1974]. *The Production of Space*, Oxford and Cambridge, MA: Blackwell. [La production de l'espace, English translation by Donald Nicholson-Smith.]

Lehtovuori, P. and S. Ruoppila 2012. 'Temporary Uses as a Means of Experimental Urban Planning', *Serbian Architectural Journal*, 4: 29–54.

Lydon, M., D. Bartman, T. Garcia, R. Preston and R. Woudstra 2012. *Tactical Urbanism: Short-Term Action, Long-Term Change, Volume 2*, The Street Plans Collaborative, March. Available at: http://issuu.com/streetplanscollaborative/docs/tactical_urbanism_vol_2_final (accessed 20 May 2015).

Scott, A. and E. Ben-Joseph 2012. *Renewtown: Adaptive Urbanism and the Low-Carbon Community*, New York: Routledge.

Stevens, Q. and M. Ambler 2010. 'Europe's City Beaches as Post-Fordist Placemaking', *Journal of Urban Design*, 15: 515–37.

Vasudevan, A. 2014. 'Autonomous Urbanisms and the Right to the City: The Spatial Politics of Squatting in Berlin, 1968–2012' in B. van der Steen, A. Katzeff and L. van Hoogenhuijze (eds) *The City is Ours: Squatting and Autonomous Movements in Europe from the 1970s to the Present*, Oakland, CA: PM Press. pp. 130–51.

Urban and Suburban Politics

Before the 1960s, city governments were powerful. In addition to people making money from control over the resources of capital and land, control of the bureaucracies and decision-making power of government was a separate means of acquiring wealth. The power to tax or regulate both land use and public services gave local government officials significant leverage over other people's money. Because of public sector services, cities are also major employers. For all these reasons organized interests have always competed with each other for influence over and control of local government. This struggle provides the drama of politics, whether it takes place in cities or suburbs.

Prior to the 1980s, typical urban regimes reflected the participation of traditional ethnic groups, such as the Irish, the Poles, Italians and Jews. More recently, this composition has changed because of the growing influence of minorities within central cities. Over 300 US cities have minority mayors, most commonly, African Americans, but now the growing power of the Hispanic community is also reflected in urban leadership. In the suburbs, which are overwhelmingly white, powerful interests are best characterized in terms of middle-class concerns rather than ethnic influences. Suburban governments are invariably controlled by real estate developers and active representatives of middle-class homeowners interested in maintaining the quality of family-oriented services and the value of homes.

The issue of who controls local government has been an important one in the urban literature. Three perspectives were argued – the elitist, the pluralist and the state managerialist. Floyd Hunter's studies of Atlanta in the 1960s established the *elitist* perspective. He argued that cities are controlled by some powerful elite. Influential leadership groups are most often composed of financial and select business interests, including real estate developers, as well as career politicians that operate from a community power base. Other analysts, such as Robert Dahl, countered this view by arguing that *pluralist* interests were reflected in local politics. According to Dahl, despite the presence of a select group of influential people, many community interests were recognized in local politics. Today we understand that local governments are most often a combination of elite and community interests. Powerful people do not need to control every decision. They only intervene when their immediate concerns are at stake. Even advocates of pluralism, like Dahl, came to acknowledge this truth of how elite power operates. Community interests are usually recognized by local government, except when these clash with the concerns of the business elite. Consequently, this mix of interests characterizes local politics best. In addition, however, another perspective qualified this view. Now we also know that government employees and administrators may have their own independent interests. This *state managerialism* perspective is also important in understanding local politics.

In the UK, Prime Minister Margaret Thatcher attempted to destroy any vestige of urban politics, as the 'urban population' represented the site of opposition to her imposition of market ordering in the 1980s. New Labour, under Tony Blair, attempted to revive cities, and the party was partially committed to regional government. However, its technocratic approach, borrowing examples from the US and trying to impose them in a British context, attempted to avoid a revitalization of urban politics. Current urban policy in the UK revolves around the *Core Cities* idea, which seeks to revitalize the urban downtowns using technocratic and managerial means to improve the competitiveness of these cities. Citizen participation and enabling communities in these cities to improve their lives, is notably absent from this scheme (www.odpm.gov.uk).

While elites are invariably entrenched, their composition does change over time as a result of different groups competing for power. There is considerable evidence, for example, that many cities today are dominated by banks and financial interests because this faction of the business community still has investments downtown, such as banking centers. Suburbs and some of the newer cities of the sun belt, in contrast, possess dominating elites with interests in real estate and local corporations. But, the succession of economic elites is just one way to look at changes in local government. Politics is a dramatic enterprise. It involves struggle, coalition building, competition and compromise.

In the 1800s, when US cities were developing rapidly, city regimes were powerful because they commanded considerable wealth. Most often a select group of politicians took control of local government and ran it in order to make money. This arrangement was called a 'political machine'. The machine used graft and corruption to amass cash that helped generate votes which kept it in power. The principal characteristic of a machine was that it functioned solely as a means of administering the city, including through giving patronage positions to its supporters that were financed by graft and corruption. This particular form of elite control did not possess any ideology of governance. The goal was the mobilization of votes in order to remain in power where favors could then be performed for business interests in return for cash. By the late 1800s, community leaders had tired of the corruption associated with this style of administration. Progressive reforms were passed at the turn of the 20th century that made local government more professional, more middle class, and more honest. Under the old machines, cities were carved up into 'wards' where local leaders provided favors to residents in return for votes. Candidates merely had to win their wards in order to advance to the seats of city government. Progressive reforms did away with this arrangement.

These reforms aggregated sections of the city into larger districts that were mixed and less dependent on favors owed to particular groups or individuals. In the extreme case, progressives made election to office dependent on majority voting from the city population as a whole. In short, reformers of machine politics changed the structure of local government by combining districts and cutting down on the way local interests could be represented. The result was a greater need for consensus building and, therefore, a more *political* local politics.

The experience of the UK and other European countries has been similar. Municipal socialism of the 1950s was a byword for corruption, particularly around building contracts. But the associated politics was about delivering local services and infrastructure for local residents and not the imagined politics of the post-1980s generation which seeks to use local office for global advancement.

At present the situation is quite the reverse. Neither city nor suburban governments are powerful. Sprawl patterns of population deconcentration have fragmented the metropolitan region and representative voting has lost its clout on the local scene (see the entries on *Sprawl* and *Multi-Centered Metropolitan Regions*). For this reason, political regimes must do the best they can to supply necessary services while dealing, at the same time, with their dwindling resources. In 1966, for example, the city of Atlanta outspent its suburban counties by two to one. Twenty years later, in 1987, however, Atlanta's spending on services accounted for only 10% of its total spend within the expanding multi-centered region. The suburban counties in that area became more powerful.

A second reason for the decline in power is that participation in local elections and in political affairs is limited. Voter turnout is low and the best and brightest people are no longer attracted to run for office. In both cities and suburbs there is a crisis in the quality of public services. This state of affairs is not helped by either the decline in manufacturing and industry within central cities or the reluctance of suburban residents to pay local taxes. As the quality of public services declines and people feel the pressure from inadequate schools, roads, economic development and tax relief, these concerns are expressed as the content of local metropolitan politics. Occasionally, discontent spills over into an organized effort seeking change. When this happens we experience a social movement.

URBAN POLITICS AND PLANNING

Often the goals of politicians are pursued through the use of planning programs that claim to benefit the whole, but really mask special interests. One example is the effort made by local politicians using federal money to revitalize downtowns, called 'urban renewal'. Most of these interventions were aimed at slum clearance and so they removed thousands of low-income residents from the center of US cities. Little was done to encourage investment in affordable housing. Instead, revitalization really meant that corporate interests supporting politicians now had a way of channeling money into downtown real estate. In the end, two decades of urban renewal programs beginning in the 1960s, left large amounts of city land vacant and most downtown department stores struggling, despite the construction of pedestrian malls and the clearance of slum housing.

In the 1960s, another kind of politically led planning appeared, one that was more reformist in nature. In response to the ghetto riots that ripped across the nation, US cities elected reformist mayors who used planning tools to affect more equitable resource allocations. One such case was the administration of Mayor Carl Stokes, the first African American elected to lead a large city – Cleveland, Ohio. Stokes announced a new regime called *equity planning* with a goal of 'providing more choices to those who have few, if any, choices'. An ideology emerged from this experience that challenged the traditional view of the urban planner as simply a technician who managed land use. Instead, Cleveland's planners, under Mayor Stokes, tried to acquire both power and resources to support the improvement of public space, housing and public transportation. This change in the profile of city planners is also called *advocacy planning*, when work is carried out with and for the benefit of local communities (see the entry on *Planning and Public Space*).

Not everyone supports this more activist role of planners in the US and it is very much a political issue, meaning that powerful interests in the private sector oppose a principal focus on equity planning in place of the more traditional one of pursuing economic growth. Yet, the Cleveland administration of Carl Stokes had one notable victory: with the city in a weakened state, a powerful private utility company sought to purchase Cleveland's publicly owned electrical company, which could only run with the benefit of continual public subsidies. The equity planners knew that once the utility was privatized affordable electricity would be forfeited and the poor would suffer. With an effective political campaign, this privatization effort was finally blocked. However, the case points out the very close connection between urban planning in the US and local politics. It is usually the latter that uses the former for its own ends, often with negative results, as profit-making is subsidized while cities continue to decline.

SUBURBAN POLITICS

Suburban politics is much more straightforward than the city variety. There is one overriding interest in suburbia – single family home ownership. Suburban politics is home owner politics and elected officials in suburban areas tend to be non-partisan managers of property taxes. The aim of their administrations is to preserve the quality of suburban life. Most often this involves appropriate road maintenance for automobile traffic, adequate crime control and the raising of money for amenities, such as parks, recreational centers and civic events. If the mayors of US cities have lost their stature over the years as political players because their populations have declined, suburban leaders have even less stature because they never did have much clout in the first place. Metropolitan regions are notoriously fragmented, meaning that town officials cannot command many votes outside their own area. Yet, suburbanites are quite satisfied with these arrangements. What their governments lack in overall political power they make up for in approachability and attention to local concerns. Suburban politics serves the people in a direct, although limited way. One issue that has mobilized suburban residents in all areas of the country is the control of growth.

THE NATURE OF LOCAL POLITICS

Is urban politics an independent force in society or is it so dependent on economics that it is totally derivative? Of course, local politics is important precisely because it is the only way that cities and suburbs have real power. They exist as political units even if the form of space has transcended their boundaries. For this reason, cities and suburbs remain relevant as aggregate actors in the regional urban array. What of the issue of power elites? Yes, they exist. But elites also change over time depending on the confluence of the most powerful interests operating in the local area at a particular phases of development. It is not always real estate elites that are the most influential. In the past, industrialists and railroad interests comprised the urban elites. Today banking and professional service interests are the ones with clout downtown. When suburbs are young, growth interests seem to control politics. Yet, as they mature, residents become more concerned about controlling growth and avoiding its problems, such as heavy traffic. Variations in influence and the contentious nature of urban interests makes local politics an excellent way of illustrating and distinguishing the real differences that action and local activities make in relation to structural factors of change in our society.

CITIZEN PARTICIPATION

Active participation by local residents of a municipality is said to be a hallmark of democracy. Some new perspectives on revitalizing the city, such as the New Urbanism, hold increased participation as a core goal (see the entry on *Planning and Public Space*). Yet, this concept, like others we have examined, has a confusing array of connotations. Sheryl Arnstein (2003) in the 1960s carried out an influential study that attempted to sort out these meanings and identify the role that participation plays in local politics. She states that:

> [C]itizen participation is a categorical term for citizen power. It is the redistribution of power that enables the have-not citizens, presently excluded from the political and economic processes, to be deliberately included in the future. It is the strategy by which the have-nots join in determining how information is shared, goals and policies are set, tax resources are allocated, programs are operated, and benefits like contracts and patronage are parceled out. (2003: 236)

Arnstein argues that there is a typology of participation, from the lowest level where people are simply manipulated, which she calls 'nonparticipation', to a second level called 'tokenism' where citizens are consulted and allowed to attend information meetings, and, thirdly, to a growing involvement that she terms 'citizen power' and which includes forms of partnership and even control.

Arnstein also shows that the desire for citizen participation has been inflected by federal policy guidelines that have often shifted as a consequence of the political ideologies of the existing presidential administrations at the time. In the 1960s, following the graphic social unrest in cities, federal legislation asked for the 'maximum feasible participation' of local residents. This imperative was implemented in the Model Cities programs run by the Department of Housing and Urban Development (HUD). Later, in the 1970s, when it was decided by bureaucrats that the communities were acquiring too much control over federal funds, new legislation was passed requiring all poverty program monies to be run through city hall. Cities were required to create a new bureaucratic arm, the City Demonstration Agency (CDA), in order to manage the funds. The CDAs reduced the participation of local citizens back down to the level of consultation and access without direct decision-making or partnership. The result was that local community boards in cities became simply advisory to the planning and execution of development strategies.

URBAN AND SUBURBAN SOCIAL MOVEMENTS

A social movement is an organized political campaign directed at government and demanding structural changes in social organization. When participants aggregate in significant numbers a social movement is born. In the past, such movements have mobilized around issues of renters' rights, community control of school boards, welfare rights, neighborhood policing and community redevelopment. More recently, the campaigns for smart growth and sustainable development could be considered social movements. Critical perspectives on planning, such as New Urbanism, also try to reinvigorate the active involvement of local residents in town planning through the discussion mechanism of 'charrettes'. (See the entry on *Sustainable Urbanization*.)

The danger is that many social movements become professionalized and formalized. In East Germany up to the 1980s, there were very few opposition groups to the former communist regime. As pressure grew for liberalization, following Gorbachev's *glasnost* program in the Soviet Union, citizen groups sprung up in East Berlin, Leipzig, Dresden and other East German cities. After unification, all these movements became subsidized or underwritten by local authorities, thereby losing their independence and legitimacy (Rink, 2000). In the UK, the squatter, cooperative and self-build movements of the 1970s have found themselves incorporated into social housing, which is now a multi-million pound business drawing on loans from international banking interests. In short, urban social movements are often co-opted precisely because they address issues that local governments – urban and suburban politics – must eventually face. However, in order to continue to fight for their particular interests, they need to remain independent. Hence, the situation of many urban social movements is a contradictory one.

REFERENCES

Arnstein, S. 2003. 'A Ladder of Citizen Participation' in R. LeGates and F. Stout (eds) *The City Reader, 3rd Edition*, London, UK: Routledge. pp. 244–54.

Rink, D. 2000. 'Local Citizen's Initiatives During the (East) German Transformation' in P. Hamel, H. Lustiger-Thaler and M. Mayer (eds), *Urban Movements in a Globalising World*, London: Routledge.

Urban Violence and Crime

When people speak of crime, they usually mean violent crime and occurrences of violence, especially random street crime. From the 1960s through the early 1990s urban areas in the US were plagued by frequent acts of violence associated with robberies, street muggings and gang-related shootings. A significant amount of property crime also occurs in both cities and suburbs.

Discussing crime, firstly, it is important to distinguish between the actual *crime rate* of a locality and the popular perception of the likelihood of crime, often linked to *fear of crime*. Secondly, the crime statistics warrant a critical eye. Not all crimes are reported to police, and there is a very significant variation regarding the types of crime reported. Rape and sexual abuse, especially, are only rarely reported to the authorities, distorting the official view on crime and its effects in society.

Popular media tends to focus on spectacular criminal acts, such as murders and robberies, often exaggerating the dangers of urban life. This obscures the fact that during the latter part of the last century and in the early 2000s, urban crime remarkably *declined*. This is true for all developed countries and almost all types of crime. In New York City between 1990 and 1995, all crimes declined by over 40%; in Los Angeles and Houston the decline was over 20%, while other cities, such as Philadelphia, Detroit and Dallas, all saw their rates drop. The same trend has continued in the 2000s. One theory for the decline is that the population of young adult and disadvantaged males had declined and this group historically contains the highest percentage of perpetrators. Another possible reason for the decline is the reduction in the use of drugs.

At present both cities and suburbs are safer places to be than they were in the 1990s. Violent crime has declined. However, the level of property crime still remains comparatively high. It is a much more troubling problem in the US than in Europe, for example. Suburbs as well as cities are afflicted with auto theft, credit card theft, identity theft, robberies and other acts that involve the theft of property. Internet-based 'cyber crimes', such as denial of service attacks, are very likely growing, but this type of crime is not reliably recorded at the moment.

Crime pushes up the security budgets of companies and households and results in billions of dollars in unnecessary medical expenses for the victims of violent actions. It can also devastate property values. In areas of the city with high crime rates, the value of property is depressed. Thus, innocent households suffer doubly in crime-infested areas because they are both victims of crime, in many cases, and also because the value of their property declines.

NATURAL SURVEILLANCE

Jane Jacobs' (1961) writings were significant in pointing to the role of pedestrians in enriching city life and securing against crime. For Jacobs, the ideal city neighborhood is one that has a mix of residences and commercial establishments open late into the night. Her model was the place where she lived in Manhattan, an area called Greenwich Village, which was a lively area of diverse people, including many single women. Jacobs observed that the streets were always filled with pedestrian traffic because of both the comings and goings of residents and also the clientele of the commercial businesses. Street crime was comparatively low in this section of the city and violent crimes were almost unheard of there. Jacobs argued effectively that this feature was the direct result of the active pedestrian scene (see the entry on *Nightscapes and Urban Escapades*). There were simply too many people out at all hours of the day and night to allow the committing of a crime. In addition, shopowners and other *public figures* kept an eye on the street life, intervening if necessary.

Jacobs believed that if the city could be made safe for single women and children, then it would be able to compete with the more family friendly places in the suburbs and people would not abandon it as they had been doing during the 1950s and 1960s when she was living in Greenwich Village. Whether or not she was correct about this aspect of her argument, she did explain why crime was low in the area. Deserted spaces allow the necessary opportunity to victimize others that criminals require. Lively street scenes filled with pedestrians at all hours not only deters crime, but are the very hallmark of a healthy city. Recently, Jacobs' ideas have been appropriated by a planning and policy movement called Crime Prevention Through Environmental Design (CPTED). While the design of the physical built environment does have a role in fighting crime and producing positive feeling about the place, many claims made under the banner of CPTED are exaggerated; especially, the so-called 'broken window theory' that links public disorder and serious crime, is simply wrong.

RACIAL VIOLENCE

US cities, in particular, have been the scenes of racial riots, often in response to racial segregation and discrimination. Despite advances in tolerance and inclusion, major disturbances have increased since the 1900s. According to Berger (1978: 267), among the major occurrences between 1908 and 1968 were:

> 1908 – Springfield, IL; 1917 – East St. Louis; 1919 – Chicago; 1921 – Tulsa; 1935 – Harlem; 1943 – Harlem, Detroit, LA; 1960 – Greensboro, NC; 1963 – Birmingham, Savannah, Cambridge, Chicago, Philadelphia; 1964 – Jacksonville, Cleveland, St Augustine, Jersey City, Elizabeth, Paterson, Harlem, Bed-Stuyvesant, Philadelphia, Rochester, Chicago; 1965 – Selma, Watts, Chicago; 1966 – Watts, Chicago, Cleveland and 15 other cities; 1967 – Detroit and 175 other cities; 1968 – Newark and 157 other cities.

TYPES OF VIOLENT CRIME

The experience of crime and violence is not the same in every city. Popular films and TV programs convey something about the variety of crime and victimization across continents: *Blade Runner*, *Gangs of New York*, *The Wire*, *Lock Stock and Two Smoking Barrels*, *City of God*, *La Haine*.

The reporting of violent events and crime is often conflated as if they had a single cause. For example, the London riots of 2011 had a number of the usual causes: alienation and adventure of the young, criminal opportunism, and so on. The riots were triggered by the shooting of a suspect by the police in North London. For the Right, the riots were a manifestation of lawlessness in the form of looting shops and malls and an opportunity for violence against the police. For the Left, the causes lay in unemployment, alienation and the institutional racism of the police and other forms of social exclusion in poorer and mainly ethnic minority suburbs. In a sense, it was a combination of all these factors, yet there were even differences between the different boroughs where this occurred (Reichner and Stott, 2011).

Yet this is small beer compared to the levels, frequency and intensity of violence and crime in a larger number of African and Asian cities. But again here there are big differences between nations and cities. Table 8 provides a useful overview of the manifold nature of urban crime and violence. But, like any template, factors that do not fit are just as important as those that do. A study undertaken of Bogotá, Kinshasa and Nairobi sets out an approach that combines similarities *and* differences in the causes of urban violence, in which crime situates itself:

> Urban space is characterised by conflict … but what is of interest to us is the way in which conflict can become violent. Violence is generated when risk factors interact in a situation of conflict. We define risk factors as *existing conditions that could potentially culminate in violence*. It is not the risk factors in themselves that are producing violence, as they are necessary but not sufficient conditions for violence to occur. For our purposes, violence is defined as *the manifestation of distorted power relationships produced by the complex interaction between risk factors*. This definition and the subsequent analysis are specifically based on urban spaces seen both as exemplary of wider processes, and as having distinctive features embedded in the urban reality. (Agostini et al., 2006: 1, italics in original, note removed)

The authors set out three structural characteristics by which they analyze the three cities:

- The Primary Nexus: Is envisioned as the point where there is a significant alignment of common processes, and the point at which the potential for violence is extremely high. These processes are: a crisis of governance, unequal access to economic opportunity, economic decline, and the naturalisation of fear and insecurity.
- Secondary Nexuses: Are the points of overlap between two of the case cities, where the potential for violence is significant, but not as likely as in the primary nexus.
- Context Specific Processes: Highlight the unique manner in which risks factors interact to produce violence in each of the cities. (Agostini et al., 2006: iii)

Table 8 Categories, types and manifestations of violence in urban areas

Category of violence	Types of violence by perpetrators and/or crime	Manifestations
Political	State and non-state violence	Guerrilla conflict Paramilitary conflict Political assassinations Armed conflict between political parties
Institutional	Violence of state and other 'informal ' institutions, including the private sector	Extra-judicial killings by police Physical or psychological abuse by health and education workers State or community vigilante-directed social cleansing of gangs and street children Lynching of suspected criminals by community members
Economic	Organized crime Business interests Delinquents Robbers	Intimidation and violence as means of resolving economic disputes Street theft, robbery and crime Kidnapping

Category of violence	Types of violence by perpetrators and/or crime	Manifestations
		Armed robbery
		Drug trafficking
		Car theft and other contraband activities
		Small-arms dealing
		Assaults including killing and rape in the course of economic crimes
		Trafficking in prostitutes
		Conflict over scarce resources
Economic/ social	Gangs Street children (boys and girls) Ethnic violence	Territorial or identity-based 'turf' violence Robbery, theft Petty theft Communal riots
Social	Intimate partner violence inside the home Sexual violence (including rape) in the public arena Child abuse: boys and girls; inter-generational conflict between parents and children; gratuitous/routine daily violence	Physical or psychological male–female abuse Physical and sexual abuse, particularly prevalent in the case of stepfathers but also uncles Physical and psychological abuse Incivility in areas such as traffic, road rage, bar fights and street confrontations; arguments that get out of control

Source: Moser (2004).

The World Bank has noted the impact of the rapid urbanization of developing economies in generating greater violence and crime, but talks little of the underlying political histories or structures (World Bank, 2010). The recent political uprisings as part of the Arab Spring and subsequent civil wars, as well as the riots in Turkey, Brazil and other rapidly developing economies, can be said to be caused by urban factors. But this confuses form and function; as in the case of the Arab Spring nations and Turkey, forces of democracy, secularism and religious fundamentalism come together in an explosive mix in urban places. It can be argued that addressing poverty, economic inequality and social exclusion would lead to democratically secular societies. Yet, the evidence of this is doubtful in the case of Turkey in that secularism is closely associated with military repression (one has only to look at particular histories, for example the role and collapse of the Ottoman Empire, in the history of Europe and its bordering regions) (Mazower, 2004). Similarly, riots in Brazil were associated with a reaction to the cost of building stadia for the 2014 World Cup, at a time when the stellar performance of the Brazilian economy was fading fast.

REFERENCES

Agostini, G., F. Chianese, W. French and A. Sandhu 2006. *Understanding the Processes of Urban Violence: An Analytical Framework*, London: Crisis States Research Centre Development Studies Institute, London School of Economics.

Berger, A. 1978. *The City: Urban Communities and their Problems*, Dubuque, IA: Wm. C. Brown and Co.

Jacobs, J. 1961. *The Death and Life of Great American Cities*, New York: Vintage.

Mazower. M. 2004. *Salonica, City of Ghosts: Christians, Muslims and Jews 1430–1950*, London: HarperCollins.

Moser, C. 2004. 'Urban Violence and Insecurity: An Introductory Roadmap', *Environment & Urbanization*, 10: 1–6.

Reichner, S. and C. Stott 2011. *Mad Mobs and Englishmen? Myths and Realities of the 2011 Riots*, London: Constable & Robinson.

World Bank 2010. *World Development Report 2010: Development and Climate Change*, Washington, DC: World Bank.

Urbanization and Urbanism

Both these terms are old and have been used for some time to describe city-based processes. Now they present a question of whether they can be extended to the concept of fully urbanized regions and the perspective of *total urbanization*, discussed by Henri Lefebvre (1991). We think they can and, in loose usage, they already have been.

URBANIZATION

This concept has been traditionally defined as the process of city formation and city growth. Urbanization involves the way social activities locate themselves in space and according to interdependent processes of societal development and change. Its analysis is often historical and comparative. Historical studies on urbanization try to answer such questions as: How did cities first form? What were the conditions that produced them? What were early cities like? Is there a necessary social organization without which urbanization cannot proceed?

Contemporary studies are divided among those addressing developed and those addressing relatively underdeveloped or developing regions of the world. In the advanced countries, especially those in Western Europe and the US, issues of urbanization often involve the question of deindustrialization and its consequences. Shifts to new, high-technology and financial services industries are important, as are their social consequences for structural changes in the labor force. The gentrification of older and formerly under valued housing is another issue that is addressed (see the entries on *Globalization and Meltdown* and *Housing*). In the less developed or developing areas of the world, urbanization studies involve the explosive growth of large cities and rural to urban migration as it affects both the city and the countryside.

The notion of urbanization as a historic process should not be confused with *urbanization rate*. The latter refers to the balance between urban and rural populations of a country at a given moment in time. In developed countries, the urbanization rate is close to 90%, but variations are relatively large, partly because of real socio-spatial differences and partly because of differences in defining 'urban' populations statistically. Globally, 54% of people live in urban conditions (2014). The growth of urban populations will continue in all global regions, but somewhat surprisingly only three countries, China, India and Nigeria, will represent a lion's share of the growth until 2050. India is projected to add 404 million urban dwellers, China 292 million and Nigeria 212 million (http://esa.un.org/unpd/wup/).

THE URBAN REVOLUTION

In the 1940s, the historian V. Gordon Childe presented a theory of city growth (see Gottdiener and Hutchison, 2000: 26). His argument, called the *urban revolution*, remains relevant today for the study of urbanization in the third world, although there have been some critiques in recent research. This theory had the virtue of defining precisely how the economies of early civilizations were able to support entire groups of people who did not produce agricultural goods. The extraction and control by a ruling elite of the agricultural surplus was the basis for the type of hierarchical social organization that supported city life.

The problem with Childe's view is that it is an *evolutionary* model. Recent evidence suggests that city growth was discontinuous and that multiple stages existed together, such as the development of an agriculturally based economy alongside the development of science and crafts. Also there is some evidence that in ancient cities, like Catal Höyuk in Turkey, commerce and trade were the key factors in providing a basis for the urban economy, rather than an agricultural surplus (Jacobs, 1969). In fact, throughout history cities were the sites of an active market serving a much larger region. It is impossible to separate the market in some form from the settlement known as a city in the ancient world, if not also today.

CONTEMPORARY URBANIZATION

At the turn of the 21st century, 2.8 billion people lived in cities, representing 47% of the world's population. In 2014, the global urbanization rate was estimated at 54%. Much of this concentration actually exists within urbanized regions, because there is often no distinction between the 'city' as a compact urban form and an expansive region of urbanization associated with a central place. In any case, by contrast, in 1950 fewer than 750 million people or 29% of the world's population were city dwellers, according to United Nation statistics (UNCHS, 1987, 2001). The rapid urbanization, on a massive scale, and over a short period of time, has been propelled to a great extent by the developing countries, while almost all population growth in the near future will take place in the cities of the developing world. The number of urban residents in the developing countries has exploded from fewer than 300 million (17%) in 1950 to over 1.9 billion (40%) in the year 2000, a figure that is expected to double in the three decades to come. The share of the world's population living in urban areas of developing countries continues to soar, from 12% in 1950 to 68% in 2000. By the year 2015, this figure will have reached 75% of the world's population and the number of urban dwellers in developing countries will be about the same size as the current world's population, 2.8 billion. In short, urbanization in the developing world is an explosive phenomenon replete with many social problems that will only grow worse in the future.

The process of urbanization in developing countries can be captured by increases in the number and size of cities. The number of large cities with a population of more than 1 million increased during the second half of the 20th century. The number of large cities increased from 80 in 1950 to 365 in the year 2000. This rise in large cities has been more dramatic in the developing countries, from 31 in 1950 to 242 in 2000 (UNCHS, 1999). Over the last two decades, the number of large cities has more than doubled. In addition, the size of cities is also rapidly increasing. In 1950, New York was the world's only megacity – i.e. a city with 10 million or more residents. Out of five megacities in 1975, three were in developing countries, and at the beginning of the 21st century 15 out of 19 were in developing countries (United Nations Population Fund (UNFPA), 2000: 6). These megacities in developing countries are expected to grow faster than those in developed countries. In most cases, however, the concept of 'megacity' actually refers to the new form of space called the Multi-Centered Metropolitan Region (MMR), despite the persisting importance of a large and built up central business district.

In contrast to the characteristics of the traditional bounded city, the new form of settlement space can be typified by two features: it extends over a large region and it contains many separate centers, each with its own abilities to draw workers, shoppers and residents. Not every country of the world is experiencing this new form of multi-centered metropolitan growth, but all countries seem to be subjected to a process of urban development that has produced gigantic cities and urbanization on a regional scale. This explosive growth implies an immense social crisis for the developing countries.

URBANISM

Urbanism is a way of life characterized by density, diversity and complex social organization. Most often the term today means the culture of cities. However, here too, analysts conflate the culture of cities with that of suburbia, although the latter is usually described in stereotypical terms (see the entry on *The Chicago School*).

Both cities and affluent suburbs are typified by high consumption lifestyles and the participation in an advanced, information-based economy. Urbanism has traditionally been associated with a greater sophistication in understanding and consuming the arts, expensive dining, sophisticated entertainment and fashion. Suburbia is typified as family and private home centered with a reliance on the automobile as the dominant mode of transportation and a daily life exemplifying the value of privatism. It is not clear whether such sharp distinctions can be made today, although it is certainly true that city and suburban living differ because of the respective modes of housing and transportation – the one characterized by high rises and public transportation; the other by the single family home and the automobile.

Discussions of urbanism often emphasize that city life is more tolerant of strangers and so-called 'deviants' than the suburbs. There are special districts in the city that come alive only at night where people engage in partying activities (see the entry on *The City* for further discussion). Cities are supposed to be more diverse ethnically, racially and with regard to class than suburbs. There is still an implicit understanding that city people are more interested in hustling for advantages in economic and social relations, while those people living in the more suburbanized areas of metro regions take a steadier view of employment, and share intimacy only with their select circle of friends.

Today it is not clear whether these sharp social distinctions can be made between urbanism and suburbanism. All areas of the Multi-Centered Metropolitan Region have become increasingly diverse in recent years. Immigrants no longer select the inner city as their place of initial residence. Subcultures abound throughout the region. The emphasis on a high consumption lifestyle seems to characterize all areas.

Historically, there is a theory that sought to characterize life within the big city as relatively unique. It was articulated by Lewis Wirth of the 1930s Chicago School (see the entries on *The Chicago School* and *The City*). There is also recent evidence that inner cities have nurtured entertainment districts which cannot be found in the suburbs on such an extended scale and which produce a street life at night that is definitely a city phenomenon (see the entry on *Nightscapes and Urban Escapades*). Finally, it must be observed that, when dealing with the truly global cities of the developed countries, their repositories of art, music, dance, fashion, design, architecture and all other aspects of what was once called 'high culture' are unprecedented in quality, quantity and accessibility, with no comparable experience offered by any other spatial form.

REFERENCES

Gottdiener, M. and R. Hutchison 2000. *The New Urban Sociology, 2nd Edition*, New York: McGraw-Hill.

Jacobs, J. 1969. *The Economy of Cities*, New York: Random House.

Lefebvre, Henri 1991 [1974]. *The Production of Space*, Oxford and Cambridge, MA: Blackwell. [La production de l'espace, English translation by Donald Nicholson-Smith.]

United Nations Center for Human Settlements (UNCHS) 1987. *Global Reports on Human Settlements*, Oxford: Oxford University Press.

United Nations Center for Human Settlements (UNCHS) 1996. *An Urbanizing World*, Oxford: Oxford University Press.

United Nations Center for Human Settlements (UNCHS) 1999. *Basic Facts on Urbanization*, Nairobi, Kenya: UNCHS Habitat.

United Nations Center for Human Settlements (UNCHS) 2001. *Cities in a Globalizing World*, London: Earthscan.

United Nations Population Fund (UNFPA) 2000. *The State of World Population*, New York: UNFPA.

CPSIA information can be obtained
at www.ICGtesting.com
Printed in the USA
BVHW01s1310230818

524938BV00014B/28/P